49-

D1713895

Culture, Ritual and Revolution in Vietnam

ANTHROPOLOGY OF ASIA SERIES

Series Editor: Grant Evans, *University of Hong Kong*

Asia today is one of the most dynamic regions of the world. The previously predominant image of 'timeless peasants' has given way to the image of fast-paced business people, mass consumerism and high-rise urban conglomerations. Yet much discourse remains entrenched in the polarities of 'East vs. West', 'Tradition vs. Change'. This series hopes to provide a forum for anthropological studies which break with such polarities. It will publish titles dealing with cosmopolitanism, cultural identity, representations, arts and performance. The complexities of urban Asia, its elites, its political rituals, and its families will also be explored.

Dangerous Blood, Refined Souls
Death Rituals among the Chinese in Singapore
Tong Chee Kiong

Folk Art Potters of Japan
Beyond an Anthropology of Aesthetics
Brian Moeran

Hong Kong
The Anthropology of a Chinese Metropolis
Edited by Grant Evans and Maria Tam

Anthropology and Colonialism in Asia and Oceania
Jan van Bremen and Akitoshi Shimizu

Japanese Bosses, Chinese Workers
Power and Control in a Hong Kong Megastore
Wong Heung Wah

The Legend of the Golden Boat
Regulation, Trade and Traders in the Borderlands of Laos, Thailand, China and Burma
Andrew Walker

Cultural Crisis and Social Memory
Politics of the Past in the Thai World
Edited by Shigeharu Tanabe and Charles F. Keyes

The Globalization of Chinese Food
Edited by David Y. H. Wu and Sidney C. H. Cheung

Culture, Ritual and Revolution in Vietnam
Shaun Kingsley Malarney

Culture, Ritual and Revolution in Vietnam

Shaun Kingsley Malarney

UNIVERSITY OF HAWAI'I PRESS
HONOLULU

© 2002 Shaun Kingsley Malarney

Published in North America by
University of Hawai'i Press
2840 Kolowalu Street
Honolulu, Hawai'i 96822

First published in the United Kingdom
by RoutledgeCurzon
11 New Fetter Lane
London EC4P 4EE
England

Printed in Great Britain

Library of Congress Cataloging-in-Publication Data
A catalog record for this book has been requested

ISBN 0–8248–2660–4 (alk. paper)

Any nation is a nation only as long as it has its own particular God and rules out all other gods in the world with no conciliation; as long as it believes that through its God it will be victorious and will drive all other gods from the world.

Dostoevsky, *The Possessed*

For my parents

Contents

List of Illustrations

Illustrations appear between pages 114 and 115

1 The Giap Nhi communal house, circa 1991, before the market was moved to a location concealed from the communal house facade.
2 The Giap Nhi communal house, circa 1998.
3 The Giap Tu communal house, circa 1991.
4 The Giap Tu communal house, circa 1998.
5 A simple ancestral altar with a poster featuring an image of Ho Chi Minh above.
6 Members of the Women's Buddhist Association chant during funeral rites for a former member.
7 A Giap Tu man delivers a funeral oration. Next to him are food prestations given by guests at the funeral.
8 A Giap Nhi funeral procession.
9 The eldest son at a funeral wearing the "straw hat".
10 Family members bid farewell at the grave site.
11 "The Fatherland Remembers Your Sacrifice" certificate and simple altar for family war dead.
12 Residents toast those killed by the French during the 1947 reconquest of Thinh Liet at the 1992 rites conducted to commemorate their deaths.
13 The spirit cabinet in the Giap Tu communal house containing the Ho Chi Minh portrait.

Preface

This is a book about cultural and ritual change. Specifically, it is a book about how the introduction of an ambitious set of cultural reforms by the Vietnamese state has affected the cultural and ritual life of one northern Vietnamese commune. Beginning in the 1940s, and reaching full form from the late 1950s onward, the Vietnamese government attempted to remake Vietnamese society and culture in order to bring them into line with official ideology. Although many of the grander manifestations of this agenda, such as the land reform and cooperativization campaigns of the 1950s and 1960s, have received extensive scholarly attention, the cultural aspects of the revolution remain largely unstudied. This monograph attempts to fill this gap by examining in detail the components and mechanics of the revolution as it has unfolded and continues to unfold in Thinh Liet commune of Thanh Tri district, just south of Hanoi. One of my aims in writing this study is historical. The analysis begins in the 1940s and examines the progression of official policies and practices with an eye to understanding not only their content, but also the issues and concerns that local officials faced when implementing them. A second aim is ethnographic. The Vietnamese revolution did not occur in a vacuum. Instead, it had to cope with a broad range of local values and attitudes. In my analyses, I attempt to show what some of these values and attitudes were, who advocated them, and how they continue to animate local cultural life. As I state throughout the text, a definitive cultural orthodoxy does not exist in contemporary Thinh Liet. My objective, therefore, is to bring out as fully as possible, the multiple ideas, positions, and definitions that compete in local debates over cultural and ritual life. My final aim is theoretical. Revolutionary cultural change represents both an empirical and theoretical challenge for the study of human culture. Building on an approach derived from the sociology of knowledge, I attempt to lay out what I consider a useful method for the study of culture in such a context. I also seek to explore why many revolutionary ritual reforms achieved only limited success and consider what the implications of this were for understanding the role of culture and ritual in Thinh Liet life.

The research upon which this study is based was conducted in and around the city of Hanoi from March 1990 to August 1992, December 1993 to February 1994, July 1996, and July 1998. Field research began in Thinh Liet commune in March 1991 and continued in all of the following periods. In order to add historical depth to the study, I conducted research in 1992 and 1994 at the National Archives in Hanoi where I consulted French colonial administrative documents. While these helped give me an understanding of the commune's history prior to 1940, research in Hanoi at the National Library and the Institute of Social Science library gave me a better understanding of the broader historical processes that have affected Thinh Liet from 1945 onward. It is important to note from the outset that this study does not claim that Thinh Liet's history of revolution is necessarily representative of the experiences of all northern Vietnamese communities. Cultural practices vary widely between communities in the region, and official documents and scholarly studies have demonstrated that the implementation and reaction to revolutionary policies also varied. Thinh Liet's experiences and unique dynamics should therefore be considered in their own right. Nevertheless, I suspect that many similarities do exist and hope that future research on northern Vietnam will bring out more fully that which is shared and that which is unique.

Fieldwork in northern Vietnam in the early 1990s presented a number of special challenges. Given that government officials did not allow me to live in a rural village, field research consisted of almost daily trips to the commune at all hours of day and night. Local residents and officials were initially somewhat suspicious about having an anthropologist nosing around their community. Residents worried because only a few years before a visit to one's home by a foreigner would have led to a visit by the police to learn what had been discussed. Official concerns related to whether my real aim was to collect intelligence for the American government, and also that something untoward might happen to me that they might have to answer for at higher levels – a concern articulated through frequent comments about young people throwing rocks at foreigners. All of these concerns were also combined with a lingering uncertainty about the fact that I came from a country that had been their main adversary for decades and whose soldiers had been responsible for the death and injury of hundreds of local people.

The initial stages of my interviewing were arranged by Trinh Mang, a retired colonel from the People's Army, who at that point served in the communal administration as the official in charge of social and cultural affairs. While he attended some of the initial interviews, after a few weeks he simply introduced me to families and let me go about my business. On the whole, most families were receptive to my visits, but Mang made it clear that for some my nationality remained problematic. My standing in Thinh Liet improved significantly after my attendance at a funeral in the autumn of 1991 when, as is common among participants in a funeral procession, I chewed betel nut after an elderly woman offered it to me. Unexpectedly, my consumption of the betel nut took me over an unknown cultural boundary. From that point on I became known as 'the American who chews betel just like us.' This act, combined with my appreciated attendance at numerous funerals, brought me into the realm of moral relationships with many residents and opened many new doors. It also marked a change in the tenor of my conversations with residents. Previously I had asked most of the questions in our conversations, but many with whom I became acquainted began asking me about myself and my country. This was particularly true of former soldiers and others who wanted to learn more about Americans and the situation in the United States during the American War in Vietnam. Many northern Vietnamese are fond of saying that Ho Chi Minh taught that the American war was a war of the US government against North Vietnam, and not a war of the American people. Although some people retained their reluctance to talk to me, which is unsurprising given the amount of suffering the war caused in Thinh Liet, I was grateful that so many looked beyond the war and opened their lives and community to me.

Numerous debts of gratitude were accumulated in the completion of this study. My foremost debt goes to my assistant, Le Van Sinh, who opened countless doors for me and was always able to understand my sometimes opaque questions and render them in an idiom that Thinh Liet residents understood. This study would not have been possible without his unflagging patience, friendship, and assistance. Professor Phan Huy Le of the Center for the Cooperative Study of Vietnam sponsored my project and tirelessly arranged for the many levels of official permission that research required. Other people who helped me in various capacities included Phan Dai Doan, Nguyen Van Chinh, Le Thi Nham Tuyet, Nguyen Hong Ngoc, Nguyen thi Bich Thanh, the family of Tran Tien and Le Mai, the staff of the National Archives, and Rob Graham. I owe a special debt to Trinh Mang and the people of Thinh Liet for teaching me so much about their lives. While still a student I had the good fortune of having teachers who took an interest in my work and helped me to rethink many aspects of my material. In particular, Robert Hefner, Peter Berger, Sherry Ortner, Ray Kelly, Norma Diamond, Martin Whyte, and Paul Dresch deserve mention. David Akin, Michael Herzfeld, Hue Tam Ho-Tai, Ben Kerkvliet, John Kleinen, Hy Van Luong, David Marr, Charles Nuckolls, Bill Steele, Alexander Woodside and Peter Zinoman either read or discussed various parts of this project with me. Their input is greatly appreciated. Any mistakes, of course, are mine. Financial support for research and writing came from a National Science Foundation Graduate Fellowship, Mellon

Foundation Candidacy and Dissertation Fellowships, the Department of Anthropology and the Horace H. Rackham School of Graduate Studies at the University of Michigan, and the Harvard Academy for International and Area Studies of the Center for International Affairs at Harvard University. I am grateful to all of these organizations for their generous assistance. My family provided solid support throughout this project, particularly when it seemed that fieldwork in Vietnam would be impossible. My final thanks go to my wife Christy and my sons Liem and Kien. They encountered this project in its later stages, but the joys of time with them helped keep my spirits up over the many months it took to complete it.

Introduction

The year 1986 marked a watershed in modern Vietnamese history. The Vietnamese government and Communist Party, after years of evidence that their collectivist economic policies were failing, endorsed the Renovation policy (*Doi Moi*) that advocated the dismantling of the command economy and allowed for the introduction of what some would eventually call 'socialism with market characteristics.' Although the policy focussed primarily on economic issues, and would over the following years produce a surge of economic growth in the country, laying deeper behind it was a profound reorientation of the party and state's role in Vietnamese life. Whereas both had previously assumed a dominant role in order to realize the goal of establishing socialism, the new policy's introduction marked a significant retreat from its earlier position and created the conditions for the emergence for non-state-directed activity in many areas of social life. As a consequence, the number of private businesses swelled, literature and the arts experienced a minor renaissance, and people even began to assert themselves, albeit in a limited way, in political affairs. Accompanying these political and economic transformations was a reconfiguration of the state's involvement in cultural and ritual affairs. Similar to their agenda to create a socialist economy, the Vietnamese Communists had attempted to create a socialist culture, with its own core of officially acceptable ritual practices. For over thirty years, they had maintained strict control over cultural life through the propaganda and surveillance activities of local party cells and mass organizations. Ritual life was similarly controlled through such practices as the insertion of officials into ceremonies, the monitoring of unsanctioned ritual specialists and locales, and even raids into local homes to confiscate forbidden ritual paraphernalia. Propaganda and legislation coming from the government today, with their requisite condemnation of ritual profligacy and the continued existence of 'superstitious' practices, demonstrate that officials have not lost their interest in maintaining cultural and ritual orthodoxy in the country. Yet, despite the intensity of official

1

rhetoric, the Vietnamese state has since the late 1980s slowly scaled back its involvement in cultural and ritual life. Whereas officials could formerly take control over practices, they now often stand on the sidelines, sometimes criticizing, sometimes tacitly tolerating, and sometimes encouraging what is taking place.

The work of numerous scholars has shown that the weakening official control over culture and ritual was followed by a significant resurgence of ritual practice in the north (see Endres 1999; Kleinen 1999; Luong 1992 and 1993; Malarney 1993; Norton 1999). Weddings, funerals, and communal house rites began returning on a scale and frequency not seen for decades. However, although such rituals were resurgent, it was also clear that the rituals people began organizing were in no way exact replicas of pre-revolutionary ritual practices. In fact, these new rituals often involved a blending of some practices common before the revolution and others encouraged during the reform campaigns. At times the rituals that resulted could be surprisingly internally contradictory, if not politically suspect. My first encounter with this occurred on 19 May 1990 in a ceremony conducted in Hanoi's Temple of Literature (*Van Mieu*). On this day, the centenary of Ho Chi Minh's birth, my teachers had invited me to watch a group of villagers from a community outside of Hanoi conduct a *le khao vong* dedicated to Ho. This ceremony was common before the revolution, but had definite elite associations as it celebrated either a scholar's success on an examination or the promotion of a mandarin. When I asked my teachers whether there was anything contradictory or even politically suspect about these villagers holding a seemingly feudal ceremony, which ended when villagers escorted a small palanquin with a framed official portrait of the elderly Ho Chi Minh out of the temple compound, they replied that there was not. The fact that Ho had helped engineer the destruction of the social order from which this ceremony came was unimportant. What was important was that Ho Chi Minh was a man of knowledge and learning, and as the ceremony celebrated such achievements, honoring Ho with it was quite appropriate. To my teachers and the assembled villagers, there was no contradiction.

When I began research in Thinh Liet commune one year later I encountered other rituals in which the form, style, purpose, and content were being created, defined, and often debated as the ritual unfolded. Indeed, it was clear that if there previously had been any orthodoxy associated with ritual practice in Thinh Liet, which itself is historically questionable, it was now gone. Local residents had embarked on a project that reminded me of the tireless *bricoleur* of which Levi-Strauss spoke (see Levi-Strauss 1962), but instead of using bits and pieces drawn from their mythical toolbox to make sense of the world, Thinh Liet *bricolage* involved the cobbling together of elements of pre-revolutionary practices with revolutionary ritual reforms, and the mixing of ideas drawn from official ideology with the very same ideas that ideology had intended to eliminate, in order to produce an innovative set of ritual practices. What also stood out about this *bricolage* was that the proper organization of some ritual practices was very important to people, but they did not always agree on what that proper organization was. This process of ritual change and contestation is the focus of this study. In the analysis that follows, I do not attempt to present an encyclopedic discussion of all attitudes about all ritual practices in Thinh Liet. Some rituals, such as those held for one month old infants, or those that mark an adult's attainment of 60, 70, 80, or 90 years old, were not areas of controversy, nor were they a focus of significant official meddling in Thinh Liet.[1] Other rituals, such as weddings, funerals, death anniversary ceremonies, communal house ceremonies, rites for war dead, and spirit medium rites, were a focus of public debate, and had also occupied an important place in the reformed ritual corpus. It is these rites that will comprise this study's analytical focus.

The resurgence of ritual raises important questions about the nature of culture and ritual in contemporary Thinh Liet. As I hope to show, instead of there being a single, unified culture shared by all, what we have is a cacophony of voices, each defining its own vision of how things should be. I seek to explore the history and nature of this innovative process in order to understand how the people of the commune – male and female, young and old, party members and non-party members, farmers and intellectuals – with their diverse and sometimes conflicting ideas of culture, tradition, morality, sacredness, and appropriateness – are attempting to recreate and redefine culture and ritual in the wake of the cultural reform campaign. As I will argue in the conclusion, I also feel that there are much deeper implications to this resurgence that bring us back to fundamental questions about the role of culture and ritual in human life. In most of the chapters, the main questions I ask are how have these ritual changes unfolded and what have their primary components been. I address the question of why people seek to conduct rituals in particular ways, but I do not address the broader question of why certain elements of the reform campaigns succeeded and others did not. I will comparatively examine this latter point in the conclusion and argue that when looked at in their totality, these changes reveal a great deal about the role of ritual in articulating diverse notions of what Thinh Liet society should be, as well as the role of culture and ritual in confronting and dealing with some of the fundamental existential concerns that residents face.

Theoretical Orientations: Culture and Ritual in a Post-Revolutionary Society

Analyzing culture in a current or former revolutionary society poses a number of significant difficulties. Unlike in non-revolutionary societies

3

where culture certainly changes, but generally in a relatively less dramatic fashion, revolutionary societies often experience dramatic ruptures in cultural reproduction and transmission. This was the case in the French revolution when revolutionary authorities embarked upon an ambitious dechristianization campaign that was combined with an effort to install a new cult of reason, liberty, and equality (see Fauchois 1989). In the socialist revolutions of the twentieth century this trend continued. Culture, in all of these cases, became an important arena for revolutionary practice because revolutionaries recognized that ideas and practices that existed in the old order had been critical for the maintenance and reproduction of that system. Thus, not only did they need to introduce new ideas and practices to define and legitimize the new regime, they also had to delegitimize old ideas and practices in order to prevent backsliding into the pre-revolutionary status quo. The existence of these new cultural elements and policies, however, did not empirically entail the elimination of all of those ideas and practices that revolutionaries opposed. This of course was the origin of Marx's famous comment at the beginning of *The Eighteenth Brumaire of Louis Bonaparte* that,

> Men make their own history, but they do not make it just as they please; they do not make it under circumstances chosen by themselves, but under circumstances directly encountered, given and transmitted from the past. The tradition of all the dead generations weighs like a nightmare on the brain of the living.
>
> (Marx 1987:15)

The scholarly record on revolutionary societies has compellingly demonstrated that in revolutionary societies, ideas and practices that antedate the revolution and those that accompanied the revolution coexist, often in states of tension if not outright conflict.[2]

The proliferation of multiple and sometimes contradictory ideas, values, and practices demands an analytical approach that can account for this wealth of diversity. The approach taken in this monograph derives from the sociology of knowledge. Culture, according to the approach taken here, is constituted by the numerous and diverse systems of knowledge that exist in social life. Peter Berger and Thomas Luckmann have commented that, 'The sociology of knowledge must concern itself with everything that passes for "knowledge" in society' (Berger and Luckmann 1966:14ff.), thus I begin with the position that any system of knowledge that exists in a particular social context can be considered as constitutive of culture. Myths, legends, moral rules, political manifestos, scientific theories, agricultural techniques, historical narratives, classifications of the natural world, religious doctrines, definitions of causality, conceptualizations of the body, justifications for inequality; in short, the complete range of collectively held or intersubjective knowledge, which is to say not the thought of only a single individual, can all be described as part of 'culture.' In the analysis that follows, I will often speak of the 'cultural realm' or 'cultural world' of Thinh Liet commune in order to emphasize that I am not speaking about a Herderian 'Vietnamese Culture,' but instead examining those ideas, values, practices, and meanings that exist in and animate the particular social context I focus on here, Thinh Liet commune.

Such an expansive approach to the study of culture requires five important qualifications. First, although it is assumed that cultural knowledge is to some measure shared, it is a mistake to assume that all members of the society or social group under study possess the same knowledge. In a fitting turn of phrase, Dan Sperber has commented that members of social groups possess a 'shared orientation' that facilitates the mutual comprehensibility of cultural symbolism (Sperber 1975:137). Indeed, some level of shared knowledge is necessary for social actors to communicate with each other through language or other media. The issue goes deeper though in that social actors also generally share what Alfred Schutz described as 'common sense knowledge of the world' (Schutz 1973:7). This knowledge includes basic propositions about how the world is, what exists in it, how it is divided up, and how to get along in it. As Schutz commented, 'the world we live in is a world of more or less well circumscribed objects with more or less definite qualities, objects among which we move, which resist us and upon which we may act' (Schutz 1973:7). Schutz notes that the majority of the assertions and propositions that constitute this knowledge are 'just taken for granted until further notice' (Schutz 1973:7). Despite this level of shared knowledge, major differences can exist regarding the distribution of knowledge. Berger and Luckmann speak of what they describe as 'socially segregated subuniverses of meaning' (Berger and Luckmann 1966:85). These are bodies of knowledge linked to specific social groups that are not evenly distributed in society nor necessarily shared with other groups. Anyone who has ever been at the mercy of an auto mechanic or sat uncomprehendingly through a physician's explanation of a diagnosis understands this point intuitively, but the ethnographic record provides many other cases such as the exclusive esoteric knowledge of the Javanese religious specialists discussed by Robert Hefner, the monopolization of sacred knowledge by men in Baktaman society discussed by Frederik Barth, or even the uneven distribution of magical knowledge in Trobriand and Azande society discussed by Malinowski and Evans-Pritchard (Barth 1975; Evans-Pritchard 1976; Hefner 1985; Malinowski 1922).[3] In each of these cases, social groups and actors bring different bodies of knowledge to social practice.

The second qualification to note is that it is through the medium of culture that social actors come to understand and define 'reality.' One of the most fundamental starting points of interpretive social science is that 'reality' itself is a social construct and social actors are progressively socialized and enculturated into their understandings of what 'reality' is. The feature of reality that requires emphasis here is that in the social world, purely social phenomena, such as ideas about gender, patriotism, or social roles, can possess what Jürgen Habermas has called 'unshakable facticity' (Habermas 1990:177) that often makes them seem to be ontologically of the same order as material phenomena. Berger and Luckmann noted in their definition that reality was 'a quality appertaining to phenomena that we recognize as having a being independent of our own volition (we cannot "wish them away")' (Berger and Luckmann 1966:1). Like Schutz commented above, many aspects of our reality seem to be common-sensical and we take them for granted. They are simply part of the world. Durkheim recognized this same point earlier when he commented that socio-cultural phenomena have what he called *chosité* or 'thingness,' an idea that asserted that these phenomena seem not evanescent but almost to have the same substantiveness as other 'things.' What is important to note here is that 'reality' includes such components as classificatory systems, basic ontological notions as to what exists in the world, ideas about what has effective influence on human life and/or matter, and how humans should conduct themselves in social life.

The third qualification to note is that while 'reality' is itself a social construction, the socio-cultural world often includes conflicting definitions of reality or other aspects of social life. The historical debate over whether the world was flat or round is an ideal example of this, but any other aspect of the cultural world, such as ideas about gender roles, moral responsibility, or the nature of causality, can also become points of contention. Berger and Luckmann note that conflicting ideas are often situated in different social locations and distinct groups or institutions advocating differing positions can become 'rival schools of thought' with each 'seeking to establish itself and to discredit if not liquidate the competitive body of knowledge' (Berger and Luckmann 1966:85ff.). The key to the successful acceptance of any reality definition, or to use Habermas' terms, the successful fusing of 'facticity and validity' (see Habermas 1998), is the establishment of its legitimacy. Legitimation is a processual phenomenon that involves the invocation of explanations to justify a particular order of things. Legitimacy is a 'contestable validity-claim' (Habermas 1979:178), and therefore subject to both challenge and discrediting. In order to achieve acceptability, assertions of legitimacy invoke specific forms of authority. This authority can be derived, for example, from tradition, what Weber called 'the oldest and most universal type of legitimacy' (Weber 1978:37), charisma, or from such modern sources as 'science' (see Habermas 1971), though other possibilities exist as well (see Habermas 1973). The legitimation process also usually involves institutional structures, such as a clergy or scientific community, that advocate and support particular reality definitions. Despite these different sources of legitimacy and the 'realities' that they justify, there usually exists one definitive or dominant construction of reality. Karl Marx and Frederick Engels referred to such a definition as the 'ruling ideas' (Marx and Engels 1970:64) and other ideas are usually measured against these.

The fourth qualification to note is that just as there can exist multiple and sometimes conflicting definitions of reality, so can different actors in the same social context have different understandings of what reality is. The existence of a dominant construction of reality, in effect, does not entail a complete correspondence between different actors' understandings of reality. One potential danger of a sociology of knowledge approach is that social agents become over-determined socially; which is to say that one can conclude from their structural position, along with its associated body of knowledge, what their understanding of reality is. For example, one might conclude that Communist Party members, with their years of political indoctrination, embrace an atheistic definition of reality. As a general tendency this is true, but in a place like Thinh Liet commune, there are party members who are ambivalent about this assertion or even reject it. A related problem works at a deeper level. While there does exist a social distribution of knowledge, and one can usually trace the different social loci that are advocating or propagating different bodies of knowledge, social actors often have knowledge of the different definitions of reality that exist in their social world. To return to Thinh Liet, both party members and non-party members have understandings of the atheistic reality definition propagated by the party and the theistic definition the party hoped to eliminate. Thus, at a subjective level, these different definitions coexist, yet actors give different weight or acceptance to the different definitions, and this relative weighting or acceptance can change over time. In such a situation, it is wise to accept Rodney Needham's admonition to not describe their attitudes toward reality as 'beliefs,' but instead recognize the potential ambivalence or uncertainty actors might have (see Needham 1972). In the analysis of Thinh Liet's cultural world, I attempt to point out the general trends in people's attitudes toward different aspects of reality, while also bringing out the variation and ambivalence that exists.

Disputes over legitimacy and the nature of reality lead to the final qualification that culture is fundamentally dynamic and subject to change over time. This point might seem trivial today, but it is important to mention in the Thinh Liet case not because it happened, but for the way it has happened and continues to happen. To a very important extent, cultural change in revolutionary Vietnam was the outcome of the naked exercise of power, defined here in the Weberian sense of the ability to force somebody else to accept one's will, by party officials. Cadres exerted tremendous pressure on people in order to force them to abandon unsanctioned practices and conduct their lives according to the new principles articulated by the party. Officials felt, however, that outright coercion would likely produce more resistance than acceptance of official views, thus persuasion became a critical part of official efforts to create the new culture. In social life, this produced a tremendous amount of argument and disputation about the true nature of reality, culture, ritual, and morality as cadres tried to convince others of their new truth. The deeper significance of this process was that the arguments and criticisms they involved mobilized their own sets of 'facts,' their own sets of true assertions about reality and how it works. Official efforts to produce what Ludwik Fleck has described as 'real fact' (Fleck 1979) involved two primary approaches. First, the party drew on the authority of science and, through the application of empirical methods, attempted to demonstrate to citizens the numerous negative consequences of unsanctioned cultural practices. Animal sacrifices did not cure illness, nor did they guarantee a good harvest, and these consequences could be empirically proven. Such 'scientific' facts were extremely important. Equally important were the 'historical' facts produced by the party. The reason for revolution was not simply because of the way Vietnam was, but because of the way it had been before. The revolutionary present had been preceded by a past that had featured numerous negative characteristics, many of them cultural. The party sought to define these negative characteristics and use them as a justification for change. The construction of these 'historical' facts also often drew on the authority of science and empirical methods in order to advance official claims. In doing so, the state hoped to reveal the detrimental character of certain practices, delegitimize them, and thereby convince the people to abandon them. These official assertions and their associated facts, however, did not constitute the totality of people's understandings of their culture and rituals. Local memories and under-standings of the practices sometimes contradicted these official versions, or acknowledged but simply ignored them, while highlighting other features. This dialectic of official and local understandings, of official and other facts, has played an important role in the evolving debates over what culture is and how to properly organize social life and ritual practice.

The formulation of culture presented here is critical to the analyses developed in this monograph because what I seek to do is not create a laundry list that describes what contemporary Vietnamese culture is, but instead to explore the multiple disputes and debates over culture, morality, and ritual that exist in one northern Vietnamese community. I also seek to examine the ideas associated with these debates, and the social actors advocating the different positions. As the ethnography presented here will show, the definition of what constitutes 'reality' in contemporary Thinh Liet is still very much open to debate, and different social groups and actors, such as men and women, young and old, and party members and non-party members, are frequently engaged in a public competition to delegitimize other definitions of reality and achieve the public acceptance of their own. What I therefore attempt to show is the divergent definitions of reality and the social actors putting them forth. One key dynamic that will become evident in the analyses are the differing notions of legitimacy that exist in Thinh Liet life. One of the main actors in this competition is the Vietnamese state and its agents, often though not universally Communist party members or veterans of the military, who frequently invoke a positivist approach to culture and who also argue that particular aspects of local cultural life, such as ideas about supernatural causality or the significant expenditure of resources involved in some ritual practices, hinder the development of a new and better society. For these actors, the defining axis of legitimacy rests on allegiance to the revolution and the creation of a progressive, advanced, and civilized society. Arrayed against these actors are a wide variety of others for whom allegiance to the state or revolution may or may not be problematic, but for whom other ties of legitimacy, such as moral responsibilities to one's family members or co-residents, are paramount. As will become clear, for many actors involved in this process, the ideas and values discussed and debated are not mere ideological window-dressing, but are instead powerful and important principles to guide their lives. Indeed, what I hope to demonstrate is how different social actors have different ideas of what is right or what is appropriate, and these ideas have an important influence on how people organize their rituals and conduct themselves in society.

Two points need to be made regarding the centrality of ritual to this study. My reason for focussing on ritual derives from reasons both empirical and theoretical. Beginning with the former, ritual practice was a critical locus for state action in revolutionary Vietnam. Revolutionary states have all treated ritual, as Christal Lane stated in reference to officially-sponsored rituals in the former Soviet Union, as 'a form of political socialization ... a way of inculcating the norms and values of the dominant ideology' (Lane 1981:19; see also Binns 1979; Binns 1980; Fauchois 1989). Just as the revolutionary French government celebrated the new cult of reason, liberty, and equality in innovative rituals practices, or the Chinese, Soviets, and other revolutionary socialist states created their own ritual corpus that celebrated socialism, internationalism, the working class, and an assortment of other values (see Binns 1979; Binns 1980; Evans 1998; Lane 1981), the Vietnamese also launched an ambitious campaign to create and define orthodox ritual practice in the revolutionary state. I have previously described this approach to ritual as 'state functionalism,' a phenomenon in which state officials employ ritual in order to advance official objectives and ideology (Malarney 1996b:540).[4] When Vietnamese officials developed their reformed ritual corpus, they always did so with an eye toward advancing certain official ideas and policies, many of which are described in later chapters. This

9

approach to ritual had an uncannily Durkheimian quality. Durkheim asserted that ritual produces a 'collective renovation' (Durkheim 1965:390) in which 'the common faith becomes reanimated quite naturally in the heart of this reconstituted group ... After it has been restored, it easily triumphs over all the private doubts which may have arisen in individual minds' (Durkheim 1965:387). The reformed ritual corpus developed by the Vietnamese Communists, and this is true of state functionalist rituals in general, were designed to serve this same purpose and create a unity of thought and values among the participants. As will become clear in later chapters, the state never successfully achieved the unity of opinion it desired, but many of the ideas put forth by the state still figure prominently in debates over ritual practice.

A second empirical reason for choosing ritual as a primary focus relates to its centrality in local debates about culture and morality. As I discovered, ritual is one of the most important contexts in which people contest and dispute the nature of public morality, individual responsibility, appropriate social practice, relations between humans and the supernatural, and even the existence of the supernatural. Disputes and disagreements about culture, morality, and tradition existed in a general or abstract way in local life, yet it was often in the context of rituals that these debates came out and became matters of public concern. Furthermore, people simply liked to talk about certain rituals. In doing so, their comments frequently revealed not only their own evaluations regarding proper ritual practice, but also their thoughts on a wider range of issues. Often their comments went beyond simple evaluation to withering critique. Given that people sometimes disagreed about how to conduct rituals, I do not attempt to provide extremely detailed descriptions of ritual sequences and para- phernalia as that would create the false appearance of a widely accepted orthodoxy, though I do describe the general structure of rituals as well as those points that people disputed. There were only two features that I felt characterized all rituals in Thinh Liet. The first was that ritual performance always involved moral action. Ritual always involved distinctions between right and wrong, proper and improper. People might dispute just what these are, but this moral dimension was always present. The second feature derived from the oft-quoted phrase, 'wealth gives birth to ritual form' (*phu quy sinh ra le nghia*). As Thinh Liet residents themselves explain, the idea behind this adage is that individuals should organize their rituals according to their means. Thus, the poor man who only presents a hard-boiled egg and a bowl of rice to the spirit of his deceased parent is as virtuous as the rich man who organizes a funeral with a thousand guests. This principle itself recognizes that people can perform the same ritual differently, but derive the same moral benefit.

These empirical points give rise to my theoretical approach to ritual. Victor Turner commented that people perform rituals in order to achieve particular goals or objectives. 'Each ritual,' he stated, 'has its own teleology. Its own explicitly expressed goals' (Turner 1967:32). Accompanying every ritual performance is a declared purpose or function, such as mollifying the ancestors, putting a soul to rest, or ensuring a plentiful harvest. Contra Durkheim, Turner also noted that 'each participant in the ritual views it from his own particular corner of observation' (Turner 1967:27), thus participants often had divergent attitudes toward, ideas about, or understandings of the ritual. The analyses presented in this study seek to extend the implications of Turner's thinking by bringing out the *multiple* teleologies present in Thinh Liet ritual practice. As will be shown, for different actors in Thinh Liet, the same ritual could be performed with very different goals in mind, such as celebrating socialism or putting a soul to rest, and for a single actor that same ritual can have multiple and perhaps conflicting goals, such as again celebrating socialism or putting a soul to rest. In the analyses presented here, I attempt to clarify not only the different social actors who participate in and sometimes control rituals, but also the diverse ideas that they bring to ritual and how these influence its performance. My approach therefore does not regard ritual as a de facto site for collective renovation, but instead as a potential site for disagreement and contestation.

The emphasis on ritual teleology links to another aspect of my approach to ritual, namely that ritual performances are a site for moral action and the expression of desire. Ritual is a form of purposive human action that is distinguished by its futurity. Rituals constitute a bridge between the present and the future, and the realization of a ritual's teleology involves the expression of a desired shape for both present and future. Rituals must be properly conducted in the present for them to attain their specified future goals, thus ritual action is moral action, but this goes beyond simple ritual propriety. Most ritual activity is social activity in that it at a minimum involves engagement with another entity, such as between a single performer and a spirit, but often in social practice ritual practice involves a much wider set of relationships. For example, the Thinh Liet rituals analyzed in this study involve a variety of actors, such as the living, the dead, the spirits, and the state. Visible in these categories are basic ontological assumptions, such whether spirits exist or not, but most importantly, also visible in the ritual process is a set of assertions or even imperatives about the proper constitution of relationships between the agents. To give another example, in a Thinh Liet funeral, the ritual process contains assertions regarding how humans should behave toward the dead, such as the rites they should perform, and also how they should behave toward each other, such as fulfilling exchange relations. This second moral dimension is extremely important because in it one can get broader glimpses of people's desires and expectations about what their society, and people's proper roles and actions within it, *should* be. Within the rituals, therefore, are definitions and conceptions of society as moral community. But given that rituals can have multiple teleologies and participants can have diverse perspectives on the rituals, the moral expectations and visions of moral community that a single ritual mobilizes can be diverse and even contradictory. This point will be explored further in the conclusion.

A final point should be made regarding the use of the term ideology in this study. Several Marxian-inspired anthropologists, such as Johnathan Friedman and Roger Keesing, have portrayed the entire realm of knowledge and ideas that constitute human culture as ultimately serving political purposes. Roger Keesing commented of human systems of meanings, 'They constitute *ideologies*, disguising human political and economic realities as cosmically ordained. Even in classless societies, cultural ideologies empower some, subordinate others, extract the labor of some for the benefit of those whose interests the ideologies serve and legitimate' (Keesing 1987:161). Although the idea is a seductive one, such a formulation is unsatisfactory because it confuses the empirical with the theoretical. Sherry Ortner summed up well the problems of this type of position when she noted in a critique of Structural Marxism that, 'the tendency to see culture/ideology largely in terms of mystification gave most of the cultural or ideological studies in this school a decidedly functionalist flavor, since the upshot of these analyses was to show how myth, ritual, taboo, or whatever maintained the status quo' (Ortner 1994:385). Louis Dumont had earlier developed a similar critique when he noted that ideology 'is not the *whole* of social reality,' and to assume that it is prevents the analyst from proving or disproving what is ideological and what is non-ideological (Dumont 1970:344). In order to avoid the problems raised by Keesing's approach, I will therefore use the term ideology in reference to ideas that can be directly traced to specific political actors or institutions, such as the 'egalitarian ideology' of the Communist Party, or the 'respect men, despise women' (*trong nam, khinh nu*) ideology of the mandarinate. This is not to deny that the consequences Keesing describes cannot derive from specific cultural ideas; this will in fact be shown at numerous points in the text. However, by clearly linking the concept of ideology to specific social agents, I hope to be able to clearly show who was advocating specific ideas and values.

The Setting

A visitor to Thinh Liet commune one hundred years ago would have found a community very different from the slowly urbanizing commune of today. French maps from the early 1900s depict the wide buffer of rice fields that formerly encircled the commune. The closest commune stood over a mile away. Communication between communes was difficult. Highway 1 was still a dirt track and residents relied as much on water to move between villages as on roads. Thinh Liet, straddling the *Set* river that runs from the north of Hanoi to the delta to the south, benefitted from water travel as traders moved up and down the river peddling fish, rice, baskets, and other wares. Thinh Liet was the most famous commune on the river, known locally as Set Village (*Lang Set*). It was particularly renowned for a breed of perch that thrived in its waters. The poet Ly Van Phuc (1785–1849) opined of Thinh Liet perch that 'no matter how long the water has dried to mud, I know that special taste will still be there' (Vu Tuan San 1989:8). Unfortunately, the Set today is a black and almost stagnant channel that serves to evacuate water from Hanoi's sewage treatment plants.

The founding of Thinh Liet commune has never been satisfactorily determined although local evidence indicates that it was already settled by the turn of the sixteenth century. Among the earliest documented residents was Bui Vinh (1498–1545), a high-ranking mandarin from the neighboring commune of Dinh Cong who settled in Thinh Liet late in life. Since its establishment, the nucleus of the commune has always been the three villages of Giap Nhat, Giap Nhi, and Giap Tu. Giap Nhi was the first settled village, where Vinh's lineage continues to live today. Over time, seven other villages were settled, each retaining the term *giap*, which implies a territorially based unit of association, followed by a Sino-Vietnamese number. At one point all eight villages existed independently. By the beginning of the eighteenth century, Thinh Liet was composed of only six villages (Vien Nghien Cuu Han Nom 1981:47). 'Third Giap' (*Giap Tam*), local legend says, was abandoned by its residents in the seventeenth century because of an epidemic and 'Fifth Giap' (*Giap Ngu*) had merged with 'Fourth Giap' (*Giap Tu*). 'Seventh Giap' (*Giap That*) later merged with 'Eighth Giap' (*Giap Bat*) in 1921. The latter two cases were the result of dwindling populations. 'Sixth Giap' (*Giap Luc*) and 'Eighth Giap' (*Giap Bat*) were part of Thinh Liet commune up through the colonial period, but both were absorbed into the 'City of Hanoi' (*Noi Thanh Thanh Pho Ha Noi*) after 1954.

Contemporary Thinh Liet commune (*Xa Thinh Liet*) consists of the three villages (*lang* in the vernacular, *thon* in administrative usage) of Giap Nhat, Giap Nhi, and Giap Tu. The distinction between 'commune' and 'village' is critical for understanding Thinh Liet's recent history. Several scholars have chosen to describe *xa* as 'village' and *lang* as 'hamlet' (cf. Popkin 1979). These terms are unsatisfactory for Thinh Liet because they impute a measure of socio-cultural significance to the commune that is absent in local life.[5] Beyond the commune's borders people do identify themselves as hailing from a specific *xa*, but the most important unit of affiliation and identity is the *lang*. This significance is reproduced in several different ways. Each *lang*, for example, has its own communal house (*dinh*) that houses the altar of the village guardian spirit. This structure serves as the primary focus for local collective ritual life with a detailed set of

13

bi-weekly, monthly, and annual rituals. Allegiance to the communal house is strong as residents of one *lang* will often not perform rites in other communal houses. The *xa* has no corresponding sacred structure, nor does it have a schedule of regular rituals. The *lang* has also historically been the critical unit for contracting marriages, as shown in the preference for village endogamy. Marriage within the *xa* was acceptable, and certainly not as problematic as marrying out of the *xa*, but the most sought after marriage was with someone from the same *lang*. Each *lang* also had its own distinctive characteristics in its ritual practices, such as the time of its feasts or the ceremonial order, that distinguished it from surrounding *lang*. Some Thinh Liet residents claim that residents of different villages speak with slightly different accents, a claim I found hard to confirm. Finally, local moral discourse is constructed with reference to the *lang* and its value system. Families speak of the *tinh lang* or 'spirit of the village,' a constellation of values that emphasizes equality, solidarity, reciprocity, and affective relations between residents. Others evaluate a person's relative moral worth according to their ability to live up to this code. Significantly, there is no such system for the *xa*. Within Thinh Liet, it is therefore important not to over-emphasize the socio-cultural significance of the commune.

Today the three villages Giap Nhat, Giap Nhi, and Giap Tu occupy approximately 294 hectares of land. 40 hectares are devoted to housing, 9 hectares are consumed by the Set river watercourse, 35 hectares are occupied by an assortment of government buildings, factories, and the 10 hectare Giap Bat rail yard. A total of 203 hectares are used for agriculture and aquaculture. According to figures collected by the local administration in 1992, Thinh Liet had a population of approximately 9,275 people living in 2,259 households (*ho*), although recent estimates by officials place that number over 10,000.[6] Figures given by the officials tended to vary, but unlike the marked predominance of women over men that has characterized much of Vietnam since the end of the American War in Vietnam, Thinh Liet's population appeared split into relatively equal groupings of women and men, with slightly more of the former. Similar to the rest of Vietnam, Thinh Liet's population is dominated by young people with over 40 percent of its population aged eighteen or younger. Less than 10 percent of its population is 60 years or older.

Economically, Thinh Liet is remarkably diversified. Agriculture is still the commune's mainstay, but residents engage in a wide-range of occupations such as factory work, handicrafts, aquaculture, gardening, petty trading, office work, government work, and entrepreneurial activities. During the cooperative years (1959 – 1990), approximately two-thirds of the residents worked as agriculturalists. Following the dissolution of the cooperatives in the early 1990s, the number of agriculturalists has declined to approximately one-third of the population. Of the three villages, Giap

14

Tu has the highest concentration of farmers, Giap Nhat the highest concentration of government and office workers, and Giap Nhi the highest concentration of factory workers and entrepreneurs. Similar to other communities near Hanoi, Thinh Liet's economy has improved significantly since the late 1980s, a trend evident in greater numbers of televisions, motorcycles, new homes, renovated sacred architecture, and larger and more expensive ritual practices. Increased incomes have not been distributed evenly throughout the commune. Giap Nhi residents, particularly those who have taken up entrepreneurial pursuits, have done comparatively better, but large numbers of very poor families remain in all villages. The latter is especially true of families confined to agriculture, petty trading, and handicraft production. Rich and poor alike, however, frequently engage in two or more pursuits simultaneously in order to make ends meet.

Giap Nhi is the commune's dominant village. It alone possesses 111 of the commune's 203 hectares of productive land to Giap Nhat's fifteen hectares and Giap Tu's 75 hectares. Giap Nhi's population also exceeds 6000 people, while Giap Tu has some 2000 residents and Giap Nhat just over 1000. Giap Nhi's dominance is evident in other fashions. Since 1954, when revolutionary authorities installed Thinh Liet's 'Communal People's Committee' (*Uy Ban Nhan Dan Xa*), the party-dominated structure responsible for administering the commune, the administrative seat has been located in Giap Nhi, as are the commune's 'Communal People's Council' (*Hoi Dong Nhan Dan Xa*), an elected assembly of 30 to 40 members that has a limited role in running the commune, and the commune's original Monument to the Revolutionary Martyrs (*Dai Liet Si*).[7] Every person who has served as President of the People's Committee has hailed from Giap Nhi, as have all but one of the Secretaries of the commune's Communist Party cell. Economically, Giap Nhi has always been the wealthiest and had the most diversified economy. During the colonial period, both Giap Nhat and Giap Tu relied on agriculture and handicraft production as the mainstays of their economies while Giap Nhi engaged in both and complemented them with trading, small-scale manufacturing, and even an illegal casino.

The greatest measure of Giap Nhi's dominance is the fact that it is regarded as the commune's most culturally and politically sophisticated village, a status that stretches back many centuries. An examination of the *Tu Dien Nhan Vat Lich Su Viet Nam* (Nguyen Q. Thang and Nguyen Ba The 1991), a Who's Who of Vietnamese history drawn from a multitude of contemporary and historical sources, lists fourteen Giap Nhi residents and none from the other two villages. Among these were poets, military leaders, and ministers. Two of the village's most famous native sons were Bui Xuong Trach (1451–1529), a man who began his life working in the ricefields, but at the age of 27 passed the mandarinate's doctoral

15

examination and began a distinguished career as diplomat and minister for the Le dynasty, and Bui Huy Bich, probably the most famous village native, who during the late eighteenth and early nineteenth century was a dominant figure at the Vietnamese court as well as a famous historian.

Giap Nhi's political and cultural ascendence carried into the colonial and revolutionary eras as well. The Bui lineage had at least one member who served as a minister in the Nguyen court. A number of other residents passed the doctoral examinations during the early years of French rule and held high positions in the administration. One man served as the financial commissioner of Hanoi. During the revolutionary era, a number of Thinh Liet residents distinguished themselves by their activities for the nation and revolution. One Giap Nhi native served as the editor of a major Hanoi daily, another served in the National Assembly, and still another met Jane Fonda on her famous visit to Hanoi. He later served as a member of the North Vietnamese delegation to the Paris Peace Talks in 1972–73. Giap Nhi also has the largest number of retired military officers, including the commune's only former general. Since the relaxation of cultural policies began in the mid-1980s, the residents of Giap Nhi have led the campaign to resurrect and reconstruct previously banned ritual practices. Villagers from Giap Nhat and Giap Tu begrudgingly acknowledge that despite the inter-village rivalries and local variations in ritual practices, Giap Nhi sets the cultural standard.

On a final point, it is important to note that at the level of everyday social life, regardless of whatever official, party, or village affiliations one might have, the most fundamental social affiliation an individual has is their 'family' (gia dinh) membership. Every individual in Thinh Liet is irrevocably part of a family, and their actions and worth are evaluated with reference to it. A family's character transcends its individual members and persists through time. Both virtues, such as talent, honesty, and industriousness, and liabilities, such as laziness, promiscuity and especially insanity, continue inexorably down through every new generation. Thinh Liet has its respected families, usually referred to as 'orderly' (co ne nep) or 'cultured' (co van hoa), because of their internal harmony, fairness, and conscientiousness toward others, as well as its marginalized families that contain confrontational, promiscuous, or insane members. A family's reputation is always contingent and can more easily be damaged by perceived inappropriate behavior by its women than by its men. Whenever misfortune strikes, local residents are often quick to attribute it to the family's character. As will be discussed later, the family is also the primary unit for exchange relations.

In social life the boundaries of the 'family' (gia dinh) can blur generationally and consist of either a nuclear or an extended family.[8] The term's semantic flexibility is evident in the fact that one's 'family' can be simply one's spouse and children, or it can also include those individuals along with parents or grandparents. Beyond kinship, the shared activities that tend to define family membership in Thinh Liet are co-residence in the same home, the joint consumption of meals by members of different generations (*an chung*), and most importantly, joint participation in ancestral rites. Kinship in Vietnam is reckoned patrilineally and brides usually settle virilocally after marriage. The common Thinh Liet pattern is for several agnatically related families to live in the same compound. Newlyweds usually live in the groom's father's home immediately after marriage, but after some time build an independent house in the family compound where they will take their own meals. The eldest son almost universally remains in the father's house and inherits it on his father's death. One of the eldest son's most important responsibilities is serving as the head of the family ancestral cult. Almost every household in the Vietnamese countryside has an altar dedicated to the deceased parents and ancestors of the household. On important days, such as on the ancestors' death anniversaries (*ngay gio*), family members congregate to propitiate the souls of the deceased and share a meal. As will be discussed in later chapters, these rites are a critical obligation of all residents. Another arena of salient ritual obligation is the patrilineage. Thinh Liet commune has several dozen patrilineages (*ho* in the vernacular; *toc* in Sino-Vietnamese) that, by definition, are exogamous. A child inherits its surname and patrilineage membership from the father (Unlike some parts of China, there is no requirement for surname exogamy). Historically, lineages played an important political role in village life, though they were never as strong as lineages in neighboring regions of southern China (Moise 1986:147). Lineages also had an active ritual life involving many members, conducted in lineage halls (*nha tho ho*), and led by the lineage head (*truong ho*), a position inherited by primogenitural succession from the apical ancestor. The political role of lineages was limited from the 1950s through early 1990s, but in recent years Thinh Liet lineages appear to be regaining political strength (see Malarney 1997).

Like most Vietnamese, Thinh Liet residents are fond of claiming that kin relations constitute a realm of warmth and affect in which people are united and can always rely on each other for help and assistance. As they say, 'a drop of blood is deeper than a pond of water' (*mot giot mau dao hon ao nuoc la*), thus they are always ready to selflessly assist their kin. In reality, people are far more ambivalent. From one perspective, this can be seen in a variety of adages, such as 'sell your distant brothers and sisters, buy close neighbors' (*ban anh em xa, mua lang gieng gan*), or perhaps the most biting assessment of family life, 'A family is like an outhouse. Those on the outside want to come in, those on the inside want to get out' (*Gia dinh la nhu mot chuong xi. Nguoi o ngoai muon di vao, nguoi o trong muon di ra*). People recognize that kin relations can become burdensome. Some kin meddle in other's personal affairs. Others borrow money, which one cannot

17

refuse, and never pay it back. Others shirk their responsibilities. And some seniors boss around their juniors. In short, conflicts break out and appear to always have broken out, a point evident in events as diverse as the August 1904 beating of a woman from one branch of a Giap Nhi Bui lineage by men of another branch after a perceived insult at a lineage death anniversary rite (Ha Dong #1704) and the repeated refusal in 1991 to allow me to watch lineage rites of another Giap Nhi lineage because, as I was informally told later, arguments kept breaking out at the gatherings that members did not want me to see. Despite these and other conflicts that occur, both family and lineage membership are important criteria for social identity in Thinh Liet life.

Chapter Summary

The chapters in this book divide into two main parts. Part One focuses on the implementation of revolutionary policies in Thinh Liet. Chapter 1 examines the conduct and consequences of the land reform in the commune. Its first section explores the new theory of society introduced by land reform cadres, its acceptance and rejection, and the methods employed for the delegitimation of Thinh Liet's former elite. The second section examines the revolutionary agenda to resignify space in the commune. It discusses the manner in which the state's assertion of control over land allowed it to desacralize the local landscape, remove the material infrastructure that had formerly supported unsanctioned ritual practices and social groups, and then further limit the emergence of other unsanctioned activities with the establishment of the agricultural cooperatives. Chapter 2 provides a detailed discussion of the revolutionary agenda to reclassify society, culture, morality, and ritual practice. It analyzes the contents of this agenda, while also examining the mechanisms used to implement it and some of its consequences in contemporary life.

Part Two focuses on the consequences of the reform campaign as seen from the perspective of contemporary Thinh Liet ritual practices. Each of the five chapters in this section is organized around a single set of ritual practices, their history, and the ideas and debates that inform their contemporary organization. Chapter 3 examines debates over whether supernatural causality exists in human life. Official propaganda attempted for several decades to rid the Vietnamese of any such notions, but many still exist in Thinh Liet life. This chapter attempts to locate socially both the opponents and advocates of these positions, as well as the different contexts in which residents invoke supernatural explanations. Chapter 4 discusses the reform of funerary ceremonies. The party hoped to simplify funerals and make them vehicles for official ideology. As the analysis shows, people vigorously objected to certain aspects of the reforms that prevented them from properly fulfilling their moral obligations to their deceased kin and co-villagers. They did, however, accept reforms that made funerary ceremonies more egalitarian. Chapter 5 examines weddings and marriage. Reforms of both of these institutions had been designed to loosen parental control over children, create equality between husbands and wives, and reduce the amount of status competition that occurred in wedding ceremonies. This chapter discusses how these reforms have led to debates over who and how to marry, what constitutes an appropriate wedding, and whether recent changes in weddings ceremonies are positive or negative. Chapters 6 and 7 examine recent Thinh Liet ritual innovations. Chapter 6 looks at Thinh Liet's experience of war and the emergence of an innovative funeral rite created by the Vietnamese state to honor and glorify war dead. Although Thinh Liet residents value these rites, they were ultimately regarded as insufficient because they could not deal with the most fundamental concern of funerary rites, putting the soul of the deceased at rest. Residents therefore created their own new ceremony to achieve this end, but as will be shown, official and local rites mobilize very different ontologies of war dead. Chapter 7 examines the resurgence of communal house rituals in Thinh Liet. While men exclusively controlled these rites in the past, resurgent rites have witnessed the emergence of important roles for women in them. The analysis looks at how women have created places for themselves in communal house rites, as well as how men and women continue to negotiate their role. This latter issue is examined in detail through an analysis of a case from Giap Tu in which male villagers attempted to install the spirit of Ho Chi Minh as the village guardian spirit. Finally, in conclusion, I will comparatively examine the successes and failures of the reform campaign in order to determine what they say about the role of culture and ritual in Thinh Liet residents' lives.

Revolution Comes to Thinh Liet

■ CHAPTER ONE ■

The Land Reform

Redefining Society and Space

The Vietnamese revolution officially began with the August Revolution of 19 August 1945 when the Vietnamese Communists and their supporters overthrew the Japanese administration that then ruled Indochina. Over the next year they began the revolutionary transformation of northern Vietnamese society through such measures as the installation of new party-controlled 'Resistance Administration Committees' (*Uy Ban Hanh Chinh Khang Chien*) to administer the countryside and the initial propagation of revolutionary cultural policies. Although significant, these early efforts were tempered first by the necessity of working with other political groups opposed to the French, and then by the French reconquest of large areas of northern Vietnam in late 1946 and early 1947. During the following eight year war, the Communist-led resistance, known as the Viet Minh, continued to implement revolutionary policies, though primarily in areas under its control. Areas under French control, such as Thinh Liet commune, saw these efforts basically stop, except in a disorganized, behind-the-scenes fashion.

Thinh Liet came under revolutionary control again in late 1954, but the decisive event that marked the beginning of its revolutionary transformation was the commencement of its land reform (*Cai Cach Ruong Dat*) in December 1955. This chapter's purpose is to examine the conduct and consequences of Thinh Liet's land reform. Similar to the experiences of countless other northern Vietnamese communities, the land reform was a turbulent period in the commune as land reform cadres overturned the former elite, broke up land holdings, and redistributed land and property in a more equitable fashion. These events were important and will be discussed. Equally important was the land reform's ideological dimension. In carrying out their campaign, the cadres propagated a new theory of society that included new definitions and evaluations of people in the community, as well as new readings of the past and how they arrived at their present. They did the same with local ideas associated with space as

23

they assumed control over all space, advanced new definitions of it, and then employed these to carry out their policies. As will be shown, the land reform, beyond simply redistributing land and disrupting previous structures of exploitation, introduced into Thinh Liet life a new way of thinking and talking about their society and the spaces around them; however, these ideas still had to cope with those that existed before the revolution.

Part 1: Recasting Local Society

The Land Reform Comes to Thinh Liet

The first land reform cadres arrived in Thinh Liet, or Unity Commune (*Xa Doan Ket*) as the revolutionary authorities had renamed it the year before, in late December. The Thinh Liet land reform, like that of the rest of Hanoi's outskirts, belonged to Wave 5 of the campaign. Wave 1 had begun a year and half earlier in Thai Nguyen, Thanh Hoa, and other areas under Viet Minh control. Over the succeeding months, the campaign had slowly worked its way toward the capital and other areas that had been under French control. The campaign's diverse objectives were evident in the legislation that had been passed to formalize the land reform. In April 1953 the government had passed Decree 149-SL that stated that the policy's goal was to 'foster the mental and material strength of the peasantry, increase production, and intensify the resistance war' (Vietnam, Government Gazette 1953:47) through such methods as a rent reduction and the redistribution of commual or abandoned land to the needy. A significant change appeared on 4 December 1953 when the National Assembly passed the Land Reform Law (*Luat Cai Cach Ruong Dat*) that declared that one of its primary goals was the 'elimination of the feudal landholding system of the landlord class' (Section 1:1). The law detailed how to deal with landlords and the assorted enemies of the people and revolution. Land reform was no longer a policy only designed to create an equitable distribution of land in the countryside. It had become a direct assault on the former elite and the system that had supported them.

The Thinh Liet land reform began in a general climate of fear and anxiety. The land reform's previous waves had been marked by numerous excesses, or 'deviations,' and news of these had been filtering back to the Hanoi area. Land reform cadres had exhibited extreme overzealousness that had resulted in bogus denunciations, errant classifications, and unwarranted executions. The main cause of the deviations was the highly-charged environment in which land reform was carried out. The land reform cadre's primary function was to elucidate the class struggle and the wickedness of the exploiting classes for the unknowing masses. Cadres

24

were quick to indict individuals as landlords or enemies of the revolution, even if they lacked sufficient evidence. As Edwin Moise noted, 'It was considered a great "achievement" to expose as a reactionary plotter or a landlord someone who had not previously seemed to be one' (Moise 1983:232). For many cadres the land reform campaign also carried the spirit of a paranoid scientific exercise. Every village was to have certain fixed percentiles of the different social classes and the job of the cadre was to smoke out the cagier members until the necessary percentiles were reached (see Moise 1983:216). On both of these points, the cadres' exuberance was assisted by local political machinations as old scores were settled, political opponents eliminated, and those associated with the former elite ostracized, humiliated, and in some cases executed. Working at a different level was the general atmosphere of terror and suspicion the campaign created. Both the cadres' conduct and the participation of the villagers required extreme zeal as the unenthusiastic risked being accused of 'lacking revolutionary spirit' (*thieu tinh than cach mang*). Such charges, although possibly groundless, could result in grave consequences for the accused as once such an accusation was made, one was generally powerless in refuting it. Trapped in this climate of excess reinforcing excess, villagers who lived through the period coined the adage, 'First the cadres, second the heavens' (*Nhat doi, nhi troi*).

Several other factors complicated the Thinh Liet land reform. During the French war, the loss of members killed in battle or by French security forces had severely weakened the party apparatus around Hanoi. The local party structure needed significant strengthening if it was to successfully meet its objectives. Another problem was the economic structure of Hanoi's outskirts (*Ngoai Thanh Ha Noi*). Waves 1 through 4 had taken place in predominantly agricultural areas. The regions around Hanoi maintained an agricultural base, but a large number of surrounding communities, like Thinh Liet, were extensively involved in other economic activities, such as fishing, handicraft production, and a host of other pursuits ranging from growing flowers to producing rice cakes. Many individuals from neighboring villages also worked in Hanoi as traders, clerks, laborers, or factory workers. This economic diversity complicated the land reform agenda because many who lived outside of the city did not fit exactly into the land reform's classificatory scheme. Others presented a different problem in that they controlled resources or businesses that officials did not want to disrupt for fear it would either create panic in the city or retard the development of North Vietnam's economy. In order to develop the north's industrial base, the party wanted to preserve the integrity of the integrated city-country economy. The cities were to provide the nucleus for future industrial expansion and the role of the outskirts was to 'produce directly to meet the needs of the city' (Hanoi, Land Reform Committee 1956:32). The committee needed to ensure that this relationship

25

remained intact and therefore implemented a set of regulations designed to moderate the land reform in Hanoi's outskirts.[1]

When the cadres from Nghe An and Thanh Hoa settled into the spacious, two story brick house that a colonial-era canton chief donated for use as the commune's People's Committee, one of first tasks before them was the propagation in Thinh Liet society of an entirely new theory of local society. Appropriating Marxist-Leninist theory, the Communists asserted the dominant characteristic of rural society was class conflict manifest in relations of oppression and exploitation imposed by the elite on the poor and dispossessed. Previous conceptualizations of society in Thinh Liet had divided the community into such groups as the mandarins (*quan vien*) and commoners (*bach dinh*), or poor families (*nha ngheo*), wealthy families (*nha giau*), Confucian families (*nha Nho*), trading families (*nha buon*) and others. The Communists installed a new system of classification derived from political and economic considerations. The most stigmatized group in the new system were the landlords (*dia chu*). One set of regulations from 1957 concisely described the essential characteristics of the landlords when it stated, 'landlords are people who own large amounts of land and do not personally engage in labor, either of the primary or secondary variety. The main source of their livelihood derives from the exploitation of peasants through either land rentals or wage labor. There are landlords who concurrently lend money for a profit, or have industrial or commercial concerns, but the primary and most common form of exploitation of the landlords is renting out land' (Vietnam, Prime Minister's Office 1957:4). Another Vietnamese scholar commented, 'Landlords generally do not engage in labor but instead live and get rich by exploiting peasants through land rents, loans, and wage labor' (Tran Phuong 1967:36). Party ideology asserted that the landlord class maintained itself through a system of 'feudal' relations that were predicated upon their control over land and their ability to collect land rentals. Landlords, in official characterizations, were non-productive citizens who lived off the sweat and toil of others.

The landlords were the main antagonist in the land reform. Official propaganda during the campaign dwelled on the evils of the landlord class, and both the print and spoken media dazzled the population with tales of rape, cruelty, murder and aggression committed by the landlords against the peasantry. For example, one official source, *The Victory of the Land Reform in the Outskirts of Hanoi* (*Thang Loi Cai Cach Ruong Dat O Ngoai Thanh Ha Noi*) noted that in the period stretching back to the Japanese occupation of Vietnam in the early 1940s, the thirty four landlords in Co Nhue commune had killed sixty seven people (including thirty two soldiers and guerrillas), assisted in the capture by Japanese and French authorities of sixty one people, beaten twenty two people to the point of crippling, beaten another 189 less severely, burned three houses, made ten people disappear, and raped eight women. And this did not include their economically exploitive activities, the conspiracies they hatched to kill cadres or hinder the land reform, or their convincing of large numbers of people to migrate to South Vietnam (Hanoi, Land Reform Committee 1956:76). Moise accurately summarized the party's attitude in his quotation of an editorial in the Party daily *Nhan Dan*, 'The more we study, the more clearly we see that all the disagreements and divisions in the rural areas are caused by the landlords' (Moise 1983:198).

Despite the aggressive policies and rhetoric against the landlords, the party also showed a certain ambivalence toward them. This tendency was most visible in the different types of landlord classifications. The worst type of landlord was the 'cruel and despotic landlord' (*dia chu cuong hao gian ac*). Individuals in this category had reputedly committed murder, rape, or actively opposed the people or revolutionary policies. Such people were often said to have a 'blood debt' (*no mau*) with the people. Below them were the 'regular landlords' (*dia chu thuong*), who received their classification as a result of meeting the criteria listed above. Slightly below them were the 'administrative landlords' (*dia chu quan ly*), people who did not necessarily own large amounts of land, but who served as a landlord's agent in administering his or her lands. Finally, in the most acceptable category, were the 'resistance landlords' (*dia chu khang chien*). The existence of this category illustrated the types of compromises the party was willing to make at the local level. Resistance landlords had the same characteristics as the regular landlords, but in the period since the August Revolution, they or their children had supported the revolution by either serving in the military, as cadres, or by giving assistance and shelter to cadres and guerrillas. Regular landlords who were active in the revolution, but whose children were not, could receive the 'democratic personalities' (*nhan si dan chu*) classification if they had long abandoned all 'feudal exploitive relations,' or the 'patriotic personalities' (*than si yeu nuoc*) classification if they had not completely abandoned such relations but were still vigorous in their support of the revolution. People with these latter three types of classifications received much better treatment than the other landlords, a compromise that helped prevent the complete alienation of those who supported the revolution but had questionable class backgrounds.

The rest of the party's class system broke down into four main categories. Just below the landlords came the 'rich peasants' (*phu nong*). Like landlord families, rich peasants often rented out land and hired wage laborers, but what differentiated them from the landlords was that rich peasants participated directly in production. In practice, differentiating between the two classes could be difficult. Cadres therefore employed a formula in which, in principle, a family needed to rent out a multiple of the amount of land they worked (either two or three times, depending on the circumstance) in order to receive a landlord classification. The next group

27

was the 'middle peasants' (*trung nong*). The members of this group engaged directly in production, often owned modest amounts of land, and sometimes supplemented those lands with rentals. The final two categories were the 'poor peasants' (*ban nong*) and the 'laborers' (*co nong*). These families represented the poorest segments of Vietnamese society who depended upon sporadically-available and poorly-paid wage labor. The latter group owned no land except that on which their houses stood. Thinh Liet residents recall that the members of these groups were so poor that they were usually unable to secure land rentals because they lacked sufficient collateral. But unlike the stigmatized landlords, it was the people in these latter two categories that the revolution valorized most highly. In carrying out the land reform, the government instructed cadres to 'Rely completely on poor peasants and laborers, unite with the middle peasants, make allies of the rich peasants, and definitively overturn the landlords, traitors, reactionaries, and cruel despots' (*Dua han vao ban co nong, doan ket chat che voi trung nong, lien hiep phu nong, danh do dia chu Viet gian phan dong va cuong hao gian ac*) (Tran Phuong 1967:115). The land reform sought to overturn rural social structure by placing the former paramounts at the bottom of the new order and the formerly dispossessed on the top.

Party ideology asserted that one main goal of the land reform was the elimination of exploitation, but at a deeper level the campaign also carried with it a rejection of the elite stigmatization of manual labor that had characterized the pre-revolutionary period. In overturning the social order, the party deliberately championed manual labor as a glorious and honorable activity, while simultaneously ridiculing those who avoided labor. The glorification of labor linked to its role in creating the new Vietnam. Following the Leninist creed that the development of heavy industry was essential for the creation of a fully socialist society, the party exhorted Vietnamese in all manual occupations, such as agriculture, light, and heavy industry, to selflessly devote themselves to production to achieve this goal. Labor became a patriotic duty, and those who worked hard could even receive such high government praise as a 'Hero of Labor' (*anh hung lao dong*) award. Unsanctioned labor, such as the stigmatized 'small peasant production,' remained vilified, but to work for the benefit of the nation was a marker of respect and dignity. The overturning of the stigma of labor illustrates the subtle understandings that officials had regarding the nature of inequality in rural Vietnam.

Overturning Thinh Liet's Landlord Class

After a brief stay at the People's Committee, the land reform cadres began the Thinh Liet campaign by moving into the homes of the poorest local villagers to practice the 'Three Togethers' (*ba cung*) of the land reform, 'Eat together, live together, work together' with the peasantry. The cadres stayed in the poorest homes for three reasons. First, the cadres needed to determine the structures of exploitation and the party felt that the former elite would undoubtedly attempt to manipulate events in their favor (the elimination of this bias was also the reason why non-resident cadres conducted the land reform across Vietnam). Second, the cadres needed to begin 'mass mobilization' (*phat dong quan chung*). In carrying out the land reform, cadres needed to demonstrate to the people the rectitude of their social vision, as well as their diagnosis of Vietnam's social ills, and then spur the masses to action. Moise describes this phase well when he comments,

> A cadre would go into a poor peasant's or laborer's home to live together, eat together, and work together with the peasant. By sharing the peasants' poverty and asking about their sufferings (*tham ngheo hoi kho*), the cadres would try to win their trust and convince them that the landlords, not fate, had caused their sufferings, and that it was both necessary and possible to attack the landlords in order to win a decent life.
>
> (Moise 1983:174)

Finally, the cadres needed to recruit a network of local residents who, themselves trained and 'mobilized,' would become 'backbone elements' (*cot can*). These individuals would then help the cadres mobilize other residents to conclude the reform.

Despite extensive mobilization in the commune, the cadres encountered a population whose attitudes did not immediately match their vision of local society. Like other cadres working in the outskirts of Hanoi, they were frustrated by their inability to convince local farmers of the landlords' true character. One official source declared with exasperation, 'In other places where the rent reduction has been carried out the peasants know what a landlord is, but here (in the outskirts of Hanoi) the masses still call them wealthy families (*nha giau*)' (Hanoi, Land Reform Committee 1956:9). In Thinh Liet and other communes in the outskirts, residents were slow to equate what they considered to be respectable wealthy families with the exploiters of party ideology. Cadres were also frustrated by the reluctance of some farmers to accept the exploitive nature of land rents. The party land reform historian Tran Phuong illustrated this shortcoming when discussing the share-cropping land rental arrangement, called *cay re* (which was also the most common rental arrangement in Thinh Liet (see Malarney 1993:235)). He noted,

> The distinctive feature of *cay re* is that the greater the harvest, then the greater the ability of the landlord to exploit the peasant. When he rents out his land, the landlord says, "You put in the work, and you put in the capital. You get bowls of rice and I get grains of

29

paddy. It works out well for both of us." When peasants have yet to
have their consciousness raised, there are yet some who mistakenly
believe that the benefits for the peasant and the benefits for the
landlord are the same.

(Tran Phuong 1967:38)

Many villagers in revolutionary Thinh Liet subscribed to this view. They
did not conceive of the land owner-renter relationship as necessarily
exploitive given the widespread use of the *cay re* rental agreement. Even
under the worst conditions, many renters felt, there would still be
something left over for the farmer. Indeed, in terms of exploitation, that
which local farmers found most exploitive was the former regime of French
taxes. Despite some tensions that still lingered between the commoners
and the former elite, people recognized that exploitation existed, yet it did
not necessarily conform to the dimensions articulated by the cadres.

According to regulations implemented by the land reform cadres in
Thinh Liet, an individual's family technically had to exist entirely on the
rented labor of others or have land holdings that on a per capita basis
exceeded three times the village landholding average to be classified as a
landlord. Cadres determined the classifications in Thinh Liet by first
mobilizing the backbone elements and others, and then arranged meetings
with the members of each village neighborhood (*xom*) to discuss and make
the determinations. The actual designation of landlords in Thinh Liet
revealed that other factors were also involved. In the villages of Giap Nhi
and Giap Tu, the cadres identified a total of nineteen landlords – fifteen in
the former village, four in the latter. Among the nineteen, eight men and
two women were regular landlords; three men from Giap Nhi and one
from Giap Tu were 'cruel and despotic' landlords; three men were
'administrative' landlords; and two men, again from Giap Nhi, were
'resistance' landlords. The Giap Tu 'cruel and despotic' landlord was also
classified as having a 'blood debt' with the people (see Figure 1.1).[2] Two
features are immediately evident in the classifications. First, large land
holdings or existing on income from land rentals did produce landlord
classifications, as shown in the case of the two Giap Nhi women and several
of the regular landlords. This exploitation factor was also the likely
motivation behind the three administrative landlords, although given the
recipients' general poverty, those classifications are puzzling. Second, the
political character of the process is also evident in many of the
classifications. Out of the sixteen men given landlord classifications, ten
had held or sought to hold positions in the former administration. Two had
served as mandarins at the level of district chief and above; two had served
as canton chief; two had been village chiefs (one of the canton chiefs had
also held this position but is not counted here); two were former members
of the Giap Nhi Mandarin Association, a group composed exclusively of

Figure 1.1: Giap Nhi and Giap Tu Landlord Classifications[3]

	Name	Landholding (Hectares)	Former Position
Giap Nhi			
Regular	Muop (F)	0.18	
	Do (F) ~	1	
	Uy (M)	3+	Village Administration, Mandarin Association, richest man in village (from inheritance and business interests)
	Cong (M) ~	1+	Village Administration, Farmer, Land Manager
	Trac (M)*	21.6	Province chief
	Tri (M)	1+	School teacher, Village chief candidate in early 1950s
	Huong (M) ~	2	Village Administration
Resistance	Quynh (M)	little	Canton chief, Mandarin Association
	Binh (M)	little	Managed aunt's land
Cruel and Despotic	Hoe (M)	0.29	Village chief, worked for French
	Tho (M)#	little	Village chief
	Thanh (M) ~	1+	Unclear
Administrative	Nga (M)	little	Land manager, rickshaw driver
	Kien (M)	none	Farmer
	Xanh (M)	none	Land manager
Patriotic Personality	Tuong (M)	8+	Province chief
Giap Tu			
Regular	Nghiep (M)*	10.8	District chief
	Bo (M) ~	little	Canton chief, father of Duyen
	Ai (M)# ~	little	Successful Farmer (Denounced by children)
Cruel and Despotic	Duc (M)^	little	Lieutenant in colonial army (Had 'blood debt,' also a 'reactionary.')

* Classification given in absentia after landlord had moved away.
^ Executed.
# Committed suicide.
~ Received reclassification.

men who had held administrative posts at the village level or higher;[4] two had served in village administration in lesser capacities; and one had been a candidate for village chief in the early 1950s. Giap Nhi's 'patriotic personality' was Bui Phat Tuong, a former province chief and large landowner in Thinh Liet. He was also extremely active in the revolution, a point that earned him a better classification, and later became a member of the National Assembly. The numbers of landlords would undoubtedly have been much greater if many members of the former elite had not sold off their land and left Thinh Liet for Hanoi or South Vietnam in the early 1950s. One can see from the classifications that land ownership was related to the ability to obtain village office, though it is important to note the men listed here as holding little land, but who still attained an office were either well educated or from wealthy families. The dynamics of exploitation aside, one can conclude from the classifications that three men received landlord classifications for overtly political reasons.[5] One man from Giap Nhi, who owned virtually no land, was given the landlord classification for having served as both canton and village chief in the colonial period. Classified as a resistance landlord, his house served as the Thinh Liet People's Committee until 1991. Another from Giap Nhi, who owned perhaps a quarter hectare of land, was given the classification for formerly serving as village chief and also for his reputation of cruelty toward the peasantry. And one man from Giap Tu, also landless except for his home, was classified as such for having served as canton chief and also for the fact that his son, as will be discussed below, politically ran afoul of the cadres during the campaign. Finally, the presence of two resistance landlords and one patriotic personality illustrate that in Thinh Liet, some prominent members of the local elite were committed to the revolution (see Luong 1992). These classifications help to illustrate that different members of the elite maintained diverse relations with the masses, and also helps to explain the reluctance of some residents to accept outright the landlords' allegedly exploitive character.

After the determination of classifications, the richest man of Giap Nhi, the largest landowners of Giap Nhi and Giap Tu, the highest ranking mandarins in the commune, and the largest absentee landlords and their representatives, had all become landlords or patriotic personalities. The next step in the process of 'overturning' the former elite stratum of Thinh Liet society was the confiscation of their land holdings and possessions. In line with the 'land to the tiller' policy articulated by the government, the land reform endeavored to equitably redistribute the landlords' and rich peasants' excess lands to the laborers, poor peasants, and middle peasants. In Thinh Liet, the cadres added up the total amount of these holdings in the commune (significantly, this was not done on a village basis), combined it with the commune's communal land, and determined that each member of the eligible families was to receive 720 square meters (2 *sao*) of land.[6] In an interesting concession to the moderately successful middle peasants, they also granted farmers who were renting land at the time of the land reform complete rights to that land. Residents commented that at the time of the distribution, land was given out without consideration of the plot's productivity, ease of access, or other factors. This originally created some discontent that was later eased by the introduction of a tax policy that gave relief to those with poor quality plots. Some ambitious middle peasants took advantage of this policy by accepting low tax, supposedly unproductive plots that they then turned into a top shelf plots through their own efforts. After the land redistribution, the formerly wealthy landowners found themselves with little or nothing, while those who had nothing found themselves with respectable land holdings.

Beyond losing their land, the landlords also had their homes and possessions confiscated and redistributed. Cadres entered landlords' homes, decided what the families did not need, such as excess furniture or wealth items, and gave them away. They also gave away any farm implements or animals regarded as excessive. In a direct attack on the former symbolism of the elite, the cadres appropriated the spacious, brick homes and large compounds of many landlords, calculated the amount of living space the family needed, and then allowed poor families to move into the remaining spaces. This produced a number of uncomfortable situations as many elite families found themselves sharing their homes with poor families they might never have spoken to before the land reform. Elite families found their homes literally invaded by cadres and strangers, some of whom simply took valuable items from their homes, while the owners were powerless to stop them. The social turbulence aside, the land reform did succeed in finding good accommodation for many of the poor farmers who had previously lived in thatch huts.

Delegitimizing the Former Elite

Almost completely stripped of their land, incomes, homes, and many possessions, the landlords and other former members of Thinh Liet's elite found themselves without the material foundation that had previously supported their status. They had been, in effect, brought down to the level of those they had previously dominated. The final step in 'overturning' the former elites was to destroy the residual prestige and legitimacy that many continued to enjoy. The previously mentioned problems of the locals' initial unreceptiveness to the cadres' lessons on the exploitive nature of the former elites, merging them instead into the somewhat benign category of 'wealthy family,' was indicative of what the cadres might have described as the peasantry's false consciousness. Despite extensive mobilization and propaganda, many residents still regarded many members of the former elite with respect and esteem. To the cadres, this itself was part of the exploitation mechanism. Destroying this residual prestige, therefore, was the only way to destroy this mechanism.

The first steps in delegitimizing the former elite were the elimination of the symbolic and linguistic forms that had separated commoners and elites. Beginning with dress, the party forbid the wearing of the immaculate clothing of the former elites, such as the tunics (*ao thung*), turbans, and shoes with upturned toes of the men, and the flowing silk tunics worn by women (*ao dai*). Villagers were required to dress simply and modestly. The most popular style of dress for men became the olive drab fatigues worn by returning soldiers. Many former commoners continued to wear the dark cotton clothing they had always worn, yet for both men and women, Western-styled shirts and trousers became more prevalent. Cadres forced the landlords to perform symbolically humiliating work. Giap Nhi landlords were required to assemble every morning and sweep out the plaza before the communal house. Cadres also banned the former styles of interaction between commoners and elites. All forms of kowtowing were forbidden. The use of honorific titles and self-deprecating forms of address, such as addressing a village chief by his title while referring to oneself as 'child', were also abolished. Titles were not to be used in social life. Instead, one was to refer to people by their name with either a kinship term or the egalitarian 'comrade' (*dong chi*). Party members in particular were to use this latter term. Thus, whereas the former canton chief was addressed as 'Mr. Canton Chief' (*Ong Tong*) without using his name, the president of the commune's People's Committee, named Son for example, was addressed as 'Comrade Son' by other committee members or perhaps 'Uncle Son' (*Bac Son*) or 'Older Brother Son' (*Anh Son*) by kinfolk or non-party member villagers. This manipulation of terms of address was taken one step further with regard to the landlords. After receiving their classifications, villagers addressed landlords by the extremely degrading and humiliating pronoun '*may*,' a term generally reserved for children or insults. The landlords, in return, had to address others as 'sir' (*ong*) or 'madam' (*ba*), while referring to themselves as 'child' (*con*). This latter change represented a complete inversion of pre-revolutionary practices and lasted for several years.

The strategy used to the greatest effect for the delegitimization of the former elites were the denunciation sessions (*dau to*) organized against the former landlords and other enemies of the revolution. In these sessions, modeled on the 'speak bitterness' sessions of revolutionary China, former elites were publically denounced by their alleged victims.[7] In Thinh Liet, the denunciation sessions for all villages in the commune were held in an open area next to a grain warehouse in the village of Giap Bat. There, the land reform cadres set up a table where land reform committee members and 'backbone elements' sat. This group included a secretary (*thu ky*) to record the deliberations and was presided over by a 'judge' (*chanh an*), in actuality the land reform team leader. Some distance in front of the table, a hole had been dug in the ground, approximately one meter deep, where the individual being denounced was required to stand. Prior to the denunciation sessions, the landlords had received their classifications in the neighborhood meetings mentioned above. Although the cadres decided on the appropriate classification, the people in the local neighborhood could offer their opinions, creating some measure of popular participation in the process. During the deliberations, the accused had to stand alone in front of the sometimes hostile crowd. Once the classification was delivered, the landlords were then sent to the denunciation sessions to determine their punishment. Former participants recall that these sessions were as equally devoted to political propaganda as they were to denunciation. When the session began, the cadres presented an open indictment of the landlord class, explaining how the multiple problems of Vietnamese society were the result of the system of exploitation the landlords had imposed upon the people. After this short course of 'ideological mobilization' (*phat dong tu tuong*), the denunciation began. The landlord was put into the hole, and villagers lined up before him to recount the abuses and injustices the accused had committed against them. The landlords were accused of rape, murder, brutality, fraud, land theft, and other crimes. In several cases, villagers were eager to carry out this task. Thinh Liet had a number of men who had been cruel toward the peasantry or had committed real crimes. Among these was the former officer in the colonial military from Giap Tu who openly opposed the revolution and had allegedly raped a local woman. Many villagers relished the chance to settle such scores.

After the few men for whom the people had true disdain, the denunciations became more complicated and divisive. While the land reform team was in the commune, a general atmosphere of fear and paranoia settled in. Villagers were afraid to visit other families for fear of guilt by association if that family received a negative classification. People were also excessively deferential toward the cadres, addressing them with such virtually groveling terms as 'honorable team member' (*thua qui doi*), an appellation as inegalitarian as others the cadres were attempting to eliminate. Hostility or a bad attitude could create suspicions in the cadres' minds. Despite not being openly forced to do so, villagers were under intense pressure to participate in both the classification and denunciation sessions. Failure to attend the meetings could in the least case lead to strong words from the cadres to never bother to attend another session, or in the most serious case to accusations that one lacked revolutionary spirit or was opposed to the revolution. Failure to denounce landlords or enemies of the revolution could also lead to public criticism by the cadres and the order to never return to any meetings. As one resident commented, 'no one could run away.'

The pressures to denounce the landlords and enemies, in the end, strained the fabric of local society and destroyed several local families. Thinh Liet had two suicides during the land reform. The first was a former Giap Nhi village chief classified as a cruel and despotic landlord. He killed himself before the cadres could do the same. The second was a Giap Tu landlord. His case was indicative of the pressures placed on villagers to denounce landlords. During his denunciation session, his children and relatives lined up and publicly denounced him. Afterwards, he went home and hung himself. Other landlords were also denounced by relatives, friends, or those they formerly trusted. Local society was also strained by the political purges carried out during the period. After the land reform began, a large number of men who had served in the party or revolutionary administration from 1945 to 1954 were rounded up and accused of subversion and espionage. This hit hardest in Giap Tu where seven men were arrested and imprisoned as alleged agents of the Vietnam Nationalist Party (*Viet Nam Quoc Dan Dang or* VNQDD).[8] Among this group, one, named Nguyen Ton Duyen, had served as secretary for the party cell of Thanh Tri district, while another had been its propaganda chief. The other five arrested included a doctor, a bicycle repairman, a former President of the revolutionary People's Committee from the late 1940s, and the father of Secretary Duyen, who, as noted above, was a former canton chief and had been classified as a landlord. The fifth man, an employee of the Hanoi Water Works, was the only one of the five to have specific charges brought against him. He was accused of committing sabotage for the VNQDD after being caught urinating into one of the holding tanks at the Water Works.

The purges increased the general sense of fear in the commune, but the resolution of Duyen's case confirmed for many that the process was veering out of control. Duyen's revolutionary credentials were impeccable and residents greatly admired him. Before rising to the rank of district secretary, he had been a party member for many years and had served with distinction in the struggle against the French. Despite his rank and activeness, he had succeeded in avoiding arrest. This fact, as some who knew him tell it, led to his downfall as it allegedly caught the attention of a high-ranking Chinese cadre sent to assist the Vietnamese. Only a double agent, the cadre asserted, could serve for so long without arrest. The Vietnamese Communists, therefore, arrested him and accused him of serving as a VNQDD agent. He was held for close to a month and at his trial in mid-January 1956, found guilty and sentenced to death by firing squad. Several days later, the land reform cadres rounded up hundreds of Thinh Liet villagers and marched them up to the neighboring village of Dinh Cong to watch the execution. There, in front of his friends, neighbors and relatives, Nguyen Ton Duyen was publicly denounced for his crimes against the revolution and executed. Witnesses recall that just before he

36

was shot he called out, 'A thousand years for President Ho! A thousand years for the Workers' Party!'[9]

Nguyen Ton Duyen was not the only man executed in Thinh Liet during the land reform. The Giap Tu native accused of rape was also executed at his trial's conclusion. The cadres had not succeeded in the complete humiliation of every member of the former elite class. Many former officials escaped with rich or middle peasant classifications, and three of the landlord classifications were actually delivered in absentia as those individuals had fled to Hanoi. Furthermore, none of the resistance landlords had to endure denunciation sessions and it appears that some of the regular landlords, notably the women, were spared as well. Nevertheless, though they may have been spared, they were still referred to as *may* by their co-villagers and all performed such demeaning tasks as sweeping out the plaza before the Giap Nhi communal house. All of the landlords and their families became socially isolated as people were afraid to mix with them for fear of negative associations. And they also became second class, dependent citizens, a fact brought out poignantly during the land reform when a man had to seek the cadres permission to hold a funeral for his deceased mother. When the cadres finally left Thinh Liet at the end of January 1956, the former elites had been definitively overturned and neutralized in communal life.

The Economic Consequences of Land Reform in Thinh Liet

The Thinh Liet land reform completely transformed the local economy, but one of its most important consequences was the rather uneven 'peasantification' of the commune. Agriculture was not the main occupation for the majority of local families before 1955. Census figures from the 1920s indicate that only around 30 percent of commune families engaged in some form of agriculture (20 percent for farmers, 10 percent for wage laborers). Other common occupations were the production of votive paper ingots that were burned for the dead (30 percent), as well as trading and other handicraft pursuits (see Ha Dong #488 and 583). This diversity and the need to maintain the outskirts economy in order to provision Hanoi created a land distribution quandary for the land reform officials. Their response was to limit the distribution to only those individuals who were engaged in agricultural production. Those who had 'stable occupations' outside of agriculture, for example factory workers, traders, or generally those with pursuits that did not require landownership, could continue their professions and were not to receive land (Hanoi, Land Reform Committee 1956:57). Although this policy worked well with factory workers and silversmiths, Thinh Liet's situation represented a special case because the commune's most common handicraft activity, the production by families of votive paper ingots, violated the party's anti-superstition policy (*chinh sach chong me tin di doan*). In party ideology, superstitions were the set of ideas and practices that asserted that a variety of forms of supernatural causality existed in human life, and these needed to be eliminated for Vietnam to advance (see Chapter 3). During the land reform, cadres shut down ingot production and converted these families into farmers. Many former traders also received land. As a result, the number of farmers in the commune increased dramatically, though many had little experience with farming. One local official claimed that at the time of the land reform, some 70 percent of those who received land in Giap Nhi had never worked as farmers before, while some 20 to 30 percent in Giap Tu had not. Some Giap Nhi families, apparently, even refused their allotted parcels, though all Giap Tu families accepted their's. This same official commented that at the land reform's conclusion, approximately 70 percent of the Thinh Liet population were farmers, 15 percent were traders, 10 percent factory workers, and 5 percent did an assortment of pursuits. In the new revolutionary society, Thinh Liet became an agricultural community.

Another peculiar consequence of the Thinh Liet land reform was the unequal distribution of land. Land reform policy was dedicated to creating an equitable distribution of land in the countryside, but the policy of granting middle peasants and below the rights to land they rented or worked before the land reform created marked inequities in Thinh Liet. After a fierce battle between French forces and local guerrillas in February 1947, many villagers, faced with the prospect of living under French occupation, had fled to areas controlled by the Viet Minh for the remainder of the war. Those who stayed behind had the pick of sizeable tracts of abandoned land to farm for themselves. Some also purchased land from those who feared they might in the future be classified as landlords. As the war wound down villagers slowly returned, but many plots of land were never reclaimed. When the land reform was conducted, those farmers who still retained occupied land or worked rental lands received them in their entirety. As a result, a number of poor and middle peasants who before land reform owned no land, but rented or occupied extensively, found that they owned as much as one hectare, a figure that might have earned them a landlord classification if they had owned it before. If these holdings seemed too big, subtle pressures did exist to give away some of the land. Such was the case of a Giap Tu middle peasant who gave back some 400 square meters of rice land. Some from Giap Nhi also claim that given the fact that historically there were more farmers in the village, Giap Tu benefitted much more from the granting of land rights to renters or occupiers.

One final point of interest was the fact that in Thinh Liet, the government agenda to make the poor peasants and laborers the paramounts of the new society at more than an ideological level bore only limited fruit. Residents recall that many families in this category struggled greatly after the land reform. Many who had never farmed before became farmers, but still did not know what to do, so their yields were low. And as the more successful like to tell it, some of these families were poor from their own lax work habits or profligacy, so no revolutionary policy could ever really help them. Whether that was true or not, what did happen was that middle peasants soon began to dominate the local administration and then the agricultural cooperatives that were established in 1959. Many of these men would have been on the border line of the wealthy families before the revolution. What qualified them for these positions was their industry, organizational ability, and success in agriculture – traits they could apply to the work of the administration or the cooperative. The domination of the middle peasants in Thinh Liet would match the national trend, assuming that Le Duan's 1961 comment that middle peasants made up 45–50 percent of the party membership was accurate (Le Duan 1965b:73). Members of some poor peasant and laborer families did later assume high ranking official positions in Thinh Liet, but their numbers never matched those of the middle peasants.

The Consequences of Revolutionary Social Classification

In August 1956 the Vietnamese Communists publicly declared that excesses had occurred during the land reform (Moise 1983:239). Many cadres had gone beyond the purview of their instructions and innocent people had suffered. In order to correct the mistakes committed during the land reform, the party launched a Rectification Campaign that again sent cadres to the villages, but this time they were charged with reviewing prior classifications and reclassifying individuals who had received errant classifications. When the Rectification Campaign reached Thinh Liet in late 1956, six of the original nineteen landlords received reclassifications. Of the Giap Nhi landlords, three of the regular landlords were reclassified as middle peasants and one of the cruel and despotic landlords was reclassified as a regular landlord. With the exception of the absent Nghiep, all Giap Tu landlords, including the father of Nguyen Ton Duyen, were reclassified as middle peasants. Two reclassifications were apparently made posthumously. All other landlords retained their original classifications. Nevertheless, even for those who received reclassifications, none was able to regain their confiscated land or possessions, although some apparently regained sections of their houses. Below the landlords, a number of rich peasants were also reclassified as middle peasants, but their numbers are unclear. All the men imprisoned as VNQDD agents were ultimately released as well.

When compared with the experiences of many other regions of the country during land reform, Thinh Liet and the outskirts of Hanoi had enjoyed a relatively smooth though not bloodless transition (see also Moise

1983:202). Party satisfaction with the results was quite evident when they declared, 'In sum, the land reform's victory in the outskirts of Hanoi has shattered the political power of the landlord class, abolished the exploitive regime of the feudal landholding system, secured political and economic victory for the working peasants, contributed to the maintenance of security and order in the city, constructed a positive relationship between city and country, strengthened agricultural production, and protected and encouraged industry and commerce. All of these have built an advantageous foundation from which to realize the State Plan of 1956' (Hanoi, Land Reform Committee 1956:72). In Thinh Liet, the feudal regime had been toppled, a new leadership ran local affairs, and a new theory of society's ills, its causes, and its cure, had become part of the local cultural world. The newly formed community, however, did not constitute an exact replica of official ideology. The poor peasants and laborers who were ideally to run the reconstituted community had been replaced by the middle peasants. Many people who formerly had little experience in agricultural were obliged to become farmers. A number of former members of the elite were not socially isolated because of their involvement in the revolution. And some residents had still not completely embraced the new concepts of stigma and exploitation. Instead of the clearly defined social structure envisioned by officials, Thinh Liet's social order had its blurry areas. Nevertheless, the main economic factors that had previously supported the elite were gone, and the government had taken the first step toward the eventual establishment of collective agriculture that would follow several years later.

Such fundamental issues of political economy aside, the creation of the land reform classification system had important consequences for people in the following decades. After the land reform, as the North Vietnamese state expanded its reach into social life, classifications became inseparable components of individual identity. Not only did people maintain their classifications for life, they also carried down through the generations. When people interacted with the government bureaucracy, they interacted with it as an individual with a particular classification. Those with bad class backgrounds, such as the children of regular landlords, found their futures and social options distinctly limited. They could not become party members, officers in the military, and had difficulty getting the best medical care or access to the best educational opportunities. Exclusion from party membership in particular closed them off from the best social possibilities and also prevented them from obtaining high positions in the local administration. Conversely, those with good classifications had numerous benefits open to them, particularly if they could enter the party. One's family's classification, in a sense, was inescapable. Interestingly, in Thinh Liet, the descendants of families classified as landlords had many more difficulties than those families that had been involved in the colonial administration or elite before the revolution, but received a lesser classification. For example, children of landlord families became undesirable marriage partners. The only exception to this was the children of the resistance landlords, many of whom were already party members at the time of the revolution. Several of them rose to high positions, such as an editorial position at a Hanoi newspaper and membership in the delegation to the Paris peace talks. But, as one observer noted, these men could attain high positions, but they could only do so outside the commune where their family background was not as immediately apparent. Today, the classifications families received during the land reform still remain salient although their importance has weakened. When filling out numerous official documents, such as a marriage registration form, individuals often must include their family's classification, but following the introduction of the market economy in 1986, new paths to advancement have emerged, markedly attenuating the state's ability to control social life.

Part 2: Resignifying Space

Space in pre-revolutionary Thinh Liet was rich in meanings. At one level, it had an enchanted quality as it divided into areas sacred and mundane. At another level, it served to distinguish between members of local society through such mechanisms as restrictions on access to particular spaces for women and commoners. And at a final level, ownership and control over space, notably agricultural land, provided an important support for the elite and a barrier to social mobility for the impoverished. When the land reform began, Vietnamese officials were keenly aware of the symbolism and consequences of local constructions of space, particularly since many of those meanings ran counter to revolutionary agendas. The remainder of this chapter will examine how cadres dealt with space during the land reform and in the following decade. As will be shown, official control over space allowed them to remove the material foundation that had supported unsanctioned rituals, social groups, and economic activities, while simultaneously giving them the opportunity to introduce a new set of meanings associated with space.

The Sacred Geography of Colonial Thinh Liet

According to ideas that predated the revolution, the Vietnamese landscape was infused with an array of spirits who guarded or controlled the land. Humans lived on and owned their villages and fields, but success in human affairs required ritual interaction with the guardian spirits of land, called most simply 'land spirits' (*tho cong* or *tho dia*). The presence of spirits in the land was evident in the ubiquity of altars dedicated to them. At the edge of rice fields, in family compounds, at shrines, in temples, almost everywhere there was human residence or activity an altar to them could be found. At these altars people performed rites to ask the spirits' permission to work or use the land and also for their assistance to achieve success in their activities. Such was the case when a farmer performed a brief rite for the spirit of his field to ensure a good harvest. Spirit control over the land was also visible in the fact that other rituals, including burials and ancestral rites, were required to begin by asking the guardian spirit's permission to allow the return of other spirits or the rite would be ineffective. There were many different types of spirits associated with place. Sometimes trees or springs had powerful spirits that dwelled within them. Open roads outside of the villages were supernaturally dangerous because malevolent wandering souls prowled there in search of sustenance. And every village had its own guardian spirit that protected and cared for the community (see also Nguyen Van Khoan 1931:107–12).

The ubiquity of these spirits related to divisions of spaces about the landscape into various degrees of sacredness and mundaneness. The most sacred sites were those in which residents propitiated spirits, though the importance of these sites varied. The simplest sacred sites were spirit shrines. Colonial Thinh Liet had several different types of shrines. Shrines dedicated to the spirits of supernaturally powerful historical figures were called *mieu*. Both Giap Nhi and Giap Tu had *mieu*, though the former was a small outdoor altar and the latter a small building. Public contributions helped maintain *mieu* and all residents could perform rites at them. Shrines owned and cared for by particular families were called *dien*. These shrines also varied in size from a single outdoor altar to a small building. *Dien* rites invoked a wide range of spirits, and were generally family-based rites devoted to healing or the acquisition of good fortune. Normally only a few related families and neighbors performed rites in a *dien*. In Thinh Liet, *dien* provided one of the main locations for the performance of spirit medium ceremonies. Similar to *dien* in worshiping a wide range of spirits, but open to all residents and cared for by them, were the *den*. *Den* were present in all Thinh Liet villages. The largest sat in Giap Nhat. Although they were more public than the *dien*, residents sometimes performed spirit medium rites at the *den* as well.

Another type of sacred site was the lineage hall (*nha tho ho*). Recollections vary, but colonial Thinh Liet had in excess of ten lineage halls where male lineage mates aged eighteen or older congregated to propitiate lineage ancestors. Local cemeteries and the graves or mausolea they contained were sacred spaces. Here residents gathered periodically, such as on a death anniversary or before the lunar new year, to propitiate the souls of the dead. The Elderly Men's Associations, a group composed of men fifty five years and older, had sacred altars for their rites. The village Mandarin Associations, a group composed of men who had served as officials at the village level and above, had sacred buildings and altars (*van chi*) where they made offerings to Confucius. Within homes, the family ancestral altar was the most sacred space. Finally, the largest sacred spaces were the communal houses of each village and the Buddhist temples in Giap Nhi and Giap Luc (though size did not determine the level of sacredness). At many of these sites, the idea of their sacredness was reinforced by a number of associated prohibitions. For example, those in a polluted state, such as those who had recently had sexual relations or menstruating women, were either discouraged, as in the case of the former, or forbidden, as in the case of the latter, from entering into or participating in rites in these spaces. Women and adolescent men were also forbidden from entering the most sacred village space, the communal house. One also refrained from defiling activities in sacred spaces. Thus, men and women were forbidden from having sexual intercourse in the area before the family ancestral altar. Finally, although all of these spaces were considered sacred, internally they often had differing degrees of sacredness. To give one example, although the communal house itself was sacred, its most sacred space was the guardian spirit's altar, while those areas furthest from the altar were less sacred. Apart from sacred sites, mundane spaces included roads, paths, fields, rivers, ponds, gardens, outhouses, and markets. A space in a field where a casket was buried, or a spot on a roadside where a young person died accidentally, could, however, become a sacred site. Colonial Thinh Liet's geography divide into spaces both sacred and mundane, but the boundaries between these classifications were not absolute and could vary over time.

Provisioning the Sacred

Beyond having spaces marked as sacred, colonial Thinh Liet's geography also had a substantial material infrastructure devoted to provisioning the rites performed at sacred sites. Land in the colonial village divided into the two categories of either private or communal land (*dat cong* or more formally *cong dien*). Communal lands then broke down into the two further categories of communal land that belonged to the village, and was ostensibly rented to the village needy, and communal land that belonged to particular social groupings.[10] Thinh Liet's total communal land holdings were roughly as follows (see Figure 1.2).

Given that Giap Nhi had approximately 108 hectares (300 *mau*) of agricultural land while Giap Tu had perhaps 82.8 hectares (230 *mau*), communal land constituted an estimated 13.6 percent and 4.7 percent of the total cultivated land in Giap Nhi and Giap Tu respectively.[11] The significance of these lands lay in the fact that their proceeds were supposed to be dedicated to provisioning the rites performed by the social group that controlled them. Those who rented the land paid their rental in kind rather

Figure 1.2: Colonial Thinh Liet Communal Land Holdings*

Village of Giap Nhi:	Hectares
Village communal land	3.6
Bui lineage, first branch	1.4
Bui lineage, second branch	2.2
Dang lineage	0.25
Elderly Men's Association	7.2
Total	14.65

Village of Giap Tu:	Hectares
Village communal land	2.5
Nguyen Cuong lineage	0.36 (rice land) 0.22 (fish pond)
Nguyen Ton lineage	0.11
Elderly Men's Association	0.72
Total	3.91
Set temple	7.2+

*One obvious question that was never answered was whether the Mandarin Associations controlled communal lands.

than in cash, and the proceeds went to subsidize ritual and other group activities. On some occasions, villages and lineages expanded their holdings through land purchases, though it is difficult to estimate the net change in communal land holdings during the colonial period because other plots were converted, both legally and illegally, to private land. One of the most common methods for their augmentation was for men without children to donate a plot of land. In accepting the land, the village or lineage agreed to annually sponsor the death anniversary of either the donor or someone the donor had selected (see also Toan Anh 1969:61). The size of these holdings could be substantial. A number of elderly men also dedicated land to the Elderly Men's Association upon joining. The main consequence of communal Land holdings in colonial Thinh Liet was that it provided local social groups with the resources necessary to carry out critical group rites. These rites not only defined the groups within the local social order, they also contributed to the maintenance of each site's sacredness.

Reconstituting Space in Revolutionary Thinh Liet

The land reform cadres' actions after entering Thinh Liet revealed that, apart from redistributing land, they also sought to eliminate unsanctioned social groups and ritual practices through the desanctification of the commune's sacred spaces. Among the cadres' first targets were the communal houses. The large-scale organization of village worship ceremonies (*te lang*) in Giap Nhi and Giap Tu had ended in 1946. Both villages organized ceremonies in early 1946, but these ceased after the commencement of hostilities with the French. The two communal houses had suffered somewhat different fates during the French war. In January 1947, the French military began its campaign to reconquer the countryside surrounding Hanoi. The battle reached Thinh Liet on the morning of 7 February (the 11th of the first lunar month). Local guerrillas had prepared for a French assault by fortifying the area near the road coming from Hanoi on the commune's western edge, but were taken by surprise when the French attacked from across the rice fields to the northeast. The superior French forces swept quickly through the commune, taking Giap Tu first, and then Giap Nhi and Giap Nhat. In the process, they killed several dozen guerrillas, including the President of Giap Tu's Revolutionary People's Committee, Truong Dinh Diem, and his younger brother, who was then serving as Deputy President. As soon as the French forces entered the commune, the guerrillas realized the impossibility of repelling their attack. Thus, in keeping with the scorched earth policy then advocated by the Viet Minh, they burned down half of the communal house of Giap Tu and damaged a portion of the communal house of Giap Nhi in order to deny the French space to billet their troops. The guerrillas' tactics of denying the French space succeeded, but both communal houses were heavily damaged.

By the end of 1956 the two villages' communal houses had not been repaired nor had there been a return to organized ritual in them. A small number of people did continue to present offerings there, but there were no feasts or sacrifices. People refrained from organized ritual in the communal houses for several reasons. First, although the French had recaptured the commune and reinstalled their own administration, a shadow Communist administration was also in place that opposed the ceremonies. Second, people were reluctant to assemble in large numbers as it could attract French forces who might mistake the ceremony for a Viet Minh convocation. Finally, the destruction in the communal houses had left their altars and ritual items in disarray. This was particularly true of Giap Tu where the scroll that recorded the identity of the guardian spirit (*sac phong*) and ritual instructions was destroyed.[12] Despite the absence of large-scale organized ritual, the communal houses were still sacred spaces and the objects and statues that had survived the battle remained under the care of conscientious male villagers.

Soon after the Thinh Liet land reform began, the cadres initiated the desacralization of the communal houses. Although never openly stated in most documents on ritual reform, the communal houses were obviously too closely linked to the former elite to be left untouched.[13] One of the

45

first moves to neutralize the communal houses was the transfer of administrative offices to other buildings. Under the French, the village had been the terminal unit of administration in Thinh Liet and communal houses had served as the seats for the village administrations. With the revolution, administrative powers were taken away from the villages and concentrated at the level of the commune, itself composed of several villages. In Thinh Liet, all administrative offices for the commune were moved to the aforementioned house of the Giap Nhi resistance landlord. The actual desacralization took more spectacular form. Many villagers were keenly aware of the multiple inequalities and indignities that had been forced on them during communal house rites. The rites had been exclusively presided over by the local educated elite; lower status men had been required to sit in non-prestigious places distant from the prestigious altars; and at the rites' conclusions, the most prestigious and sought after items went to high status men (see also Malarney 1993:154–64). Thus, when the cadres gave them the opportunity to damage these structures, a number responded with extreme vigor, particularly in Giap Nhi. Zealous villagers tore down many of the symbols of the old order. Wooden planks adorned with poetic couplets (*cau doi*) written in Chinese characters (several of which had been written by famous villagers) that hung vertically in the communal house were taken out and smashed. Sacred items, such as altar pieces, were broken into pieces. Several prized statues were either destroyed or thrown down wells. And what was not smashed, was often stolen and later kept or sold. Given that most of the Giap Tu communal house was already destroyed, the activities in Giap Tu were less effervescent than in Giap Nhi. The communal house desacralization reached its apotheosis with the abolition of its exclusive, male-dominated symbolism. The cadres discarded the previous prohibitions that had barred the entry of women and young men, and allowed all to freely enter. The party also banned the performance of any ceremonies in the communal houses. In one stroke, the party succeeded in eliminating the multiple forms of social differentiation, as seen in the entry prohibitions, seating order, distribution of food items at feasts, access to the sacred, and rights to ritual officiation, that communal houses had previously reproduced. But not only were the large ceremonies banned. Cadres prohibited villagers from making even small offerings on the altars.

The Buddhist temples were another focus of activity for the cadres. Set Temple, the main temple of the commune located in Giap Luc, was not significantly affected by the events of the period. It was regarded as a historically significant temple, thus villagers and cadres refrained from damaging it. However, given official hostility toward Buddhism, almost all villagers stopped attending ceremonies there. Tam Phap Temple, a small temple that Giap Nhi residents had built in the 1920s, was not as fortunate. Before the land reform began several brass statues of the Buddha were stolen from the temple. Once it started, cadres forced the villagers to empty out the statuary and dismantle the temple's altars. Later, villagers moved the remaining statues and other ritual items to Set Temple for storage. Neither villagers nor cadres defaced or vandalized Tam Phap temple, but by the land reform's conclusion the former temple was just an empty building.

The lineages halls (*nha tho ho*) of Giap Nhi and Giap Tu were also affected by the assault on religious architecture. Party and government documents do not contain directives banning the congregation of lineage members for the communal worship of lineage ancestors, but, beginning with the land reform, cadres closed down the lineage halls and forbid the conduct of large-scale rituals on their premises.[14] The destruction of altars and ritual objects that characterized the treatment of other types of religious architecture was absent in the case of the lineage halls. Nonetheless, several lineage halls, and this was particularly the case in Giap Tu, were converted into living space for lineage members. In Giap Nhi, the ancestral hall of the second largest lineage, the Le lineage, and in Giap Tu, the ancestral halls of the Nguyen Ton and Truong Dinh lineages, became family residences. The two large Bui lineages of Giap Nhi were not forced to house lineage mates in their ancestral halls, probably a result of their lingering political influence in the commune. Despite these conversions, in none of the cases were the altars destroyed or defaced. The altar remained the dominant feature in the homes. Families used the areas to the sides of the altar as their living space. The area before the altar was either vacant of furniture or turned into a sitting area. This space was never a sleeping area as that would offend the ancestors. The lineage halls that were forcibly converted into residences were also not given to lineage mates at random. The family of the lineage chief (*truong ho*) always occupied the hall and these men frequently continued to surreptitiously execute their ritual obligations to the ancestors, even though they could not organize large-scale rituals and feasts.

The most violent conversion of sacred village space occurred at local shrines. Spirit shrines were a focus of widespread destruction during the land reform across the North Vietnam because of their association with superstitions. Cadres and villagers were free to destroy superstitious sites with great vigor. In Giap Nhi and Giap Tu, all *den* and *dien* were either vandalized or destroyed. Their sacred objects were taken out and smashed, and their structures defaced. The *mieu* of Giap Tu was vandalized, rid of its sacred objects, and turned into a house for a poor village family. The most famous episode occurred in Giap Nhat when eight local men completely destroyed a *den* with an intensity that people remember to this day. Also destroyed with intensity were the *van chi* of Giap Nhi and Giap Tu that had served the Mandarin Associations, and the shrine in Giap Nhi and altar in Giap Tu that had served each village's Elderly Men's Association. All were destroyed because of their elite associations. By the land reform's end, all former shrines ceased to serve as foci of public ritual activity. Most were heavily damaged or destroyed, but for those that were still somewhat intact, such as several *dien* in Giap Nhi, the communal administration began an intensive surveillance program. Later, officials periodically entered and searched the sites to ensure that neither renovations nor rituals were being carried out.

At the same time as the cadres were leading villagers in the destruction of local sacred sites, they were also confiscating the lands formerly devoted to these sites. The cadres redistributed all of the communal lands that had supported communal house rites as well as the lands controlled by the local Elderly Men's Associations. Instructions published in 1955 by the Nguyen Ai Quoc School on how to resolve practical issues when carrying out the land reform noted that cadres should confiscate the lands belonging to churches, temples, and lineages. However, they were obliged to leave aside a small amount for the conduct of rites (*viec tho cung*) by churches and temples. If the people consented, the cadres could also leave aside a small amount of land for lineage rites (Nguyen Ai Quoc School 1955:16). In Thinh Liet, neither of these principles appears to have been respected, and the temples and lineages lost all of their lands. The practical consequence of these confiscations was that the cadres completely removed the material infrastructure that had formerly supported cultic activities at the sites. In one quick stroke, not only did the cadres desacralize and close down the sites, they also denied a foundation for their possible return.[15]

Completing the Desanctification

In the years after 1956, the only openly sacred site in Thinh Liet was Set Temple. The *den*, *mieu*, and *van chi*, as well as the sacred sites of the Elderly Men's Associations, had all become mundane spaces. The lineage halls were putatively mundane, but local officials turned a blind eye to covert sacred activities in their confines. The *dien* were also putatively mundane, but as residents continued to clandestinely performed rites in them, officials periodically raided them. The spaces that remained in a liminal state were the communal houses. Local officials forbid the conduct of any rituals in their confines, but instead of tearing them down or converting them to other uses, they simply left them abandoned. The reluctance of local cadres during these years to do anything definitive with the communal houses was evident in the treatment of Giap Nhi's communal house. While Giap Tu's communal house was still severely damaged from the French battle, the Giap Nhi communal house was in relatively good repair, despite the depredations of the angry villagers during the land reform. Significantly, the inner sanctum that contained the guardian spirit's altar remained untouched. Cadres, for reasons that remain unclear, never cleared out this inner room. They simply closed it up and left it alone.

The final stroke in the state's effort to resignify space began in 1959 with the establishment of agricultural cooperatives across Vietnam. The Land Reform Law had declared the establishment of the 'land ownership regime of the peasantry' (Article 1) as one of the land reform's primary goals. As discussed above, this policy had enormous implications in Thinh Liet as dozens of families that had owned little or no land received private plots. Although the redistribution had succeeded in eliminating the inequities in land holdings that had characterized the pre-revolutionary order, party officials were troubled with the direction of change that soon followed. 'The Land Reform,' as one Vietnamese scholar commented, 'had only eliminated the feudal land tenure regime, while the regime of individual private property in productive implements – the foundation of class differentiation and class oppression – still existed as before' (Dinh Thu Cuc 1976:37). As a result, 'exploitation' in its various forms soon re-emerged (Dinh Thu Cuc 1976:37; Vietnam, National Peasant Liaison Committee 1957:7). In the period between 1954 to 1960, rice yields in the Red River delta soared, in some areas even doubling those from before the Second World War (Vu Huy Phuc 1993:19), but some peasants struggled and ended up selling off land to pay debts or became tenant farmers for more successful families. A number of local markets also remained vibrant. Some of the more entrepreneurial peasants, after receiving their land, later sold it to use as start-up capital for trading enterprises (Tran Thanh 1958:7).

In the context of these events, the party began its campaign to collectivize agriculture. This campaign began in Thinh Liet in 1959 with the establishment of a cooperative in Giap Tu. Over the next three years, cooperatives were established in all Thinh Liet villages and by 1965 all but a handful of Thinh Liet farmers had joined them. Farmers ostensibly entered the cooperatives voluntarily although many recall that those who did not enter faced substantial pressures, particularly accusations of lacking patriotism, or not loving socialism or 'the movement' (*phong trao*). The critical act in entering the cooperative was the donation of one's land. The symbolic significance of this donation lay in the fact that it marked the abandonment of individual family production for collective production. Similar to what had occurred with the confiscation of lands for the sacred sites, people lost the material foundation that provisioned their independence. In doing so, land became another publically held asset intended to serve both production and the creation of socialism. And like virtually everything else in the commune, land became a proxy of the state and its policies.

The state's position as the dominant entity empowered to define the meanings and uses of space was marked in other ways as well. Starting in

1958, the communal administration began making use of the abandoned buildings within its confines. Pursuant to the overarching strategy of developing the national agricultural economy, the communal houses were put to practical use. The brick arches and lotus pond before the Giap Nhi communal house were respectively torn down and filled in to create an area for drying paddy. Then, the administration repaired the communal houses of Giap Nhi and Giap Tu, and converted them into rice warehouses. The small room that housed the guardian spirit's altar in the Giap Nhi communal house was still left untouched, but the rest of that communal house and the entire communal house of Giap Tu were converted into functional village buildings. In 1964 the local administration again opted for practicality to develop local agriculture and the former Tam Phap Temple became a rice warehouse. At some point in the early 1960s, the administration tore down the brick arches that had formerly marked the entrances into the villages in order to widen local roads. And on several occasions, officials moved local cemeteries in order to accommodate the construction of housing complexes or factories. State control over land was marked most clearly in 1967 when the Thinh Liet cooperatives eliminated all of the barriers that had formerly separated the rice fields in order to create larger, more rationally planned fields.

Officials made it amply clear to those who either left or did not enter the cooperatives who controlled space in the commune. If a family asked to leave the cooperative, they had the right to receive the same amount of land as they donated when they entered, but not the exact same plots. If they had donated a pond, however, they received nothing in return. When people asked to leave, the administration made matters difficult for them by giving them poor quality plots or plots that were surrounded by cooperative lands. This latter tactic allowed for the continued harassment of independent farmers by having cooperative members deny them permission to cross cooperative lands to get to their own, or by denying them water for irrigation. Land in Thinh Liet commune was for collective, not individual, production.

Conclusions

By the mid-1960s, space in Thinh Liet commune had been significantly transformed. The previous realms of the sacred had contracted and the realm of the mundane expanded. Communal houses and a temple had become warehouses, spirit shrines had been defaced, and the shrine to Confucius destroyed. It is important to note the differences in the conduct of the desacralization of religious architecture. Those structures which were either associated with the former elites, such as the communal house and *van chi*, or whose ritual activities were considered superstitious, such as the *den* and *mieu*, underwent the most violent transformation. Conversely, the transformations of those spaces whose ritual activities focused on kin, ancestors, or Buddhism, were much less violent. Some ancestral halls became residences, but their altars were never destroyed, and cadres never destroyed family ancestral altars, although there was strong social pressure to simplify ostentatious altars. Through the transformation and appropriation of space, the state prepared the foundation to implement its policies to constrain heterodox ritual practices and unsanctioned social groups, while simultaneously embarking upon the construction of the collective socialist economy.

Although the state's definitions of space were predominant in Thinh Liet, not all residents completely accepted their definitions. This could be seen in the continued conduct of rituals at spirit shrines. From the 1950s to the late 1980s, a large number of residents continued to covertly carry out rites. These actions angered local officials, who periodically intervened to shut down the rites, but people usually returned to them as soon as official consternation had quieted. Some people also felt that the behavior of officials toward the sacred sites would bring supernatural punishment to them. A more significant manifestation of the rejection of official ideas was the difference in effort cooperative members put into work on the cooperative lands and their own lands. According to official regulations, five percent of the cooperative's land was to be set aside for individual families to work as they wished, so long as their efforts 'did not interfere with the cooperative's management of labor' (Fforde 1989:32). Families could also freely dispose of the products of this 'five percent land.' Much to the chagrin of the cadres, cooperators worked harder on the five percent land than the regular cooperative lands. As early as August of 1962, Le Duan noted that 55.5 percent of the average cooperative member's income derived from the subsidiary household economy (*kinh te phu gia dinh*) and other sources, while only 44.5 percent came from the collective economy (Le Duan 1965a:283ff.). Moreover, the total estimated value of the five percent land's output was in the range of 60–70 percent of the value of the total output of the cooperative economy, which was obviously produced on the other 95 percent of cultivated land (Le Duan 1965a:284). Thinh Liet witnessed a similar difference in effort and productivity. Collectively held land may have been critical to the creation of socialism, but when ranked in terms of its value, that which was of the family was most important. Indeed, as residents like to state when commenting on why work on and care for collective lands was so poor, 'No one mourns for the father of everyone' (*cha chung khong ai khoc*). All the same, these points of divergence aside, revolutionary process in Thinh Liet did lead to a tremendous expansion of the lands controlled by the state, while also profoundly reconstituting the meanings associated with space.

CHAPTER TWO

Redefining Culture and Morality

Karl Marx and Frederick Engels declared in *The German Ideology* that,

> each new class which puts itself in the place of one ruling before it, is compelled, merely in order to carry through its aim, to represent its interest as the common interest of all the members of society, that is expressed in ideal form: it has to give its ideas the form of universality, and represent them as the only rational, universally valid ones.
>
> (Marx and Engels 1970:65–66)

Marx and Engels recognized the basic point, reiterated later by many critics of symbolic anthropology (see Asad 1980; Bloch 1986; Keesing 1987), that cultural values often support the interests or superiority of particular individuals or groups in society. The revolutionary's task, therefore, is to destroy or neutralize those cultural elements that reproduced the old order, and replace them with new ideas and values to create a new order. The veracity of Marx and Engels' conclusion was not lost on the Vietnamese Communists. As soon as they assumed power in August 1945, they embarked upon an ambitious program to create a new, socialist culture for Vietnam. For the officials, this project carried with it a strong sense of urgency. As many often quoted from Lenin, 'old habits and customs of people are the things of which one should be the most frightened' (Ninh Binh, Cultural Service 1968:6), thus Vietnamese society and culture needed a major reworking. Implementation of this project began in 1945, but like other policies, it was disrupted by the French war and did not see full-scale implementation across the north and in Thinh Liet until late 1954.

This chapter examines the nature of the new culture created by the Communists and the different mechanisms employed for its propagation. Anyone who spends time in the northern Vietnamese countryside is quick to recognize that the ideas, terms, and categories introduced by the revolution, far from being abstract ideas divorced from everyday life, profoundly structure and influence the way in which people conceive of and talk about society, culture, ritual, morality, politics, and numerous other aspects of social life. Discussions of morality, for example, almost always involve references to the 'revolutionary ethics' introduced by the party, or when people discuss those elements of ritual practices abandoned since the revolution, they often attach the labels 'feudal' or 'backward' to them. The objective of this chapter is to bring out this set of ideas and valuations introduced by the party when reconstituting socio-cultural life, and explain the techniques and mechanisms employed to achieve this reconstitution. At one level, this chapter constitutes a history of ideas associated with revolutionary culture, particular the assorted 'facts' and assertions the party produced to justify its agendas. Yet it is also a study of revolutionary rhetoric and how people employ that rhetoric today. As Needham commented, the employment of rhetoric does not necessarily entail that the individuals employing that rhetoric necessarily 'believe' what they are saying (see Needham 1972), yet it is nevertheless reveals the ideas and categories people employ when discussing and conceptualizing their socio-cultural world. By introducing these ideas and categories at this stage in the monograph, the reader should gain an introductory understanding of the revolutionary process in northern Vietnam that will help render more comprehensible the analyses presented in the remaining chapters.

Ho Chi Minh and the Redefinition of Morality

One key assumption of party ideology was that the 'old morality' had served to legitimize the old regime. In a paraphrase of Marx and Engels' famous statement in *The German Ideology*, one official source commented, 'We know that the ideology, morals, rituals, and practices of people are not created de novo. They are primarily the products of the exploiting regime. Marx has said: "the class in society that has power over material resources also has power over culture"' (Vietnam, Government 1962:4). To create the new socialist society, the old morality had to be 'swept clean' (*quet sach*) and a new morality created. The individual who played the key role in this process was Ho Chi Minh. Not unlike the pre-revolutionary emperor who periodically released hortative tracts to reinvigorate morality within his domain and ideally served as the 'moral arbiter of his society' (Woodside 1971:189), Ho took it upon himself to define the new morality. He argued that, 'if you do not have ethics, you do not have a foundation' (Ho Chi Minh 1984: 467), and engaged in a life long effort to articulate a new moral code he described as 'revolutionary ethics' (*dao duc cach mang*).[1]

Early indications of Ho's interest in elaborating a new moral code for Vietnamese society trace back to 1926 with his writing of the volume *The Revolutionary Road* (*Duong Kach Menh*) in which he detailed the 'behavior of a revolutionary' (*Tu Cach Mot Nguoi Kach Menh*).[2] This list of desired behaviors included a number of themes he would reiterate throughout his life, such as frugalness, self-sacrifice, steadfastness, impartiality, disinterest in material perquisites, the rejection of arrogance and status-seeking, and the abilities to ask questions and recognize one's mistakes (Ho Chi Minh 1988:7–8). Ho's next major statement on morality was the October 1947 publication of the pamphlet 'Correcting the Way We Work' (*Sua Doi Loi Lam Viec*). This ninety one page document, largely directed toward cadres, was interesting for several reasons. First, its content is extremely expansive, covering, among other things, such issues as methods of criticism, personal behaviour, experiences to follow and avoid, the problem of selecting and training cadres, styles of leadership, and the need for conciseness in words and actions. Second, the rhetorical devices employed reveal Ho's ideas about how to present compelling moral instruction and persuasion. One device he employed a number of times, and which he would use on numerous occasions later in life, was to ask a question and then supply a succinct answer followed by further elaboration. He asked, 'For whom do we work? To whom are we responsible?' He answered,

> 'If we ask a cadre "For whom do we work? To whom are we responsible?", certainly many would reply, "We work for the government or party, we are responsible to our superiors." This reply is only partially correct. If we ask, "The government and party work for whom? And who are they responsible to?", unfortunately many cadres cannot reply. The government and party are only responsible for liberating the people. Because of that, all tasks are carried out in the interests of the people and we are responsible to them'.
>
> (Ho Chi Minh 1984:458–59; see also Tan Sinh 1977)

This style served to help cadres present the new principles in a forthright, easily comprehensible fashion.

Perhaps the greatest significance of 'Correcting the Way We Work' lays in the fact that it contains one of Ho's first statements on 'revolutionary ethics' (*dao duc cach mang*). Drawing from Vietnam's Neo-Confucian legacy that valorized the five cardinal virtues of 'benevolence' (*nhan*), 'righteousness' (*nghia*), 'ritual' (*le*), 'knowledge' (*tri*), and 'sincerity' (*tin*), Ho enumerated the five cardinal virtues of revolutionary ethics: benevolence, righteousness, knowledge, 'courage' (*dung*) and 'incorrupt-ibility' (*liem*). Although Ho maintained three Neo-Confucian virtues, he semantically recast their meaning. Benevolence became unswerving compassion for one's comrades and the masses, and also the commitment not to perform any actions that would have negative consequences for the people or the party. Righteousness entailed forthrightness, an unwavering commitment to carrying out one's orders, and the devotion not to do anything that contradicted the party's interests. Knowledge involved the awareness and ability to successfully carry out one's work and avoid negative outcomes. Of the two new virtues, courage entailed having the strength and fortitude to carry out difficult tasks, even if it required the sacrifice of one's life, and incorruptibility enjoined one not to covet status, money, happiness, or praise (Ho Chi Minh 1984:466–7).

The primary impulse that informed these changes, and the theme that ran through both Ho's later voluminous writings on morality and other official proclamations, was the desire to rechannel people's loyalties and obligations away from their own parochial interests to the party, the revolution, and the collective (*tap the*). As party officials saw it, pre-revolutionary society manifest a number of detrimental tendencies that one source summed up with the statement: "'the strong win, the weak lose," "the clever live, the lesser die," or the way of life in which "disadvantage for others, advantage for me,' "I only know myself and don't care for others," these things were all considered natural' (Vietnam, Government 1962:4–5). Officials grouped these tendencies under the title of 'individualism' (*chu nghia ca nhan*) and designated them as socialism's main enemy. To overcome them, the people needed to internalize and behave according to the principle of 'all for one and one for all' (*minh vi moi nguoi, moi nguoi vi minh*). By the 1960s, officials began encapsulating the revolutionary ethics agenda in the popular adage apparently written by Ho Chi Minh, 'Industry, thrift, incorruptibility, and righteousness. Public spirit and impartiality' (*Can, kiem, liem, chinh. Chi cong vo tu*). At this time, efforts to solidify the new morality took on a sense of urgency given the difficulties the government experienced in trying to persuade people to enthusiastically engage in collective production for the agricultural cooperatives (see Vickerman 1986). Official discourse asserted that 'everything serves production' (*tat ca phuc vu san xuat*), including morality, but the stigmatized 'small peasant production' (*san xuat tieu nong*) persisted and people still preferred to produce for themselves. In 1961 Ho summed up the problem and the transformation needed in the following terms, '*Individualism*, an advantage for me, debility for others, disorganized, undisciplined, and other bad qualities that are the dangerous enemy of socialism. The people who are masters of their country must tend to the affairs of the nation as they do the affairs of their own home. Factory workers must prize their machines as they prize their own children, farmers must treat the buffalos and cows of the cooperative as their dear friends. Everyone must know how to care for that which is of the collective, and must carry out the work of the collective, just as they take care of the affairs of their family' (Ho Chi Minh 1988:50). During the American war years, the moral emphasis turned toward encouraging people to defend the country and increase production to supply the troops. The party asserted that by following the new principles, not only could the war be won and production increased, but a truly new, just, and egalitarian Vietnamese society could be created. As Ho Chi Minh stated in summation of the revolutionary ethics, 'These are new ethics, great ethics, they are not for the glory of individuals, but instead for the interests of the party, the people, and humanity' (Ho Chi Minh 1984:467).

Ho continued to write about morality virtually until the time of his death in 1969. Only seven months before he died he published the short piece 'Raise Up Revolutionary Ethics, Eliminate Individualism' (*Nang Cao Dao Duc Cach Mang, Quet Sach Chu Nghia Ca Nhan*) in which he again castigated individualists for their retrograde ways (Ho Chi Minh 1988:97). Although Ho constituted the leading figure in articulating the new morality, by the early 1960s the party had constructed a vast edifice for propagating the new moral system. Other leading officials, such as Truong Chinh, Le Duan, and Pham Van Dong, contributed to this process, along with official party organizations, such as the Ministry of Culture and the Institute of Philosophy, and official publications, such as the party journal *Hoc Tap*. After his death, the party continued to appropriate the person of Ho Chi Minh as the legitimate definer of morality. For example, in 1970 the People's Court of Ninh Binh province published a document on the organization of the New Year celebrations entitled, 'A Frugal, Wholesome *Tet*, Carried Out According to Uncle's Words' (*Tet Tiet Kiem, Lanh Manh, Lam Theo Loi Bac*) (Ninh Binh, People's Court 1970). Later official publications on morality almost always included at the beginning of the text lengthy Ho quotations, such as his famous comment, 'If you want to build socialism, before all else you must have socialist people' (*Muon xay dung xa hoi chu nghia, truoc het can co nhung con nguoi xa hoi chu nghia*). Ho's salience as moral paragon was also visible in a 1973 volume *Our Party Discusses Ethics* (*Dang Ta Ban Ve Dao Duc*) (Vietnam, Institute of Philosophy 1973). Apart from literally hundreds of Ho quotations in the volume that cover everything from the proper morality for party members to children, the introduction of the volume includes such statements as 'President Ho taught us to be faithful to the nation and filial to the people' (Vietnam, Institute of Philosophy 1973:8), or 'With regard to the problem of teaching the new morality, the party constantly brings forth the shining example of President Ho' (Vietnam, Institute of Philosophy 1973:9). Beyond textual usages, Ho's quotations were also placed on posters and banners displayed in public places.

Although the state took an intense interest in advancing the image of Ho as moral paragon, he nevertheless fulfills this role among everyday people in contemporary northern Vietnam (see also Malarney 1997). Part of this is due to the fact that after he returned to Vietnam in 1941, he took it upon himself to consistently set a moral example that both cadres and non-party members could follow (Marr 1981:100). He dressed simply, lived in a simple house, maintained an unassuming manner, and apparently did not engage in corrupt practices. Some say that he never married because he was 'married to the revolution,' although he himself commented that his was not a trait for others to emulate (Marr 1981:100). He was also a master of appearing as a man of the people. Despite his transcendent position, he interacted with the people on an intimate, egalitarian basis. He ate, lived, and mixed freely with common people, spoke of all Vietnamese as being 'children of one home' (*con cua mot nha*), and addressed people with kinship or intimate terms, such as 'friend' (*ban*) or 'dear brothers and sisters' (*Anh chi em yeu qui*). Most famously, he usually forewent the popular and prized term 'comrade' (*dong chi*) that was used for other high-ranking party members, and preferred the intimate, respectful, and slightly affectionate 'uncle' (*bac*).[3] The combination of all of these factors fortified the idea that Ho 'took the entire people as his family' (Marr 1981:100), and also gave greater credence to his moral pronouncements. He was 'loyal to the country, pious with the people' (*trung voi nuoc, hieu voi dan*). Granted, the new morality's articulation did not mean that people necessarily followed all elements within it, but it did become a benchmark for social life. Thus, in conversations about political morality, both party members and others frequently make reference to Ho's sayings as representations of the proper morality, particularly Ho's declaration 'Industry, Thrift, Honesty, and Industrious. Public Spirit and Impartiality.' Most interestingly, one also regularly hears the invocation, 'As Uncle Ho said ...' (*Nhu Bac Ho da noi ...*) preface comments about morality. This practice's social salience was revealed to me once in somewhat amusing fashion when, after being rudely treated by a Hanoi policeman, a friend encouraged me to write a letter explaining the incident to a local television program and conclude with the question, 'Is this the way Uncle Ho taught our policemen to behave toward foreigners?' Indeed, the rhetoric of revolutionary ethics, with their emphasis on probity, selflessness, and working for the good of the people and not oneself remains prominent. As I have argued elsewhere, Ho's role as moral arbiter is heavily symbolic and does not necessarily entail that Ho was all the things that have been attributed to him (see Malarney 1997:907), yet his thoughts, though imperfectly followed, remain a benchmark for morality.

Culture Redefined

Beyond reworking morality, the revolutionary state also attempted to create a new culture. Like their position on morality, cadres argued that many of the cultural ideas and practices of the pre-revolutionary period had negative consequences in Vietnamese life. As one set of regulations asserted in 1968,

> The habits of respecting men and despising women, living and
> working carelessly, disorganization, producing for oneself, the lack

of hygiene, discipline, planning, and science, following superstitions, the lack of democracy and equal rights in the family, etc
... these are all products that the exploiter's culture has left behind.
(Ninh Binh, Cultural Service 1968:19)

Ho Chi Minh stated the problem more concisely when he commented that
the mandarinal and colonial authorities had employed cultural values in
order to 'keep the people stupid.' Writing under the name Nguyen Ai Quoc
he stated, 'Keeping the people stupid makes them easy to rule over;
therefore those who hold power in our colonies eagerly employ a keep the
people stupid policy there' (Ngo Van Cat 1980:12). The revolution
required a dramatic reconfiguration of the people's socio-cultural habits
and practices in order to shatter this linkage between culture and the
former elite, and to make the people the masters of their own destinies. To
do so, the party launched a 'cultural and ideological revolution' (*cach mang
tu tuong va van hoa*) that would redefine and/or purify existing cultural
elements, as well as create new ones.

The party began its task of building a new culture in the 1940s, but
could not fully implement it until after taking power in 1954. In party
discourse, officials regularly spoke of the 'new culture' (*van hoa moi*), but
in the early 1960s they also spoke of 'mass culture' (*van hoa quan chung*)
and later the term 'socialist culture' (*van hoa xa hoi chu nghia*) became
prominent. The rhetoric of the 'new' squared with an important trend in
official ideology. Officials spoke of constructing a 'new person' (*con nguoi
moi*), a 'new society' (*xa hoi moi*), and a 'new culture family' (*gia dinh van
hoa moi*). In the former case, the 'new person' would manifest a number of
important traits such as a love for their country, peace, labor, the people,
socialism, and science. At different periods of Vietnam's revolutionary
history, the new person would also embrace a readiness to produce for the
cooperatives or bear arms for the country, but it was to always live up to the
standards of the newly articulated morality. The new society championed
these same principles and as it was a socialist society, the main principles
that theoretically guided its organization were egalitarianism, democracy,
collective labor, order, and discipline. All the same, the party still reserved
for itself the exclusive role of political leadership and did not encourage
debate about its proposals.

Party ideologues employed a number of specific terms to describe the
new culture and often contrasted them with their pre-revolutionary
opposites. One of the most prominent terms was 'progressive' (*tien bo* or
tien tien), which became a marker of prestige in local discourse. It was
contrasted with two of the most stigmatized terms in official discourse,
'backwards' (*lac hau*) and 'feudal' (*phong kien*). This latter term, which
found expression as early as 1925 in the writings of Ho Chi Minh (see
Pham Xanh 1990:165), assumed tremendous significance from the 1940s

onward. Feudal was a catch phrase used to describe any idea or practice that either reproduced relations of inequality or asserted the existence of non-empirically verifiable causality in human life. At a general level, party ideology defined all aspects of the culture and ideology of the pre-colonial social order as feudal as they validated the inequalities of pre-revolutionary social life, such as husbands over wives or mandarins over commoners. Feudalism's sinister quality was that it made the former paramounts domination and their inferiors' obedience seem natural and just. Other terms employed to describe different characteristics of the new culture were 'collective' (*tap the*) or 'shared' (*chung*) as opposed to the 'individual' (*ca nhan*) or 'private' (*rieng*), 'wholesome' (*lanh manh*), 'beautiful' (*tham my*), 'happy' (*hanh phuc*), 'cheerful' (*vui tuoi*), 'humanitarian' (*nhan dao*), 'patriotic' (*yeu nuoc*), 'proletarian' (*vo san*), of the 'people' (*nhan dan*), of the 'ethnic group' (*dan toc*), 'egalitarian' (*cong bang*), 'liberation' (*giai phong*), and 'science' (*khoa hoc*).

The latter two terms merit special attention. As noted above, the Communists held that the feudal elements had played a critical role in keeping the people stupid and unaware of the realities of their own oppression and exploitation. As Le Duan commented, 'The people have become so completely accustomed to this that they think it is completely natural, but it is in fact the consequence of thousands of years of control by the royal exploiting class' (Vietnam, Government 1962:4). The new culture would teach people the realities of socio-political life so they could liberate themselves from their bondage and become the masters of their own political destiny.[4] On a different level, the new culture would also liberate them from retrograde ideas and practices, particularly those related to ideas regarding supernatural causality, that kept people cowering in fear in their daily lives or spurred them to engage in potentially harmful practices, such as divination or spirit-based healing techniques (see Chapter 3). The element that would affect this latter change was the application of science. At the rhetorical level, science or scientific is one of the terms most frequently applied to the new culture. Vietnamese intellectuals began developing a strong interest in science in the 1920s. The idea of science was very alluring for not only was it associated with progress and provided a mechanism for escaping subjectivity and determining objective 'truth' (*su that*), its methodology 'seemed to be at the heart of man's capacity in recent centuries to break conceptual barriers, to smash myths that had held him back for so long' (Marr 1981:344). Communists ideologues carried over this same idea, asserting that science was the key for economic and cultural advancement. With it, that which was backwards would be discarded and that which was progressive would be attained. Nevertheless, officials to a certain extent fetishized the idea of science. Like the colonial era intellectuals described by Marr, for the cadres, 'there was more than a hint of religious fervor in these intelligentsia arguments (about the benefits of science). The old spirits who had helped to explain the world previously were in effect to be replaced by the single god of Science, who would not only explain but liberate' (Marr 1981:346).

Two other aspects of the new culture require mention. First, although Vietnamese culture contained retrograde elements, the new culture's creation did not entail an absolute break with the past. Instead, officials wanted to maintain those elements they considered to have positive value. For example, an official declaration from the Fifth Party Congress in 1981 declared that, 'The new culture both crystallizes and raises up to a new high level the most beautiful elements from the 4000 years of the Vietnamese spirit and culture,' but also combines them with other elements drawn from socialism, international proletarianism, contemporary scientific culture, and human civilization (Ta Van Thanh 1990:43). Certain former elements, such as the practice of villages maintaining communal lands or the history of struggle against foreign invaders, received ready acceptance, but as will be shown in later chapters, deciding what other elements were worthy of retention or elimination was often subject to dispute. Finally, officials saw the new culture as playing a deliberately functional role in creating the new society. The Vietnamese revolution broke down into three different revolutions: the revolution in science and technology, the revolution in productive relations, and the cultural and ideological revolution. Of the three, the first two revolutions took precedence as they would provide the actual material improvements in Vietnamese society, such as increases in agricultural productivity, a rise in the standard of living, and industrialization. Officials recognized, however, that as it would ultimately require people to achieve these goals, they needed to learn the value and importance of these goals so they could achieve them. Officials commented in 1962 that the task of the cadres was to 'eliminate the old culture, build a new culture, a new morality, and new ways that correlate with the new regime' (Vietnam, Government 1962:2). This idea of correlating with the new regime received even clearer emphasis when in 1981 another official stated, 'Building the new culture and carrying out the cultural and ideological revolution both have the principal goal of building the new socialist person' (Tran Do 1986:144). By building this newly enculturated person, all of the other revolutionary agendas, such as fighting against foreign aggressors, renouncing individualism, making people 'masters of the collective' (lam chu tap the), increasing production, raising living standards, and others, could be realized. The new culture, therefore, constituted a critical ligature that tied the various revolutionary agendas together within the new person. It also played an important supporting role for the other two revolutions in the creation of the new socialist society.

60

Introducing the New Ways

While the rhetoric and concepts associated with the construction of the new person and culture did filter down to the level of communes and villages, the subtle nuances of such issues were slightly removed from the everyday concerns of local cadres and confined primarily to party ideologues in Hanoi. The main concern of cadres carrying out cultural reforms at the commune level was the implementation of the 'New Ways' (*Nep Song Moi*) or 'New Life' (*Doi Song Moi*), the main local cultural transformation project.[5] The New Ways' significance lay in the fact that they represented in concrete terms the types of social, cultural, and behavioral changes the party sought to produce in Vietnamese society. Unlike the abstract admonitions about culture or morality coming from the higher reaches of official ideology, the New Ways directly engaged specific personal behaviors and were also the forum in which the party described the intended reforms of ritual practice. Indeed, although the 'cultural and ideological revolution' was included as one of Vietnam's 'three revolutions,' the New Ways represented the actual mechanics for changing local social, cultural, and ritual life.

The campaign to implement the New Ways began on 3 April 1946 with the formation of the 'Central Committee for the Propagation of the New Life' (*Ban Trung Uong Van-Dong Doi Song Moi*). Early statements on them, such as Kim Phong's 21 June 1946 volume, *What is the New Life* (*The Nao La Doi Song Moi*) declared that the New Ways were 'progressive ways' (Kim Phong 1946:11), ways that made it 'easier to breathe' (Kim Phong 1946:14). From the beginning, the New Ways were to play an important role in realizing the broader agenda of creating the new society and culture. Kim's volume, for example, devotes four pages to defining what officials meant by 'Industry, Thrift, Honesty, Righteousness;' declared that the three principles animating the New Ways were 'the people' (*dan toc*), 'democracy' (*dan chu*), and 'science' (*khoa hoc*); and explained how the New Ways ushered in an era in which fairness, equal rights, and respect for the citizenry prevailed (Kim Phong 1946:10). The volume also laid out other themes that would become prominent in later years. In a ten point list, Kim noted that people should work hard; be prepared to make material sacrifices to help the nation; reduce expenditures for weddings, funerals, and temple and mausolea construction, and devote the savings to communal benefit; maintain good health so one can work hard; practice military drills to protect the nation; study to increase one's technical expertise so one could perhaps assist in the construction of society; learn what it meant to be a new person; learn how to participate in communal endeavours and eliminate practices devoted to only family and kin; abandon gambling, the burning of votive paper items, and wasteful feasting; propagandize on elements essential to life, such as hygiene,

61

science, and other basic knowledge; and maintain an attitude of incorruptibility and righteousness in one's work (Kim Phong 1946:24–5).

As is clear, Kim's list was quite exhaustive, and as the years passed, party ideologues examined all facets of social life and broadened their list of recommendations regarding how Vietnamese should behave in the new society. Throughout, the general goals of the New Ways were summarized in the 'Industriousness, thrift . . .' adage, yet a number of other themes also remained prominent, such as conducting one's interpersonal affairs with honesty and impartiality, particularly if one held public office; working hard; being punctual and respectful of work hours; living frugally; and eliminating wasteful habits as profligacy weakened the nation. Citizens were also encouraged to 'love labor, peace and socialism' (Kim Cuc 1960:3). Other personal habits also came under scrutiny. Certain retrograde elements of Vietnamese social life, such as wife-beating and the tormenting of daughters-in-law by their mother-in-laws, were to stop. Hygiene was a major concern. Cadres regarded poor sanitation and personal habits as a root cause for the disease and miserable conditions that afflicted many Vietnamese. People were therefore encouraged to practice good personal and public hygiene in order to reduce disease and maintain good health.[6] Some recommendations were quite particular, such as admonitions not to have sexual relations in front of other people, a potentially unintended possibility in small Vietnamese houses, or write profanity on historical sites (Ninh Binh, Cultural Service 1968:50 and 60). Issues of increasing and strengthening collective production aside, the basic thrust of many elements in the New Ways was to make public life more genteel, clean, polite, and orderly. People were to dress neatly and modestly, stop getting drunk in public, and stop arguing and fighting with each other as well. One writer had a number of his own suggestions on what merited elimination from public life. He commented,

> There are some thoughtless people who, having any dirty things in their house, simply throw them out into the street, such as dead rats or chickens, or the excrement of their children. There are others who have their children relieve themselves at the curbside as if it were completely natural. There are some places on the sidewalks which are congested with places where people throw their garbage and others where people spit. The scene on the street of people spitting at their convenience is both offensive and unhygienic. Still there are yet others who consider the act of urination something that can be done in any spot or in front of anyone. Such people do not know embarrassment.
>
> (Kim Cuc 1960:44)

Beyond attempting to change how people conducted themselves in society, the other major component of the New Ways was the agenda to reform and modify ritual practice. That the Communists would want to reform rituals was not remarkable. New emperors ascending the throne in the pre-modern period often embarked upon campaigns to clean up ritual practice in their domain (see Tran Trong Kim 1954: 243–6, 436–7). During the colonial period, urban intellectuals, from whose ranks many party ideologues were drawn, had also produced numerous critiques of village ritual practices. The common theme in these expositions was the alleged waste involved in their conduct and the need to reform (*cai luong*) them in order to help the peasantry escape the cycle of poverty that oppressed it (see Murray 1980:387; Phan Ke Binh 1990:134; Truong Chinh and Vo Nguyen Giap 1974:21).

The party officially began its implementation of ritual reforms in 1945, but again the uniform implementation of the agenda across the country did not begin until late 1954.[7] The party completely banned some rituals, notably communal house ceremonies or those involving attempts to contact or manipulate the spirit world, but they sought to reform those they allowed to remain. The cadres involved in reforming rituals and writing up the new ritual regulations had a very sophisticated understanding of the way in which rituals could reproduce ideas and practices unsanctioned by the party. Cadres also understood that when reforming ritual, they could not change them to such an extent that they became meaningless and people rejected them. As officials commented with regard to funeral reforms, all new rites needed to 'respond to the worthy psychological and sentimental demands of the masses' (Vietnam, Ministry of Culture 1975:31). Thus, in reforming rituals, the general strategy employed by the party was to selectively remove certain parts, give greater emphasis or meaning to other preexisting parts, and sometimes add new components. One vital mechanism for carrying out this project was the application of a new evaluative rubric created by the party. Like the reclassification of specific elements conducted in the creation of a new culture, the implementation of the New Ways included its own redefinition and reclassification of cultural elements. Part of this included employing the feudal, progressive, or backwards labels mentioned above, but party ideologues also embarked on a more ambitious campaign to reclassify 'customs' into three main categories. The first category, which retained the pre-revolutionary term, consisted of the commendable 'customs and practices' (*phong tuc, phong tuc tap quan*). All items that fell under this title were regarded as worthy of praise and retention. More ambiguously, the second category consisted of the questionable 'out-dated customs' (*hu tuc*). Elements in this category needed reform, but were not necessarily in need of immediate elimination. The final category consisted of the malignant 'bad practices and corrupt customs' (*doi phong bai tuc*). Anything in this category was considered to have socially harmful effects and merited immediate elimination. When applied to weddings, funerals, death anniversaries, and other customs, these categories provided a device for evaluating different elements within them, and then selectively retaining, eliminating, or modifying them. By carrying out this agenda, the party hoped that it could succeed in making all ritual practices fit with socialist ideology.

The New Ways described in extremely detailed terms the manner in which individuals were to conduct themselves so they and the new society could advance and grow stronger. As with the case of both morality and culture, officials asserted that by following them, all Vietnamese would be united in the goal of building the socialist nation. In introducing one of the early tracts written by a member of the Central Committee for the Propagation of the New Ways, Ho Chi Minh stated, 'I hope that everyone among the masses has a copy of this book *The New Ways* to read, understand, and use to guide them in the realization of the New Ways. This way, we are certain to progress' (Tan Sinh 1977:9).

Mobilizing the Masses I: Institutional Structures and Texts

In order to get its message of the new culture and ways across to the people, the party employed an extensive network of official organizations, each frequently charged with a specific task in the new culture's propagation. The full-scale establishment of the new revolutionary administrative system across North Vietnam after 1954 had resulted in the disbanding of unsanctioned social organizations and their replacement by officially approved and controlled social organizations that served to protect and reproduce official interests and ideology. The dominant organization in this new system was the party, which functioned at the local level in the commune's party cell (*dang bo*) that was headed by a secretary (*bi thu*) and composed of all local party members. All party members shared a special responsibility to serve as 'models' (*guong mau*) for other residents to follow. Drawing on the Confucian principle of *chinh giao*, party members had to provide lived examples of the new morality and customs, thus realizing in one fashion the popular slogan, 'Party members go first, the nation follows' (*Dang vien di truoc, lang nuoc di sau*). Those who failed to do so could be subject to official criticism and dismissal from the party. Beyond individual members, the party also employed the array of mass organizations that operated under the umbrella of the 'Fatherland Front' (*Mat Tran To Quoc*). As a national organization, the Fatherland Front was first established in 1955 (Beresford 1988:121). It has never had an executive role in local administration, but was nevertheless critical as it answered directly to the local party apparatus and served to coordinate the dissemination and implementation of official policies. Today it consists of a total of some twenty five different associations, such as the Women's Association, the Ho Chi Minh Young Communist Pioneers, the Peasant Association, and others.

Following the departure of the land reform cadres in early 1956, cadres from Thinh Liet assumed full responsibility for implementing the new policies. Although precise figures are impossible to obtain, Thinh Liet party membership has likely followed national trends and never exceeded 5 percent of the population (see Porter 1993:69). Today it is under 3 percent with some 300 members (these numbers vary annually). Historically, the vast majority of party members have been men, who in turn have also tended to occupy the leadership positions. Since its establishment, the Thinh Liet party cell secretary has always been male, as have the leaders of most other organizations. Women have obviously headed the Women's Association, and there was an interesting exception of a woman serving as Commune President in the 1980s, but women have been marginal compared to men. Thinh Liet's earliest party members came from elite families who joined in the late 1940s. With the intensification of the French War in the early 1950s and the subsequent land reform, the local party membership's composition changed. Party members from the former elite became marginalized and the local apparatus came to be dominated by people from middle peasant, poor peasant, and laborer backgrounds. Especially prominent were men from agricultural families who had served in the army and entered the party there. These men returned to Thinh Liet after service and came to control most of the executive positions in the apparatus. As residents recall, many also provided the most vigorous examples of revolutionary fervor.

Over the following decades, Thinh Liet's party membership changed further. During the relatively peaceful years from 1957–64, and later from 1975 onward, residents who joined the party usually did so through membership in official organizations, notably the Youth Association (*Doan Thanh Nien*). This route was open to both men and women, but was demanding as consideration for membership required enthusiastic participation in the collective economy, the public display of support for official policies, years of attendance at political and indoctrination sessions (which took place at least once a week), and participation in propaganda or educational sessions for other residents. Despite the party's monopoly on power, entrance into it was actually difficult and only achieved after years of effort. This obviously screened out the less committed, but as this emphasis on commitment to party ideals was necessary for all prospective members, regardless of which organization they joined through, the extremely small percentage of party members in the general population becomes more intelligible. Thinh Liet had another important dynamic that developed from the early 1960s. With the gradual increase in factory and office workers, a number of residents joined the party through cells in those organizations, but despite their membership in the Thinh Liet party cell, they normally did not occupy executive positions in the commune cell. Instead, the cell was dominated by members of the local agricultural cooperatives, though especially those with middle peasant backgrounds. Here again, the middle peasants benefited the most from revolutionary policies. The outbreak of the decade long American War produced a final transformation in party membership and recruitment as large numbers of residents became party members while serving in organizations devoted to the war effort. A number of women became party members while serving in volunteer groups that assisted the military or conducted civilian projects, such as repairing roads, while a number of men became members while serving in the military. Party membership was optional for lower-ranking soldiers, but obligatory for officers. After the war, many former officers returned to Thinh Liet to become active in the local administration. Most Communal Presidents in the post-war period have been former officers. The Thinh Liet party cell has included members from all lineages and with the exception of some former landlord families, all segments of society, though it is fair to say that it has been dominated by agriculturalists with middle peasant backgrounds. In terms of enthusiasm, many former officers strictly propagated the party line, but several of the most strident cadres and party cell secretaries have been farmers who have never lived outside of the community. This was particularly true from the late 1950s to the early 1980s when many of the formerly disenfranchised achieved significant power and influence in the community.

When Thinh Liet cadres began implementing the reformed ritual policies, the two official organizations that played the dominant roles were the Youth Association and the Elderly Association (*Hoi Phu Lao*). The reason for their dominance related to their age-set character. Membership in the Youth Association was confined to men and women aged eighteen to twenty eight, while one became eligible for membership in the Elderly Association at age fifty five. These age groups correlated sociologically with the three main foci of ritual reform. First, couples tended to marry in their late teens and early twenties, thus the Youth Association assumed primary responsibility for propagandizing about the new marriage regime and implementing the reformed wedding ceremony. Second, the majority of funerals were performed for elderly people, and older women performed the majority of unsanctioned 'superstitious' rites, thus the Elderly Association assumed the preeminent role in propagandizing against superstitious rites and implementing the funeral reforms. It should be noted, however, that while these organizations took the lead in these reforms, the party cell and other associations participated in reinforcing their efforts. Indeed, the party's mobilizing apparatus and propaganda were a visible part of local life.

The instructions used by local organizations to reform rituals generally had their origins in orders or directives issued from the highest reaches of government, but despite the stated objective of producing a uniform socialist culture for all Vietnam, there was a striking amount of variation in ritual reform. The two organizations that laid down the parameters for ritual reform were the party's Central Committee and the Ministry of Culture. A common pattern was for one to publish 'instructions' (*chi thi*) that were then transmitted to the relevant authorities throughout the country. These then became the basis for more detailed regulations issued at the city, province, district, or even commune level. For example, on 15 January 1975, the Central Committee published Instruction #214, entitled 'On the Realization of the New Ways in Weddings, Funerals, Death Anniversaries, and Festivals,' which included a prominent section on the elimination of superstitions. Then, on 7 February 1975, the municipal government of Hanoi published its own communique, 'On the Work of Prohibiting All Occupations Related to Superstitions, Divination, Astrology, Spirit Mediumship, Votive Paper Objects . . .', which follows up the original instructions but with particular reference to Hanoi's specific concerns (Hanoi, Cultural and Information Service 1975:3–8). The ritual regulations, dozens of which were consulted for this monograph, are interesting for two main reasons. First, although they present a general outline of the types of ritual reforms the party wanted and how they envisioned their implementation, they also show that the party did not impose a universal model on all localities. Instead, a review of the regulations reveals that local officials were free to tinker with the smaller details of reforms in their areas, thereby producing numerous differences in actual reforms. Second, the regulations are surprisingly frank about some of the reforms' failures. Alexander Woodside has commented that in the nineteenth century, officials did not manipulate factual content in their reports to their superiors. Instead, conflicts and problems were recorded, and the 'emperor was supposed to reveal his worth not by suppressing them but by publishing them, answering them, acting upon them and thus transcending them' (Woodside 1971:324). Officials composing ritual regulations retained this practice of presenting both the problem and the appropriate solution to it. The regulations therefore provide a number of important details about the campaign's history, such as the numerous difficulties they had in trying to eliminate feasting and superstitious practices, as well as other items of historical significance. For example, regulations make it clear that the reforms were easier to implement during war time than in peace, specifically when the American military was bombing the north, and that elderly women remained the most difficult to convince of the reforms' merits. The fact that official organizations continued to publish the regulations for over thirty years indicates that although cadres in the communes received definitive statements from above regarding how they should reform rituals, the job of persuading the people to fully carry them out was very difficult.

Mobilizing the Masses II: The Nature of Propaganda

When embarking upon the process of achieving public acceptance of the new morality, culture, and ways, the party recognized that they faced two related obstacles. First, in order to prevent outright rejection, they needed to avoid 'commandism' (*loi menh lenh*) in their presentation. Instead, cadres were instructed to 'persuade' (*thuyet phuc*) the masses. This persuasion could involve 'mobilization' (*phat dong*), 'agitation' (*van dong*), or the activity most frequently encouraged, 'education' (*giao duc*). The ideal way to communicate the message was to educate the masses through a process of clarifying the virtues of the new regime and criticizing the shortcomings of the old, thereby causing the people to voluntarily reject the latter and accept the former. Indeed, the idea of voluntary acceptance was the universal ideal goal. To achieve it, however, cadres encountered their second obstacle: the need to present their message in a manner that would resonate with the people. The demands of this second concern influenced the nature of propaganda the party developed in that it carried the stamp of both the Confucian heritage of many high-ranking cadres as well as the methods of moral persuasion that existed in Vietnam.

Like their Neo-Confucian predecessors, one of the most popular vehicles for propaganda in revolutionary Vietnam was the slogan. Virtually every new official policy had a slogan attached to it, and Vietnamese who have grown up in the north have the capacity to recite numerous official adages. Many of the most famous were written by Ho Chi Minh, such as his call to fight, 'There is nothing more precious than independence and freedom' (*Khong co gi qui hon doc lap tu do*), or the 'Industry, Thrift ...' adage of revolutionary morality. Other commonplace slogans include 'A Thousand Glorious Years For The Vietnamese Communist Party' (*Dang Cong San Quang Vinh Muon Nam*), or one that has been widely used since Ho's death, 'President Ho Chi Minh Lives Forever In Our Work' (*Chu Tich Ho Chi Minh Song Mai Trong Su Nghiep Cua Chung Ta*). Older people who lived through the Land Reform effortlessly reel off the slogan, 'Rely completely on poor peasants and laborers, unite with the middle peasants, make allies of the rich peasants, and definitively overturn the landlords, traitors, reactionaries, and cruel despots.' And those who lived through the American War easily reproduce such slogans as 'Resolve to defeat the American Invaders' (*Quyet Tam Danh Thang My Xam Luoc*) or 'Everything for the front lines, everything to defeat the invading American enemy' (*Tat Ca Cho Tien Tuyen, Tat Ca De Danh Thang Giac My Xam Luoc*). Many of these slogans were repeated by word of mouth, or in large rallies or convocations, but following the Confucian practice of appropriating public spaces to propagate moral teachings, slogans were often displayed on public banners or billboards, particularly on important national holidays, such as the National Day (2 September), Founding of the Party Day

(3 February), or War Invalids and Martyrs Day (27 July). At an everyday level, other messages are still displayed in other public spaces. Anyone who rides through contemporary Hanoi or Thinh Liet will quickly notice numerous slogans on walls or billboards that exhort residents to live frugally, practice good hygiene, prepare for floods, increase production, have only two children per married couple, stamp out social evils, practice safe sex, prevent the spread of HIV/AIDS, and redouble efforts to build socialism.

Shorter slogans were also popular. These often followed the Confucian practice of assembling groups of related ideas into one category and identifying them with a number, usually three. The pre-revolutionary period, for example, had featured the 'three relations' (*tam cuong*) that articulated the three critical relations of the Confucian social system (subject and king, father and son, husband and wife) or the 'three obediences' (*tam tong*) that instructed women to follow their fathers when they were young, their husbands after marriage, and their sons after becoming widows. Revolutionary officials copied this same style. Thus, the revolution divided into the 'three revolutions.' Land reform cadres in the mid-1950s had to practice the 'three togethers' of the land reform. Women during the American War were encouraged to carry out the 'three responsibilities' (*ba dam dang*): responsibility for the household, for production, and for fighting in place of men. Soldiers had to practice the 'three readies' (*ba san sang*): ready to fight and die, ready to enlist or re-enlist, and ready to serve anywhere. People in the emulation movements needed to follow the 'three resolves' (*ba quyet tam*). To improve the physical environment, cadres hoped people would implement the 'three eradications' (*ba diet*): eliminate mosquitoes, flies, and rats. Other slogans included the 'three goods' (*ba tot*) of the new culture family: produce and fight well, develop the spirit of 'collective mastery,' and build the new ways of the new culture; and the 'four beautifuls' (*bon dep*): beautiful fields, beautiful villages, beautiful families, and beautiful people. Cadres frequently sought the implementation of many of these slogans in emulation campaigns (*thi dua*). The party launched these campaigns with great regularity, generally in order to increase production, but they were also employed to increase participation in the military or step up the eradication of bad customs. Emulation campaigns usually encompassed the entire nation or large areas, such as a province or group of provinces. Those who performed best in the campaign received an official certificate from the government and press coverage. Thinh Liet distinguished itself in early 1946 for its successes during the literacy campaign and in the 1980s for its agricultural cooperative's high productivity.

Another popular method for spreading propaganda, and one championed by Ho Chi Minh himself, was the use of poems and songs. Poetry has long been a national obsession at all levels of Vietnamese society. Elite scholars composed poems with obscure classical illusions in Sino-Vietnamese characters according to the requisite 'six eight' (*luc bat*) meter, while common people possessed a rich oral tradition of 'people's' poetry (*dan gian*) that described legendary tales, humorous stories, and solutions to moral conundrums, often in earthy and bawdy terms. Ho composed hundreds of poems during his lifetime, and often presented the people with a new poem at the lunar new year. Vietnam also had its own 'poet of the revolution,' To Huu. When propagandizing, poems often had a fortifying or didactic quality. A 1947 poem by Ho Chi Minh called 'The Forest Landscape in Viet-Bac' (*Canh Rung Viet-Bac*) illustrates the use of a poem to illustrate the glories of the struggle:

> The Viet Bac forest is splendid,
> Bird songs and gibbon cries fill the day
> Our guests eat fresh corn roasted with rice,
> And after the hunt we toast our roasted forest meats,
> Green mountains, blue waters, we stroll til contentment,
> Sweet spirits, fresh tea, we drink til we're sated,
> When the resistance has triumphed we'll return,
> The moon becomes old this spring.

> (Ho Chi Minh 1984:545)

Life in Viet-Bac, where the Vietnamese Communists were living in caves, was in fact quite harsh, but such poems helped fortify morale. Ho also had a preference for short phrases. In the pre-revolutionary period, brief adages were a popular method of transmitting official morality or idealized visions of Vietnamese society. Ho carried on this tradition with such phrases as:

> If you want to build socialism,
> Before all else you must have socialist people.

Or:

> In the interests of ten years one must cultivate a tree,
> In the interests of a hundred years one must cultivate people.

The party also employed poems to illustrate how those who followed unsanctioned practices suffered. This was particularly the case in poems used to criticize older cultural practices and describe the new forms popularized by the party. One poem on funerals began:

> Make hygiene a respected part of every funeral
> Fill your heart with love and respect
> At death when the eyes close all is finished
> Mourning headbands or other such items, they mean nothing.

> (Thanh Hoa, Cultural Service 1975:25)

Another poem lamented the fate of a second wife:

> The life of the second wife is hard
> I transplant, I plow, she notices nothing
> At night she keeps him all to herself
> And I sleep on a mat outside the house
> Come morning she shouts, 'Number Two! Number Two!
> Get up and make rice, potatoes, and duckweed!'
> My parents were poor,
> I slice duckweed and potatoes.
>
> (Thanh Hoa, Cultural Service 1975:17)

One final method for propagandizing was the use of didactic stories. Like the poems, these stories usually served to illustrate the suffering of those who did not follow the revolution, or the positive consequences for those who did. A fitting example of this style was the pamphlet 'Giang Bien Rids Itself of All Bad Marriage and Funeral Customs,' written by officials of Giang Bien Commune in Gia Lam district of Hanoi, and published by Hanoi's cultural service in 1973. As declared in the introduction, Giang Bien had achieved many 'preliminary successes' in the campaign to eliminate retrograde customs, thus other localities should consider their experiences as a 'lesson' (Hanoi, Culture and Information Service 1973:3). The text covers all of the standard criticisms, such as mentioning that prior to the revolution, the problem of competitive feasting was so bad that some people had to sell off family goods in order to cover funeral expenses, or were in debt many years before paying off brideprice (1973:7). The text also takes an extremely self-critical tone and notes that, despite revolutionary policies, the problem of large-scale feasting returned during the war years (likely after the cessation of bombing). This led to a number of difficulties for residents, such as work left unfinished because people were 'busy at feasts,' the excessive slaughter of pigs, and the inflation of pork prices on the open market (1973:8). Nevertheless, through the effective reasoning of local cadres, people voluntarily abandoned wasteful practices by 1971. The text also includes a passage by the President of the Commune's People's Committee, Nguyen Van Duong, in which he details how one resident went bankrupt after trying to organize a large funeral, while on another occasion an enormous feast was set upon by masses of flies, leading to a cholera outbreak in the village that killed three residents. In a manner similar to national officials, President Duong concluded that folk songs (*ca dao*) were an extremely effective method of transmitting propaganda to the people. With regard to marriage, the authors note that the official plan to conduct weddings in the village communal house had been vigorously opposed for fear that such weddings would bring misfortune to the couple, but in an example of 'cadres go first, the nation follows' (*can bo di truoc, lang nuoc di sau*), the chairman of the agricultural

71

cooperative married his wife there. One year later, both he and another couple married there were blessed with baby boys, the ideal first child. The officials concluded the reforms brought with them a corresponding reduction in social conflict. As they stated regarding the former competition in funerals, 'Now we have a 'filial association' (*hoi hieu*) that arranges everything. Everyone is like everyone else, we all live equally, and at death we are equal again. No conflicts follow!' (1973:30). This style of document, with its case-based explanations of factual problems and factual benefits, was an extremely popular way of taking official propaganda to the people.

Officials in Giang Bien also commented that they had to 'propagandize all the time' (*tuyen truyen thuong xuyen*) (1973:16), but the best method was still persuasion. The government's view echoed this position, thus they encouraged local officials to set up libraries, make use of local recreational clubs (*cau lac bo*) to shows films and plays, or simply hold instructional sessions in which cadres would 'analyze, criticize the negative effects of the problems of the old society so everyone will voluntarily oppose them' (Ha Tay, Cultural Service 1967:22). And if some individuals or families severely lacked revolutionary enthusiasm, they might be taken aside for more intensive mobilization. From the beginning of their implementation to the present, propaganda and ideas drawn from official ideology have been ubiquitous. Indeed, it is perhaps unjust to describe many of these ideas as propaganda because they constitute a vital component of the lived experience of northern Vietnamese in general and Thinh Liet residents in particular. When describing their world, or their past, phrases drawn from their revolutionary past are frequently employed to encapsulate that time or experience. Thus an elderly man when asked about the land reform will likely mention the slogan regarding who to rely on and who to destroy during the land reform. A soldier when asked about what he was prepared to do as a soldier might note how in those days soldiers had the 'three readies.' And an official when asked about the importance of developing people for revolutionary success might say, 'As Uncle Ho said . . .' and note how you cultivate a human in the interests of one hundred years. These poems, slogans, and stories are not confined exclusively to the world of detached propaganda, but are instead part of the stock of rhetorical devices and sanctioned knowledge to describe the experience of revolution.

Mobilizing the Masses III: Civic Ritual

Beyond reforming extant ritual practices, officials also sought to create new civic rites that celebrated the socialist state's virtues. They hoped that through the conduct of these rituals, Vietnamese would internalize specific components of official ideology, such as patriotism, a readiness to fight for the country, a love for socialism, and the motivation to work hard for the collective and increase production. The main holidays championed by the state were the Founding of the Party, International Workers' Day (May 1), War Invalids and Martyrs Day, the anniversary of the August Revolution, Vietnam's National Day, and after his death, Ho Chi Minh's birthday (19 May). Lesser holidays included International Women's Day and International Children's Day, but the government also encouraged officials to organize civic rites on other non-calendrical occasions, such as completing the economic plan, finishing the harvest, concluding an emulation drive, seeing off young men for military service, or even the more prosaic sessions of communal cleaning and sanitation. In Thinh Liet commune, one of the most popular civic rites was the 'Unity Meal' (*Com Doan Ket*) that cooperatives organized for their members after harvesting the tenth month rice crop. Another popular new rite, also derived from officials instructions, was the tree-planting *Tet* (*Tet Trong Cay*). The *Tet* holidays were among the most important pre-revolutionary calendrical rites, but the revolutionary government only actively encouraged the celebration of the Lunar New Year (*Tet Nguyen Dan*) and the Mid-Autumn Festival for children (*Tet Trung Thu*). Ho popularized the new tree-planting Tet as a way to develop and beautify the country. After his death, the government further linked this day to Ho by changing its name to the 'Tree Planting Festival to Remember Our Moral Debt to Uncle Ho' (*Tet trong cay nho on Bac Ho*). (Vietnam, Ministry of Culture 1975:79).

Party officials hoped that the new civic rites would have 'a deep educational effect on the people' (Vietnam, Government 1962:14). To ensure that this happened, they asked officials to set aside time during the rites to talk about the reasons for commemorating that day and elucidating the lessons the people could draw from it for the conduct of their daily lives. Thus, officials might discuss the new morals, the new person, socialism, and the necessities of hard work and frugality, while also criticizing the many bad things they still had to rise above. When trying to instill patriotism or an eagerness to fight for the nation, they might also ask local heroes who had fought to recount their own experiences, or discuss the biographies of officially sanctioned heroes, such as Tran Phu, Nguyen Thi Minh Khai, Ly Tu Trong, or Hoang Van Thu.[8] Some localities erected shrines to fallen heroes where rites could be conducted. The government declared the ideal outcome of these rites as follows:

> At the same time as we struggle against destructive old customs, all the cultural organs for the masses, especially the recreational clubs, must attentively organize new activities for the people. All the commemorative holidays for our people's heroes of must be organized with a new meaning. They must pursue the goal of educating the people on our ancestor's tradition of heroic struggle so the people can learn their examples of patriotism and fortitude

73

in realizing the responsibilities before them ... These worthy activities will improve the lives of the masses and have the power to increase production and inspire people to work hard in fulfilling their responsibilities.

(Vietnam, Government 1962:14–5)

Like their pre-revolutionary predecessors, the new civic rites created by the party were designed to create unity among the people, but instead of uniting them in a parochial village community, they would unite them in a shared national, socialist community that they were eager to participate in, work for, and defend.

Mobilizing the Masses IV: Literacy for the Masses

The final aspect of the local revolutionary cultural transformation that requires mention is the literacy campaign of the 1940s and 1950s. Pre-revolutionary society featured a high rate of illiteracy. Exact numbers are difficult to give, but most estimates range between an 80–95 percent illiteracy rate (see De Francis 1977:240). Concerns about and solutions to the illiteracy problem began to be articulated by Vietnamese intellectuals from the 1930s onward (see Marr 1981:178ff.). The Communists were sympathetic to this agenda, particularly because they regarded illiteracy as part of the elite's 'keep the people stupid policy.' Literacy, in party thought, was a vital component in making people their own masters.

The first stirrings of a literacy campaign in Thinh Liet appeared in 1944 when three young Giap Nhi men, all with elite backgrounds, organized a 'propagation of quoc ngu' (truyen ba quoc ngu) campaign in the commune.[9] This group included a former village chief's son who had studied at the elite 'School of the Protectorate' (Lycee du Protectorate); another who had studied at the famous Thang Long school; and another who was a teacher in Giap Nhi. All had links to the Communist Party, though it is difficult to say to what extent their effort was orchestrated by the party or simply the product of their own volition. Nevertheless, their campaign generally failed and popular attendance was low, notably among women and older people.

The next phase of the Thinh Liet literacy campaign began in late 1945 and went under the name of 'Mass Education' (binh dan hoc vu). Local enthusiasm at this stage was greater than before, a change usually attributed to some people's genuine interest to learn to read and write, some residual sympathy for the party because of famine relief efforts it organized in Thinh Liet in 1944–45, and the active persuasion of the reluctant by members of the revolutionary administration. The 1945 stage also involved more classrooms (one per village neighborhood (xom) instead of one per village), a course duration of two to three months, more than thirty teachers (including five women), and students of all ages and genders. The first eight months of 1946 represented the peak of Thinh Liet's campaign as hundreds of local residents learned rudimentary literacy. Like other North Vietnamese communes, public pressure to participate was very strong. At different spots in the commune, literacy campaign teachers forced passing villagers to spell words. If a villager still could not spell a word after several attempts, they were allowed to pass, but the fear of public humiliation, or a few strong words from the teachers, encouraged many to attend the classes. Thinh Liet's achievements in increasing its literacy rate earned it praise and a public celebration at *Set* temple in September 1946 that included Nguyen Van To, the former head of the Association for the Propagation of *Quoc Ngu*. Given its success, Thinh Liet never again required the organization of another large-scale literacy movement.

Literacy instruction during this period took place in the romanized *quoc ngu* script. The techniques devised to teach reading and writing were quite remarkable (see Marr 1981:33), but also significant in this process was the usage of lessons to advance officially sanctioned ideas, such as the desirability of studying hard, thrift, respect for parents, and good hygiene. Propaganda during the period portrayed becoming literate as a patriotic duty (see Ngo Van Cat 1980:45) and stigmatized those who avoided doing so. One poem read:

> If you can read, go to the gate marked 'glorious,'
> If you cannot, go to the 'gate of the blind.'
> Young girl, strong, pretty, and fresh,
> You can't read a letter, you creep to the blind gate,
> Dear girl, that gate, what shame.
> (Ngo Van Cat 1980:53)

In another, a young girl lamented an illiterate husband:

> You've left, but I couldn't go
> I lay on my back writing a line to a poem
> For I've just learned 'i, t'
> Marrying a man who can read sends one forward,
> Marrying one who can't leaves one in debt.
> (Ngo Van Cat 1980:49)

Official sources estimate that by the autumn of 1954, some ten million North Vietnamese had become literate (Ngo Van Cat 1980:104). The literacy campaign's success rightly deserves recognition as one of the revolution's great accomplishments. Whereas illiteracy had been a critical mechanism for maintaining the inferiority of many citizens, revolutionary practice had significantly weakened this function, though it did not completely eliminate the problem because a minimal level of literacy was not the same as the educational level necessary to obtain important social or political positions. The campaigns had also succeeded in advancing numerous revolutionary agendas. A Ministry of Education publication later noted that mass education had succeeded in,

> propagandizing about the resistance, putting the guidelines and policies of the party deeply into the hearts of the people, teaching patriotism and fortitude to fight and win, strengthening the efforts to eliminate the enemy hunger, defeating foreign invaders, implementing all production policies, establishing revolutionary bases, instructing cadres in the countryside after the land reform ... at every level of important revolutionary change, the campaign helped to strengthen the revolutionary efforts in every manner, and registered many impressive accomplishments.
>
> (Ngo Van Cat 1980:102)

Conclusions

The implementation of the new cultural campaigns profoundly changed the cultural landscape in Thinh Liet commune. The revolutionary apparatus not only overthrew former institutional structures, they also created a new set of structures and practices to propagate the new culture and morality while simultaneously producing a new set of facts and assertions about extant cultural practices and their benefits or liabilities. Some were labelled as regressive, others as progressive. In line with what officials in Ha Tay province stated at the height of the American War, the building of the new culture and morality was carried out 'in order to serve all revolutionary responsibilities, particularly production and the struggle' (Ha Tay, Cultural Service 1967:27), yet it also carried down to the most intimate details of people's lives and how they should behave in society. In retrospect, the consequences of this campaign have been remarkable. Although people have rejected or are ambivalent about many elements within the campaign, the state did succeed in reframing the issues. As will be shown in the remainder of this monograph, the official policies, agendas, and ideas discussed in this chapter are now a critical part of the framework in which people discuss and debate culture, ritual, morality, and other aspects of socio-cultural life. Official positions and assertions have, in effect, become part of Thinh Liet social reality.

PART TWO

The Consequences of Revolution

■ CHAPTER THREE ■

Defining Causality

In *Witchcraft, Oracles, and Magic Among the Azande*, E.E. Evans-Pritchard introduced the concept of 'socially relevant' causality (Evans-Pritchard 1976:25). Evans-Pritchard recognized that in analyzing different ethnographic contexts, it is imperative to comprehend how the members of those societies construct valid causal explanations. As he showed, for the Azande the most compelling causal explanation for misfortune was usually witchcraft, yet ethnographic data illustrate that concepts of socially relevant causation vary widely. In Japan a woman who encounters misfortune after an abortion might interpret those events as the result of the soul of her aborted fetus exacting vengeance upon her (LaFleur 1992:187), while an American women would likely not make that same linkage. Similarly, in rural Thailand the sudden onset of illness in a frightened person might be interpreted as the 'life soul' (*khwan*) fleeing the body (Tambiah 1970:58), while an American would likely search for the material factors that led to illness. Interpretation of events and the construction of a socially compelling explanation in each of these cases involves reference to basic ontological concepts. The Azande, Japanese and Thai explanations are all predicated upon the notion that there are supernatural entities or substances that exist and directly influence human life, while the American interpretations point to the pre-eminence of material explanations and that fact that supernaturally-based explanations are generally considered more speculative or irrelevant.

Evans-Pritchard's invocation of the notion of socially relevant causation has important implications for the study of Thinh Liet cultural life. Looked at in the abstract, the Vietnamese revolution represented an attempt by the state to redefine the ontological assumptions and legitimate causal explanations of the Vietnamese people. Embracing a muscular positivism, revolutionary ideology rejected all notions of supernatural causation in human life and attempted to convince the people to similarly reject such notions and replace them with an empiricist worldview. To their

79

chagrin, this agenda never received total acceptance. It did, however, change the boundaries of debate and threw open to dispute such questions as whether there are non-empirically-verifiable forces or entities that influence human life, what causes misfortune, and what constitutes a valid causal explanation. This chapter will analyze how these debates have played out in Thinh Liet. As will be shown, residents continue to employ non-empirically-verifiable causal explanations to make sense of particular events in their lives. However, there is no single universal system of explanation that all residents employ. To the contrary, such explanations tend to occur in specific contexts, and tend to be made and/or disputed by specific social actors. Throughout the analysis, an effort will therefore be made to clearly define those contexts in which residents employ non-empirical explanations, while also trying to locate sociologically the different social actors most likely to make and dispute such claims. As will become clear, important differences as to what constitutes a legitimate causal explanation exist between men and women, young and old, and party-members and non-party-members.

Secularizing the New Society

One of the most important components of the New Ways was the campaign to secularize Vietnamese society and culture. Like other socialist revolutions, the Vietnamese revolution championed atheism (*chu nghia vo than*) and rejected the notion that anything other than empirically-verifiable causality existed in human life. Feudal culture and ideology had been predicated upon a complex of 'superstitions' (*me tin di doan*), such as ideas regarding vengeful spirits, omens, and auspiciousness, that left the masses powerless in a world of fear and anxiety. Party ideologues rejected outright this system of ideas. To remake individual consciousness, revolutionary practice instituted a radical program of secularization that took the form of a 'policy against superstitions' (*chinh sach chong me tin di doan*). This policy, which can also accurately be described as a campaign, was designed to not simply eliminate by edict those superstitions that had formerly structured socio-cultural life. It also attempted to empirically invalidate their existence through the application of science and rationality. As one government document noted, 'Backward practices and superstitions are the children of feudalism, capitalism and the inadequate understanding of science' (Vietnam, Ministry of Culture 1975:1). Getting rid of them was 'a problem of human liberation' (Vietnam, Government 1962:6). As one 1968 primer put it, 'When the masses still believe in the heavens, spirits, and fate, they will be powerless before natural changes and the difficulties that the old society has left behind. People will not be able to completely be their own masters, the masters of society, nor the masters of the world around them' (Ninh Binh, Cultural Service 1968:6). Through the New

Ways, revolutionary cadres hoped to inculcate a 'scientific spirit' (Vietnam, Government 1962:11) that would rid the people of superstitions and backward practices, and make them their own masters in constructing the new society.

The most basic starting point of the secularization campaign was the reclassification of time. Time in the pre-modern period was organized according to two main principles: the year of the emperor's reign and a twelve month lunar calendar. With the abdication of the Bao Dai Emperor in 1945, any possibility of using the year of reign ended, though the Communists had already rejected it before. One distinctive feature of the lunar calendar system was its division into alternating periods of auspiciousness and inauspiciousness. It was commonly held that rituals had to be conducted at auspicious times for them to be effective. Certain days were considered so inauspicious that some individuals apparently remained in their homes to avoid disaster. The party sought to dispose of the lunar calendar and introduce the solar calendar as the benchmark for time. The solar calendar was not tainted by inauspiciousness, thus individuals would never feel fear nor reluctance to fulfill their assigned roles in production and the construction of socialism due to the date on the calendar. All ritual activities were also to be conducted according to the solar calendar, even if they fell at an allegedly inauspicious time. On a somewhat contradictory note, the government did retain the lunar calendar for such important Vietnamese holidays as the Lunar New Year celebration (*Tet Nguyen Dan*) and the mid-autumn celebration for children (*Tet Trung Thu*).

The secularization campaign also redefined the corpus of acceptable ritual practice, particularly with what the party labelled as 'superstitious' practices. Superstitions included any idea or practice that asserted that supernatural forces, causes, or entities exercised a demonstrable influence on human life. Party officials regarded superstitions as one of the greatest obstacles to the development of the new society. Apart from being a form of mental bondage that prevented the masses from taking complete control over their lives, they had other more immediate deleterious consequences in that they wasted resources, retarded production, and sometimes led to injury. In order to combat superstitions, the party vigorously banned several formerly prominent ritual practices in which the living attempted to contact and influence the supernatural world. Included here were the calling of spirits (*goi ma*), the calling of souls of the dead (*goi hon*), spirit mediumship (*dong bong*), the use of protective magical amulets (*bua*), the burning of votive paper objects (*hang ma*) for the dead, and all forms of divination (*boi toan*).

The party's campaign to eliminate superstitions proceeded through two main channels. On the aggressive side, the party prohibited all religious specialists who had formerly conducted superstitious ceremonies, such as spirit priests (*thay cung*), diviners (*thay boi*), and spirit mediums (*ba dong, ong dong*), from conducting or participating in such ceremonies. Given the destruction of many of the sacred sites where these rites were previously performed, enforcing this prohibition was not very difficult. Nevertheless, local authorities still placed these individuals under surveillance and periodically called them in for questioning. They also banned the production of votive paper objects (*hang ma*) burned by families in rituals. These objects, fashioned of colored paper wrapped around bamboo frames, represented gold (the *vang ma* formerly produced in Thinh Liet), money, clothing, or other items for use by the dead in the 'other world' (*the gioi khac*). They were offered during rituals, and then burned to transmit them, via the smoke, to the other world. Party ideologues considered the paper objects the physical manifestation of superstition, and vigorously objected to the money people spent to purchase them.

The agenda to forcefully eliminate superstitious practices was also accompanied by an extensive propaganda campaign. The party's main goal during the campaign was not simply to prohibit individuals from conducting the questionable rituals. They hoped to raise popular consciousness through education and propaganda so people would voluntarily abandon the practices. This component of the campaign in Thinh Liet commune was arranged by the commune's party cell while the subtler aspects of enforcement were delegated to the party's mass organizations, such as the Women's Association, the Youth Association, and the Elderly Association. The role of the latter group was particularly important as the party regarded elderly villagers, especially women, as the most sympathetic to superstitious practices. Working through the groups, the party sought to demonstrate why these practices were backwards and retrograde so the people would voluntarily abandon them. As one provincial primer noted regarding the method for implementing the New Ways, 'Mobilization to realize the New Ways is a continuation of the strengthening of the cultural and ideological revolution. It involves the resolution of problems in the realms of ideology, sentiment (*tinh cam*) and habits. Thus we cannot demand to solve all of these problems in one instant ... We must deeply and thoroughly propagandize, making the cadres and the people clearly understand the benefits and necessities of the reforms ... One must also avoid commandism, stand firm, yet be flexible, using persuasion and education as the main tools' (Ninh Binh, Cultural Service 1970:15).

One of the prime strategies used to undermine ideas about spirits was to demonstrate that claims of supernatural causality could not be empirically verified. Popular ideas held that spirits exercised a powerful influence over the world of humans, particularly in causing illness and misfortune. Many Vietnamese therefore attempted to cure illness through rituals that mollified angry spirits. The party emphasized the importance of modern medicine for treating illness.[1] Official propaganda regaled villagers with stories of the repeated ineffectiveness of spirit doctors in curing sickness. One family was reported to have sacrificed twenty one pigs, twelve goats, seventy five chickens and an indeterminate number of ducks in order to save a fever-stricken family member. Predictably, the woman died (Lao Cai, Culture and Information Service 1964:15). In another case, a women with a heart condition died after attempting to treat it with offerings to the spirits (Ha Nam Ninh, Cultural Service 1976:35). Officials also attempted to discredit spirit practitioners by portraying them as parasitic exploiters of the vulnerable. In official propaganda, spirit practitioners were self-interested (*truc loi*), unscrupulous extortionists who took advantage of peoples' concerns for their own personal gain. The alleged confession of a physiognomist (*thay tuong*) to a group of officials in Ha Nam Ninh province provides a fitting example of this tactic:

> Let me tell all of you, it's true, our profession is one of swindling. But getting money out of people isn't easy! You must make people move from astonishment to admiration if you're going to live off of it. You must also know how to deal with headstrong people, even those who ridicule you, and see you for what you are from the first minute.
>
> (Ha Nam Ninh 1976:36)

He then went on to describe how he would secretly collect information about people who visited him, such as a story of a lost item, and then when they later came to him he would exclaim how they looked as if they had lost something (Ha Nam Ninh 1976:37). In these and other stories, spirit practitioners were unprincipled proponents of a belief system that had no empirical substantiability and served only to separate the people from their already scarce resources. By prohibiting the performance of superstitious rites, and augmenting it with a positivist educational campaign, the party hoped to encourage the masses to voluntarily abandon ideas and practices that allegedly held them down. Such was the theory. Realization in practice often turned out to be quite different.

Implementation and Resistance

Officials began implementing their cultural reforms in areas under Viet Minh control during the French War and did so with increased vigor across the north after 1954. Although documented cases are scarce, it appears that resistance existed from the earliest years. One official source mentioned the performance of unsanctioned practices at the same time as the 1956 *Nhan Van Giai Pham* affair (Vietnam, Government 1962:11). At the Third Party Congress in 1960, the party declared that it 'must train the people to embrace a scientific spirit and overcome superstitions' (Vietnam, Government 1962:11). Over the following decades, the persistence of superstitions and the difficulties cadres encountered in suppressing them remained a constant theme in the ritual primers published by government, provincial, and district offices, giving proof to the public's scepticism regarding the anti-spiritist agenda. Many of these primers provide unexpected insights into the period. To give one example, a 1971 primer from Nam Ha province includes the full text of a 15 January 1971 directive from the Ministry of Culture to regulate local festivals (*hoi he*) across North Vietnam. In the directive, the Ministry of Culture noted that following the cessation of American bombing raids against North Vietnam in 1968, 'tens of thousands of people from all provinces, cities, and places have been going to participate in festivals. The most crowded locations have been the city of Hanoi, Hai Phong, and all of the provinces of the delta and midlands of northern Vietnam' (Nam Ha, Cultural Service 1971:6). This unexpected outburst of popular religiosity in the springs of 1969 and 1970 troubled the party because many of the participants openly engaged in superstitious practices. Officials still needed to 'patiently help those who still follow superstitions to gradually release themselves from the influence and demands of the heavens' (1971:6) and convince the masses that superstitious practices 'were a dishonest trick and a part of the keep the people stupid policy of the previous colonialist feudal regime' (1971:9). If they did this, 'slowly the ills of superstitions can be removed from the festivals' (1971:10). The text clearly shows that despite official surveillance and other tactics, a range of practitioners, such as diviners, and male and female spirit mediums, were still active in North Vietnam.

Thinh Liet residents also retained superstitious practices during this period. A small number of spirit practitioners remained active in their trades, often conducting their rites secretively at night. The most visible manifestation of residents' engagement with the supernatural was the clandestine production of votive paper ingots. The official crackdown on these items seriously limited trade networks, but both production and distribution carried on continuously, with traders slipping off at night to remote spots to sell their wares. The administration periodically responded with sweeps through homes suspected of ingot production. Cadres confiscated all of the ingots found, placed them in a large pile at a central point in the commune, and burned them before the offending producers. These fires were also accompanied by hortative talks on the wastefulness of production and the many negative qualities of the practices in which the ingots were employed. Seizures by the authorities, the last of which was carried out in 1982, usually did result in a temporary halt in production. However, after the situation calmed down, production quietly resumed again. Although the ingots had been destroyed, the hidden infrastructure of knowledge and skill for their production remained, requiring repeated reinvigorations of the campaign when production became too visible again.

By the mid-1990s, superstitious practices had undergone a significant resurgence throughout northern Vietnam, causing the former Prime Minister Vo Van Kiet to declare in 1994 that the Vietnamese people should redouble their efforts to eliminate them. Kiet's exhortations, however, rang hollow for many. The remainder of this chapter will focus on the nature of the resurgence of practices in Thinh Liet commune in which people employ supernatural or non-empirically verifiable explanations to explain difficult to understand or seemingly inexplicable events in human life. Part of the discussion will focus on a critical contradiction in official policy that effectively left the door open for the retention of ideas regarding supernatural causality in human life, but the main focus of analysis will be on the different contexts in which people employ supernatural causal explanations, the reason why such explanations are employed in such contexts, and the broader sociological attitudes toward these explanations. As will be shown, though 'superstitious' practices have enjoyed a resurgence, attitudes toward them often differ between young and old, and men and women.

The Contradictions of Tet

The most significant annual event in the social and cultural life in Thinh Liet is the celebration of the Lunar New Year (*Tet Nguyen Dan*). The Vietnamese lunar calendar features a total of seven different *Tet* holidays, such as the third month grave-cleaning festival (*Tet Thanh Minh*) or the previously mentioned mid-autumn festival devoted to children, but in common conversation when people speak of Tet they speak of the celebrations associated with the new year. Observers of Tet celebrations in northern Vietnam have accurately described them as 'something akin to Americans trying to compress Christmas, New Year's, Thanksgiving, and everyone's birthday into one giant holiday' (Hiebert 1996:44ff.). It is the main occasion for families to reunite, usually congregating in the parents' home, and the entire pace of life slows down as work is put aside and conviviality put at a premium. The days leading up to Tet are usually marked by frenzied activity as families rush to clean up their homes and the graves of their ancestors, obtain the necessary items of food and drink, and prepare their best clothes. On New Year's Eve, activity carries on throughout the afternoon and temporarily quiets down in the early evening as families settle in for the year's final group meal. Families wait until the stroke of midnight and then regale each other with the words 'Happy New Year' (*chuc mung nam moi*) as well as other stock phrases such as 'may you have ten thousand wishes granted' (*van su nhu y*) or 'may all be well for you' (*moi su tot lanh*). After the congratulations have finished and a small set of ancestral rites performed, drinks are often passed around along with envelopes containing small amounts of money, and people embark on the serious business of 'welcoming spring' (*don xuan*).

In common conversation, one often hears that Tet is the quintessential Vietnamese holiday that represents all that is good and glorious in Vietnamese culture. The idea of the singular Vietnamese-ness of Tet has widespread currency among the general population, but from the 1950s onward the party and state also sought to appropriate Tet for their own purposes. For the government, Tet Nguyen Dan was regarded, as one primer stated, 'an ancient festival of our people' (*ngay hoi co truyen cua nhan dan ta*) (Ninh Binh, Cultural Service 1970:3), but they still wanted it celebrated in very specific fashions. As early as 1958, the then Prime Minister Pham Van Dong published instructions on the proper organization of Tet celebrations. They needed to exhibit the character of 'unity, enthusiasm, labor, and thrift' (*doan ket, phan khoi, lao dong, tiet kiem*), and be rid of any 'backwards customs' such as gambling, time-wasting, profligate spending, and superstitions (Vietnam, Government 1958:31–2). They were to remain 'fun' (*vui ve*) and retain elements 'that have a good meaning,' such as the commemoration of national heroes (Vietnam, Government 1958:32), but cadres were to propagandize on the necessity of reforming Tet so it did not waste resources or interfere with production. They were to make the people understand that the new style of celebration 'was good for the country, and good for their families' (*co ich cho nuoc, co loi cho nha*). The government's lack of success in achieving these goals is evident in the fact that in 1959 and 1960 they issued further circulars and instructions that reiterated similar themes. The government designated Tet in 1959 as 'Victory Tet' (*Tet Thang Loi*), and urged the maintenance of such positive cultural and artistic elements as the presentation of poetic couplets (*cau doi*) and the production of ink blocks, but cadres were again instructed to strengthen their efforts to eliminate the holiday's perceived waste and distractions from production. Although the government gazette contains no further references to Tet, in 1967 and 1970 Ninh Binh province, and in 1971 Nam Ha province, published local directives on the proper organization of the ceremonies. Ninh Binh officials were perhaps the most honest about the official agenda when they commented that '(Tet) constitutes days of celebration for the people. It must be carefully organized with seriousness and respect. It must create a fun and enthusiastic atmosphere for everyone, simultaneously protecting the full meaning of those days as well as their political goals' (Ninh Binh, Cultural Service 1970:26). In later years, the government made an attempt to weave Ho Chi Minh into the celebrations. The last Tet Ho celebrated was that of February 1969. Every year Ho issued greetings to the people of North Vietnam at the new year, often over the radio. In 1969 he composed the following poem:

The past year saw glorious victory . . .
This year the front lines will certainly achieve more
Because of independence, because of freedom
Beat the Americans til they flee, beat the puppets til they fall
Go forward soldiers and people
A reunited north and south will make spring ever more glorious!

This spring is greater than those just past
Victory and good news spread throughout the homeland
North and south compete to defeat the American enemy
Go forward!
Bring us total victory!

After his death, people were encouraged to recite this poem to welcome the new year. Some historians claimed that Hanoi residents regularly recited this poem (Tran Quoc Vuong, Le Van Hao, and Duong Tat Tu 1976:104). Many Vietnamese still know the words today.

By highlighting Tet as a critical event in the approved cultural life of the Vietnamese, the government tapped into the holiday's legitimate popularity; however, by preserving Tet, they also retained an expanse of other associated meanings that ran counter to official ideology. Looked at analytically, the defining feature of Tet in both its ritual and social aspects is the restatement and reinvigoration of relations between individuals, families, and the broader social and supernatural world around them. The Tet ritual cycle begins on the 23rd of the 12th lunar month with the performance of the 'Sending the Kitchen Spirit Off to Heaven' rite (*Le Tien Ong Tao Len Troi*). Every home has a spirit that dwells in the kitchen, generally referred to as either 'the kitchen spirit' (*Ong Than Bep*) or more formally, *Ong Tao Quan*.[2] Spatially, the kitchen is not a prestigious or sacred area of the home. Associated with women, kitchens are normally on the side of the home, away from the prestigious central male area near the family ancestral altar. Nevertheless, some restrictions on activities in the kitchen do exist such as a prohibition on killing chickens within them. Watching over and protecting the kitchen and household is the kitchen spirit. This male spirit lives in the hearth, reportedly in the legs of the tripod upon which pots and pans were placed for cooking in earlier times. In addition to his protective role, the spirit also keeps a list of the meritorious and demeritorious actions family members perform during the year. Prior to the rite's commencement on the 23rd, family members carry out the annual cleaning of the family altar, removing all but five to seven burned-down incense sticks from their incense urns, and replacing old votive items with new ones. They also place a live on carp on the altar. The carp plays a central role in the kitchen spirit rite for after a brief propitiation of the spirit at the main family altar, the carp symbolically becomes a horse that Ong Tao Quan will ride up to heaven. Once there, he meets the King of Heaven (*Ngoc Hoang*, literally the Jade Emperor), reports on the family's behavior for the year, and asks the king to give the family peace and security in the coming year. Sending the spirit off, which occurs through the release of the carp immediately after the propitiation, has a slightly jovial side to it. The image of the carp captivates small children, who are often seen first catching carp that will be used in the ceremony, and then releasing them into ponds and streams so that Ong Tao can make his journey. Once the fish has been released, some families return home to eat a small meal of chicken, glutinous rice, and fruits.

Although the kitchen spirit occupies an important role in the ceremonies, the most important supernatural entities involved in Tet are the family ancestral spirits. At Tet, the spirits of the living and dead temporarily reunite in the home of the living. All Vietnamese ancestral rites share a similar structure in that prior to the rite family members tidy up the ancestral altar and place food items upon it. During the rite the main officiant, usually the household's senior male, lights three sticks of incense and delivers a brief invocation to invite the ancestral spirits back to the altar to consume the offerings, transmitted to them through the incense smoke. During such common rites as the annual death anniversary ceremony (*gio*), the ancestral spirits only briefly linger around the home. At Tet, family members invite the ancestors to return on the evening of the 30th of the 12th month, and they will generally stay for a period of three to seven days, depending upon the family's desires. When invited back at Tet, ancestors receive special treatment. Families thoroughly clean their homes before the year's end in order to provide a clean and pleasant atmosphere for the visiting spirits, and also prepare a number of special food items. These include boiled chicken, fried spring rolls (*nem*), shredded carrot and green papaya salad (*nom*), some variety of spirits, or perhaps beer or champagne in wealthier homes, glutinous rice prepared with lotus seeds, fruit, and other dishes of the family's choosing. Some families also put out a 'five fruits' tray (*mam ngu qua*), consisting of grapefruit, mandarin oranges, kumquat, sapodilla plums (*hong xiem*), and watermelon, that remains on the altar until the end of the ancestors' visit. The quintessential Tet food item is the *banh trung*. This square-shaped cake, usually some six inches by six inches and one to two inches high, is made of glutinous rice stuffed with mung beans and fatty pork wrapped in special leaves. After assembly, the cakes are boiled in water where the flavor is augmented by the scent released from the leaves. Some families make their own banh trung, but most buy them from skilled makers. Banh trung are consumed heavily at Tet and an average family will probably go through somewhere around five to ten banh trung during the first weeks of the new year. Vietnamese do not eat banh trung at any other point during the year. Many wryly comment that they eat them only once a year because they eat so many around Tet that they need a whole year to reacquire a taste for them.

The family meal on the evening of the 30th is one of the most important convocations of the year. Family members usually arrive late in the afternoon or early in the evening. Given the patrilineal emphasis of Vietnamese kinship, married women do not return to their natal home on the 30th. Instead they stay at the home of their husband or his parents. However, in the days leading up to Tet, a daughter and her husband are obliged to visit her parents to present them with a small set of offerings, such as uncooked glutinous rice and spirits, and propitiate her family ancestors. A child who does not intend to celebrate Tet at his parent's home must also pay a similar visit. By the time most of the guests arrive on the 30th, all of the cooking is finished and the altar is bedecked with flowers, candles, in some cases votive paper objects, and as many plates and bowls of food as possible. Before the living can begin eating, the family ancestors are invited back for Tet in the manner described above. Family members must wait to eat until all of the incense sticks have burned down. The more superstitious in the family monitor the progress of the incense for sticks that burn down completely without stopping. This is an auspicious sign while one that burns incompletely is inauspicious. The conclusion of the incense's burning indicates that the ancestors have finished eating. At this point, any votive paper items on the altar are taken out and burned for the ancestors. Also, the food offerings on the altar have now become sacralized. People refer to such items as *loc,* and eating them brings good fortune to the individual. The final meal is a warm, jovial affair, usually complemented by humor, toasting, and a palpable sense of anticipation of the excitement to come.

In the hours leading up to midnight most individuals have returned to their homes and the streets are surprisingly empty. The climax of the evening comes with the turning of the new year at midnight. The moment when midnight strikes is referred to as *giao thua.* In the minutes before midnight, several male family members congregate outside before the home. Before the Vietnamese government declared fireworks illegal in 1996, members of this group would string up a belt of red firecrackers, usually in an area before the main entrance to the home. At the exact stroke of midnight, a family member lit the firecrackers, producing long moments of cacophony as the firecrackers exploded. Given the close proximity of houses in rural Vietnam, the simultaneous explosion of thousands of firecrackers produced an extraordinary roar. Many families would later light more than one belt, causing the roar to carry on for fifteen to twenty minutes. Explanations vary as to why firecrackers were ignited at midnight. Those with a supernaturally-oriented tendency explain that the lighting of the firecrackers, similar to the lighting of firecrackers before other rituals, scares off or kills any malevolent spirits lingering around the area, thereby protecting the outcome of the family's rites. The authors of the 1976 volume *Spring and Vietnamese Customs* (*Mua Xuan Va Phong Tuc Viet Nam*) optimistically noted that 'this religious meaning no longer exists.' Instead, they offered up the more prosaic explanation that, 'Today we light firecrackers to say goodbye to the old year and welcome in a better, more progressive new year. Firecrackers explode to further emphasize the historical stages we have already passed, and fire with enthusiasm our aspirations, our path, and our successes in the new year' (Tran Quoc Vuong et al 1976:104). Thinh Liet residents noted that they lit firecrackers to scare off spirits or 'welcome the new year,' but never did they include explanations as grand as the latter.

Giao thua's arrival brings with it expectations about the upcoming year. Apart from its general celebratory character, giao thua is also a sacred though potentially dangerous moment as the unfolding of the first hour after giao thua can influence a family's fortunes for the following year. Although one generally sees a great deal of celebration after midnight, in many homes one family member, usually a senior woman, slips away right after midnight to propitiate the family ancestors, or in some cases, to present the guardian spirit of the family compound with a tray of offerings that includes a boiled female chicken, glutinous rice and monordica (*gac*), flowers, areca nuts and betel leaves, a glass of rain water, and possibly other items. This altar is located outside of the home, usually next to the wall of the compound, and the tray would have been placed by the altar before midnight. In both cases, the immediate propitiation of the spirits is performed in order to enlist their help in bringing good fortune to the family for the year. When addressing the spirits, individuals ask for a year in which family members will be happy, and that there be no accidents. Sometimes the propitiant will perform a brief divinatory rite called 'asking the yin and yang' (*xin am duong*). This rite involves asking the spirits whether one's requests for the year will be granted and then flipping two dynastic coins, covered with lime on one side and left bare on the other. If they land with different sides up, which symbolically represents the yin and yang, one's request will be granted. If the sides are the same, the request is denied. Those who first receive an unsatisfactory answer will often flip the coins again, but three negatives in a row definitively indicates that the request will not be granted.

The concern with good fortune in the new year is also evident in the performance of the 'first visit' (*xong dat*) rite. Prior to the turn of giao thua, families often contact a specific individual and ask him or her to be the new year's first visitor. The ideal candidate is someone who is well-liked, healthy, prosperous, and has many children, though a graduate student from a prosperous country will also suffice. Among the worst candidates are the ill, those with bad marriages, and those with troublesome personalities or social relations. Those in mourning are prohibited. The

90

logic for selecting the desired individuals is that in entering the family compound first, the individual's positive qualities are transferred to the family for the year. In some cases the person remains stationed outside of the family compound's gate as giao thua turns, coming in immediately afterward, though generally the appointed guest will wait and come by in the first hour. Often there is an unstated anxiety before the first guest's arrival as families do not want an undesirable guest to appear unannounced and bring potential misfortune to the home. Humans aside, if a cat is the first through the gate, the family will have a difficult year, but a dog will bring the family wealth. Once the human guest arrives, families are relieved and get on with the business of celebrating.

The days after the turning of the new year are filled with visits to friends and relatives in their homes. Vietnamese describe the first lunar month as the month for 'eating and playing' (*an choi*). Tet usually falls in either January or February of the solar calendar, thus the weather in the Red River delta is often cool, and families have time to relax between the harvesting of the tenth month rice crop and the planting of the next in the second or third. Sociality is at a premium in the first few days of the year. The commune's pathways are full of groups walking to friends' homes and one's own schedule is often filled from the early morning hours until late evenings with visits and meals at others' homes. Paying visits on these days is critical for the maintenance of social relations. To visit someone's home is at a minimum considered a nice gesture by the host, but to deliberately avoid someone constitutes a strong negative statement on that relationship. Thinh Liet residents comment, probably with some exaggeration, that in the past all village families visited each other. Today, given the population's size, that is impossible, but people generally do visit dozens of homes in the first few days. Although the rounds of visiting can be exhausting, people revel in the warm and uplifting atmosphere. The government has repeatedly attempted to get people back to work soon after Tet, but little work or official business ever began in Thinh Liet until the end of the first week.

The state's decision to foreground Tet as the quintessential Vietnamese holiday in revolutionary Vietnam entailed an inherent contradiction. The state wanted Tet to serve as a commemorative holiday that highlighted the positive aspects of Vietnamese tradition, but the celebrations themselves centered around relations between humans and the spirit world, particularly the ancestors. Interestingly, although the government attempted to limit consumption activities during Tet, and ban other rites in which humans contacted the spirit world, nowhere in official ritual primers was there any mention of removing ancestral rites from Tet celebrations. To the contrary, officials regarded ancestor worship as a positive, respectful activity that represented one of the most important aspects of Vietnamese culture. Officials from Ha Tay province, in a paraphrase of Communist Party General Secretary Le Duan, noted that 'The Vietnamese Tet is a day of celebration between the people and the heavens; worshipping the ancestors is the foundation upon which the people of today remember the people of the past, or one can perhaps say that on that day the past unites with the present' (Ha Tay, Cultural Service 1967:26). One Giap Tu officer and party member commented in a view similar to the state's position, 'propitiating the ancestors is a legitimate religious practice of our people (*tin nguong dan toc*). The rest of the spirit world is all superstitions.' For many Thinh Liet residents, this subtle distinction between the ancestors and other spirits was a misrepresentation of reality. One worshipped ancestors, not simply because of what they did when they were alive, but because they did exist, and they were simply one type of supernatural entity that exercised an influence on human life. Indeed, many residents maintained different ontologies and associated sets of causal explanations. As will now be discussed, these they employed to explain their lives and world, particularly when they encountered misfortune or the seemingly inexplicable.

Transgression, Supernatural Punishment, and Fate

One of the most common supernatural causal explanations employed in Thinh Liet is that supernatural entities punish the living for moral transgressions. This is particularly true of the ancestors (*to tien*). Humans are locked in a reciprocal relationship with their ancestors. If they care for them properly through regular ritual action and the observation of moral rules, the ancestors reward the living with good health and fortune. If humans break the rules or neglect them, the ancestors issue a suitable punishment. As one Giap Nhi votive paper manufacturer commented, 'The ancestors both support and punish.' Of the two types of transgressions, ritual neglect is more frequently invoked as a cause of misfortune. The reason for punishment in such cases is that the dead depend on the living to give them, through ritual, the food, money, clothing, and other items needed to survive in the other world. Without them the ancestors suffer. One Giap Nhi woman's family encountered repeated misfortune, including illness among her children and severe financial difficulties. When her problems would not end, she contacted a spirit medium to determine their origin. After consulting the spirits, the medium stated that a distant patrilineal ancestor was punishing her family for neglecting to conduct its death anniversary ceremony and provide it with its life essentials. In another case, a spirit contacted by a medium declared that it was punishing the living because they failed to provide it with dollars, the spirit world's new currency. On another occasion, a dead soldier's spirit was angry because it needed a new uniform and pith helmet, but his relations had not provided it. Through the mediums, the spirits detailed their needs, and afterwards the families delivered the necessary items through ritual. The latter two cases also illustrate how ideas about the supernatural have kept pace with changes in contemporary society.

Village guardian spirits are another category of spirit that has punitive powers. These spirits can be a positive force in human life, but if offended, they can also bring harm. In contemporary Thinh Liet, the guardian spirits' malevolent side comes out most clearly in reference to those who have treated the communal houses in an inappropriate or offensive manner. In recent years Giap Nhat has reportedly seen a decline in the number of male children born in the village, a fact many Giap Nhi residents attribute to the fact that the communal house faces onto a busy street, which upsets the guardian spirit. During the same period, Giap Nhi has experienced an increase in illegitimate children, a trend some link to the construction of the commune's war memorial facing the communal house entrance. Similar to Giap Nhat, the memorial's placement offended the guardian spirit. Guardian spirits also punish those who damage or insult the communal house. The most celebrated case was a young man's inability to relieve himself for several days after urinating on the Giap Tu communal house (see Chapter 7). A more serious case involved the death of a twenty two year old Giap Nhi woman who sold meat in the morning market before the Giap Nhi communal house. When she unexpectedly fell ill and died, other market women interpreted her death as punishment by the spirit for selling meat in that location. Subsequently, a number of women stopped selling meat in areas visible from the communal house. Fear of retribution by the guardian spirit was also evident in early 1992 when a local man returned to the Giap Nhi communal house a number of brass altar pieces he had stolen during the land reform.

The most interesting cases of spiritual punishment in Thinh Liet relate to the misfortunes of those involved in the destruction of the Giap Nhat spirit shrine (den) during the land reform. Although accounts of the incident differ slightly, apparently three young Thinh Liet men with strong revolutionary backgrounds orchestrated the shrine's destruction, with some four or five other men looking on or helping out. When they destroyed the shrine, they defaced the structure, smashed a number of sacred objects, and some report, perhaps with a measure of hyperbole, either urinated or defecated on the site. Afterward, all of the men met with a similar pattern of misfortune. The three ring-leaders all died at relatively young ages. The first died of a malaria-type illness contracted in the mountains of northern Vietnam only a few years after destroying the shrine. He died in his twenties, and apparently suffered quite severely. The next to die, a Giap Nhi native, was killed by an American missile in 1972 when he was 38 years old. The last to die, a Giap Tu man, went mad and died around the age of 50 in the late 1980s. The latter two men also had extremely difficult family lives. The wife of the Giap Tu man suffered from severe mental illness before her husband, while the wife of the Giap Nhi man gave birth to a deformed child. Several of the others who watched or only helped out in a minor fashion have also died, and all experienced family difficulties such as divorce or poverty. Many villagers are quick to assert that the angry spirit caused their misfortune and suffering. Even a former colonel who has been a party member for over three decades noted, 'They all died because the spirit caught them.' Some villagers liked to employ these comments as part of a broader critique of the land reform's excesses and the party's misapprehension of reality's true nature.

Another agent of supernatural punishment in Thinh Liet life is the Buddha (*Phat*). Thinh Liet attitudes towards Buddhism are colored by the dominant Mahayana Buddhism of northern Vietnam. Unlike the distant Buddha of Theravada Buddhism, such divine entities as the Buddha or the Boddhisatva Avalokitesvara (*Quan The Am*) are generally regarded as living entities that intervene in local life, often in rather non-doctrinal fashions. Older residents like to comment that 'the heavens have eyes' (*troi co mat*) and are always on the look out for people's moral violations. This idea is linked to a broader system of causality in which the children of those who live moral lives will prosper, while the children of the immoral will suffer. The most frequently cited examples of this are the families of Thinh Liet butchers who, as a result of engaging in an immoral trade that involves taking life, have reportedly all come to ruin. The Buddha will also punish the immoral with an early death. The unexpected death of an immoral person is interpreted by some with the expression, 'fined by the Buddha' (*Phat phat*). The Buddha also intervened to punish those who behaved immorally during the land reform. One Giap Tu man threw a statue of the Buddha down a well. Later, his wife became mad, an event that many attribute to the Buddha's punishment. A number of Thinh Liet residents also falsely denounced other villagers during the land reform. None of these people enjoyed long lives and all were dead by 1994, a fact one elderly Giap Tu woman summed up as 'the Buddha tried and punished them' (*Phat trung tri*).

Beyond these easily identifiable spirits, other more generic forces also punish violators of moral rules. This type of force is most commonly invoked in such circumstances as an individual dying a slow, painful death or someone dying violently outside the home in an accident. Many Thinh Liet residents hold that a person of good moral character will die quickly and painlessly, while those who have been cruel or committed many moral offenses will experience a painful, lingering death. In one Giap Tu case, a male villager who had strongly supported the anti-superstition agenda was extremely ill and lingering on his death bed. He became extremely concerned about possible criticisms and assertions that he had 'lived cruelly' (*an o ac*). He therefore asked his wife, who was active in clandestine religious practices, to bring in her friends from the Buddhist Association to

94

chant and conduct rites that would assist him in his transition to the other world. He died the day after the rites. Concerns about an individual's character can also be raised when they die violently in an accident. As one elderly Giap Nhi man stated, 'Those who die out on the road, in a car, or in a boat have committed many bad acts (*toi ac*).'

A violent death can raise potentially troubling questions that the deceased was of questionable moral character. However, in some cases those who suffer death or misfortune are of indisputably good moral character. In these circumstances one encounters a final and extremely common explanation for misfortune, fate (*so phan*). The idea behind fate is that at birth the heavens (*troi*) give each person a fate that will determine their life course. Whether their life is rich and satisfying, or poor and miserable, all is determined by fate. A person can have a 'black' or bad fate (*so den*), or a 'red' or good fate (*so do*). In conversation one often hears these terms applied to others. The miserable, impoverished farmer who fails at everything has a black fate, while the visiting American anthropologist is frequently said to have a red fate. One can also have a 'heavy fate' (*so nang*) that produces misfortunes during a specific time frame, such as a lunar month or year. Thinh Liet residents invoke fate to explain a variety of events that appear undesirable or inexplicable. It provides a ready explanation for poverty, repeated failure, and the inability of some women to bear children. The most important domain for its invocation is to explain arbitrary misfortune or an early death. One of the most poignant stories I encountered in Thinh Liet was of the son of a former colonel who was killed at nineteen when a bullet struck him in the head after a rifle accidentally discharged in his army barracks. When trying to explain why he had died, particularly since he was considered to be a nice young man of good moral character, people regularly attributed it to fate. He had been fated to die young, thus he did. Recalling the funeral, his father commented that hearing his co-residents attribute his son's death to fate made his grief feel lighter, even though he did not think there was such a thing as fate. Interestingly, given his good moral character, villagers only employed the fate explanation and never any that involved an idea of supernatural punishment.

Engaging the Supernatural: Curing Illness, Eliminating Misfortune

Although many Thinh Liet residents employ supernatural causal explanations to explain misfortune, this system of ideas does not necessarily imply a fatalistic attitude. To the contrary, people regularly engage the supernatural world in order to effect change in this world. It should be noted though that the existence of such ideas also does not imply a Levy-Bruhlian mystical communion with the world. Despite some official portrayals to the contrary, Thinh Liet residents do demonstrate a 'scientific spirit' in understanding their world. They have no aversion to the use of modern medical procedures, regularly take pharmaceuticals, accept that the vast majority of illnesses have some empirically verifiable cause such as exposure to a virus or bacteria, and are also ready to point out that a lack of effort will produce a bad harvest. Alternative systems of explanation are invoked in three main circumstances: the sudden onset of some form of mental illness or eccentric behavior; situations in which there is a pattern of frequent and repeated physical illness among family members; and cases of lingering illness in which a person does not respond to treatment. In any of these contexts, people might begin to suspect and engage the supernatural.

When a person who is normally placid and calm suddenly begins to act strangely, the dominant suspicion for the cause of the transformation is that the individual's body has been 'invaded by a ghost' (bi ma am). Linked to the realm of benevolent ancestors and guardian spirits is a range of hungry, angry ghosts (con ma). These spirits, who sport horrible visages, roam the countryside in search of sustenance. They are created when a person dies and fails to receive proper funeral rites, thereby leaving them stranded on earth without living relations to care for them. Although ghosts are more likely to try to invade and occupy a family's ancestral altar, thereby denying the ancestors sustenance and bringing misfortune to the family, ghosts also have the capacity to invade the human body. Such invasions are most likely to happen when a person is in a vulnerable situation, such as alone in the rice fields at night. Looked at comparatively, women are more prone to invasion than men.

The ghost's presence in the body causes bizarre behaviors, such as the screaming of obscenities, jerky body movements, nonsensical speech, or perhaps total silence. A possessed person is sometimes referred to as being 'crazy' (bi dien). When possession occurs, Thinh Liet residents employ a number of different therapies to force the spirit's departure. The simplest is to hold the victims arms back and beat the possessed person with a stick. Although the blows strike the person's body, some assert that only the ghost is hit and the resulting pain forces the ghost out. The application of this therapy had tragic consequences in Thinh Liet in the late 1980s when an elderly women accidentally beat a young girl to death (She was placed under house arrest afterwards). Another recent therapy attempted to scare a ghost out by laying a possessed person on the floor, surrounding her with piles of votive paper money, and lighting the money on fire. Unfortunately, the young patient was severely burned on a large portion of her body.

The inability to force a ghost from a body through a simple treatment indicates that the invading spirit is of the extremely angry or tenacious variety. Such a failure places the possessed person in the same position as someone whose family has experience repeated or extended illness: a more sophisticated treatment is required in order to identify the angry spirit, learn its demands, placate it, and persuade it to end its nefarious activities. In Thinh Liet, these next steps entail the enlistment of one of a hierarchy of progressively more powerful healing specialists. The first specialist a sufferer would likely contact is a diviner (*thay boi*). Diviners, who are almost universally men, practice their craft through a number of techniques, such as the examination of hands and faces, geomancy, numerology, or astrological techniques. They come to their craft either by exhibiting some extraordinary talent, such as the ability to accurately predict the future, or through study with an established master. Upon confronting the client, a diviner determines the offending spirit's identity, often an angry family ancestor, and prescribes a method to appease it so it will leave. This usually involves a ceremony conducted by the diviner on behalf of the family in which specific offerings are presented, though a diviner might also suggest a more complicated response such as rearranging family graves or items around the home. Many Thinh Liet residents assert that the ministrations of a diviner are usually adequate for ending interference by a relatively good-natured spirit. A good diviner is quick to recognize, however, when the solution is beyond his powers and will counsel the family to seek a more powerful specialist. This is particularly the case with spirit possession because diviners do not have the power to cast out spirits.

The next category of specialists consists of spirit mediums (*ba dong* or *ong dong*) and spirit priests (*thay cung*). In practice, spirit priests can work independently of mediums, but mediums virtually always conduct their ceremonies with the assistance of spirit priests. Both groups have special relationships with the spirit world that make them powerful assistants in resolving supernaturally caused problems. Spirit priests, like diviners, can come to their trade by exhibiting a sacred talent, but study with an established master is a vital component in their training. Thinh Liet spirit priests are all men, the majority of whom learned their art from either their father or father-in-law, though some studied with masters of no relation. Thinh Liet's oldest spirit priest is a man of more than eighty years from Giap Tu who studied under his father and has subsequently taught several of his sons. A spirit priest's speciality is the propitiation (*cung*) of spirits. A skilled spirit priest will have mastered a broad range of invocations, usually recorded in Sino-Vietnamese characters, although some newly-trained spirit priests learn the texts in romanized Vietnamese script with Sino-Vietnamese pronunciation. Families invite spirit priests to participate in rites in which specific spirits need to be persuaded or compelled to perform certain actions. Spirit priests therefore often play an important role in a number of funerary ceremonies in which the living attempt to ensure the deceased soul's safe passage to the other world. Spirit priests are consulted in cases of illness or possession because of their ability to identify the offending spirit and arrange the appropriate solution. The spirit priest can achieve the latter through the powerful incantations he delivers. This he

97

does through the writing of a 'petition' (*so*) that describes the date, location, name of the afflicted individual, and a request for the spirit to leave or desist. The spirit priest sits next to the victim or before a family altar, reads the petition, says further prayers, delivers a set of offerings, and sends the petition to the spirit world by burning it. Thus delivered, the spirit should be compelled to leave or desist.

Although some families exclusively consult a spirit priest to solve an illness or possession problem, those who seek supernatural solutions to their problems generally consult them in conjunction with spirit mediums. In Vietnam, spirit mediums are usually female, thus the common expression for a medium, *ba dong*. A small number of male mediums do exist, but mediumship is such a heavily gendered pursuit that they are often described as 'effeminate' (*dong co*). Mediums can be any age, with many beyond their child-bearing years. The common path to mediumship generally begins with participation in the decidedly unofficial 'spirit medium group' (*hoi dong bong*). This group's membership consists largely of women both in and beyond their child-bearing years. Many women become involved in the group when they face some sort of family crisis, such as illness, poverty, or some other form of hardship, while others are brought in by friends or family members. The age at which females are involved in medium groups often links with the structure of their family responsibilities in life. Those with relatively light responsibilities, notably the young and unmarried and the very elderly, are unlikely to participate in medium activities. Instead, it is those who carry a heavier burden to care for their children, husbands, parents, in-laws, and others who most frequently seek out medium groups, often to help them gain control over the indeterminacies of their lives.[3] Most women's involvement in the medium groups consists solely of attending the sessions, which are organized when needed by a member or on calendrical holidays, such as the 'entering summer' (*vao he*) ceremony on the tenth of the fourth lunar month. A small number of women experience some sort of dream or possession experience that indicates to them that they should become a medium. In these cases, there is no requirement for training or study, but the women must go through an initiation rite that marks her ascension to mediumship.

The medium's special skill lies in her ability, while in a form of ecstatic trance, to allow spirits to enter her body so the living can talk with them. In Thinh Liet, most spirit medium rites take place in family shrines (*dien*) although larger shrines, such as the *den*, are also used. What sets the activities at shrines apart from those at temples and communal houses is that ceremonies in the former are devoted to the common good, such as village welfare, while those at shrines focus on the needs of specific individuals. Spirit medium rites are usually organized at the request of an individual with a particular problem, such as illness or spirit possession. Prior to the session's commencement, which is normally held late at night, the organizer assembles a large and expensive set of offerings, and invites the medium(s), a spirit priest, a small group of three or four male musicians, and the other members of the spirit medium group.[4] The spirit priest and musicians will perform together as the spirit priest intones the invocations to the accompaniment of the music and the group members' chanting, most of whom know the invocations from memory. During the rites, the medium will have an array of spirits enter her body in a standardized order. These will include the spirits of famous historical personages, such as Tran Hung Dao, considered by many in Thinh Liet as a particularly powerful spirit. Spirit mediums also have a special affinity with the female spirit Ba Mau. Some Thinh Liet residents assert that she is the highest ranking spirit in the pantheon and is the 'foundation' (*nguon goc*) for all activities associated with mediumship, an interesting correspondence between a female deity and a largely female set of practices.[5]

Once a spirit has entered the medium's body, the assembled participants begin asking it questions. The first and longest questioning is given by the organizer, who will ask the spirit questions to determine the identity of the offended spirit causing this illness, misfortune, or possession, and what actions initiated the punishment. Once she receives a reply, her next step is to learn what remedies are necessary to end the tormenting by the spirit. These generally include the presentation of specific types of offerings, particularly food and votive paper items. A typical resolution to this problem was mentioned above when the dead soldier's angry soul requested the new items for its use. After the organizer's questions conclude, the other participants are free to ask the spirit further questions related to their own concerns. During the night, participants ask the spirits in the medium dozens of questions. Most of the responses they receive will involve angry spirits that require propitiation, but in some cases the medium will declare that the afflicted individual suffers from a 'heavy fate' (*so nang*). Ridding a person of such a fate will require a separate 'release from misfortune' ceremony (*le giai han*), conducted by a spirit priest. This will transfer the negative fate to a human-like paper doll (*hinh nhan*) that is later burned. During the early 1990s, these ceremonies became increasingly popular in Thinh Liet, particularly after an elderly Giap Tu woman, who was active in spirit medium activities and whose family compound has a large dien, was diagnosed with a heavy fate. She ignored the diagnosis, but then early in the year suffered a serious injury when struck by a motorcycle in a local market. This confirmed, for many, the reality of fate.

The sequence of questioning the spirit and performing the prescribed remedies is normally adequate for ending cases of possession, illness, or misfortune. As one Thinh Liet man commented, 'all spirits have the capacity to rescue people,' and by enlisting their help, humans can usually persuade spirits to desist. Like other systems of supernatural causality, the Vietnamese system has its own built-in failure mechanisms, usually related to the improper performance of ritual. At the conclusion of a medium ceremony, participants often perform the 'ask yin and yang' rite to confirm whether their requests have been answered. Many flip the coins repeatedly until they get a positive answer, each time praying slightly longer between flips. Nevertheless, consistent negative answers can indicate to the participant that not all went as hoped. Common causes of failure can include conducting a ritual on an inauspicious day; having a ritually impure participant present, such as a menstruating women or one who had sex the day of or day before the ritual; or failure to: present the proper offerings; to properly invite the spirits back to the ceremony; to properly write out the petition; or to properly propitiate the spirits when present. Literally dozens of reasons can be invoked to explain why the rites failed without jeopardizing the integrity of the system. One last explanation is that the spirit(s) causing the misfortunes were too powerful, malicious, or tenacious for the spirit priest and mediums. A spirit priest's power rests simply on his ability to placate and persuade. In rare cases, the spirit is immune to persuasion, and the only remaining option is to kill the spirit. This requires the recruitment of the only supernatural specialist capable of doing so, the Taoist master (*thay phu thuy*). There are no Taoist masters in Thinh Liet, although some residents reported going to visit one in Nam Ha province.

Engaging the Spirits: The Search for Economic Success

One last arena in which Thinh Liet residents engage the supernatural is the propitiation of spirits for prosperity and economic success. The correct propitiation of spirits, particularly the ancestors, has the capacity to bring the living good fortune. Although primarily rendered in the form of family harmony and general prosperity, ancestors and a number of other spirits can also be propitiated to achieve success in particular economic endeavours. The linkage between ancestors is evident in a commonly heard adage, '*lam an duoc do mo do ma*,' which literally translates as 'one makes a living because of the graves,' but more generally means that one succeeds economically by maintaining a proper relationship with one's ancestors.

Since the Renovation policy's introduction in 1986, Thinh Liet families have become economically independent and therefore responsible for their own economic well-being. Whereas previously they could rely on their cooperative or factory for some measure of assistance, families are now basically on their own. Correspondingly, the amount of ritual activity devoted to enlisting the spirit world for economic assistance has increased. This trend is most clearly visible among local women who work part-time as petty traders in Thinh Liet and other local markets. On the first and fifteenth of every lunar month these women crowd into local shrines and temples to present offerings and request supernatural assistance in their endeavors. Traders comment that they would never neglect a visit to the temple on these days for fear that misfortune might strike. Women who own shops or permanent stalls in markets are similarly meticulous about conducting rites on the first and fifteenth. Many also maintain special altars dedicated to spirits that can bring them good fortune. Thinh Liet residents, particularly men, are fond of stating that female traders and shop keepers are the most superstitious people in local society. Some men will rather cruelly play on this attitude by showing up early in the markets and haggling fiercely. Many traders hold that the first customer sets the tone for the day, thus an argumentative confrontation with a customer bodes poorly for the day's business. It might even require a brief rite after the customer leaves to get the day back on track.

The harnessing of spirits for economic success finds critical expression today in the adage, 'buying and selling spirits' (*buon than ban thanh*). Most Thinh Liet residents who actively engage the supernatural for economic success conduct their rites locally, but in recent years many have begun organizing annual visits to sacred sites in the Red River Delta that are regarded as particularly efficacious for generating wealth. Some visit the 'Fragrant Temple' (*Chua Huong*), a Buddhist temple in Ha Tay province, but the most popular destination to ask for success in commercial affairs is the shrine of the 'Goddess of the Treasury' (*Den Ba Chua Kho*) in Bac Ninh province northeast of Hanoi.[6] The Goddess of the Treasury is the spirit of a woman born of a poor family in Bac Ninh who later married a Ly king. During her life she was very popular with the people of the area after she persuaded the king to implement policies that brought them prosperity. After her death, local residents began worshipping her spirit on the 10th of the first lunar month, highlighting during the rites her ability to create prosperity. In recent years, the link between her spirit and prosperity has grown stronger and taken on a highly transactional character different from the more generic supplications people make at temples or their homes. At the beginning of the year, thousands of visitors go to the shrine to present offerings to the goddess and 'borrow' money from her. In receiving this money, which does not take material form but is still exactly stipulated, the borrower simultaneously enlists the goddess's assistance in their endeavours for that year, and also incurs a debt that must be paid by the lunar year's end. Paying off the debt entails returning to the shrine and presenting offerings to the goddess. Critically, the amount borrowed with interest must also be presented in the form of votive paper gold or money. Following the propitiation of her spirit, visitors go out to an area behind the shrine to burn the votive paper objects. Although still considered superstitious by the government, the rear area is blanketed in ash and smoke. The shrine is busiest during the first and twelfth lunar months, and has a constant stream of motorists with Hanoi licence plates during these two months.

Accepting and Rejecting Supernatural Causality

Thinh Liet society features a wide array of spiritist and fate-based explanations, but despite their prevalence, there also exists a wide degree of variation regarding their accuracy and acceptability. The variability that exists ultimately breaks down at an individual level, but there nevertheless are some general sociological conclusions one can draw. With respect to their acceptability, one can fairly state that women are more likely to employ such explanations than men. Many men, in fact, are extremely hostile to such ideas. But there also exists another level of variation in that it is generally among older men who came of age during the 1950s and 1960s that one finds the greatest antipathy toward such ideas, though it should also be noted that some men in this age bracket do advocate supernatural ideas. This unique pattern raises the question of why such variation exists. The best answer can be found in the life-experiences of the advocates and opponents.

The Vietnamese revolution attempted to profoundly change Vietnamese society, but despite its ambitious plans, one fact of life that never changed for most women was that they bore the main responsibility for their families' well-being. Men may have exercised a dominant role in public life, but women had to shoulder the burden of caring for their families and solving many of the crises they encountered. Historically, one set of agents that women could draw upon to help them achieve this goal was the spirit world. Women thus engaged in practices to ensure their family's health and prosperity, and also called upon the spirits to eliminate misfortune. This trend was apparent in Nguyen Van Khoan's 1930 article on cultic activity in Vietnam, and it was clear during the reform years that the majority of women never renounced these ideas and in many cases secretly engaged in associated practices. It was also clear that such acts of religiosity were often at their most intense during the years women were raising their children. Women, in effect, retained these ideas and practices in spite of the revolution. And unlike men, who often were more deeply integrated into the party and therefore subject to its disciplines, women remained largely outside of the power structure and could keep such ideas and practices alive without fear of major repercussions. The disparities in skills and knowledge about how to properly interact with the supernatural that exists between men and women in some Thinh Liet families today is so great that the father, who serves as head of the family ancestral cult, will perform a basic rite to begin an ancestral propitiation, but will then turn the rites over to his more skilled wife in order to guarantee their success.

The individuals who are the most vigorous opponents of supernatural causality are usually men, though particularly those with backgrounds in the party or military. At a general level, it is fair to state that one element in Thinh Liet constructions of masculinity is the rejection of many spiritist practices. Indeed, some contemporary men, of both party and non-party backgrounds, state outright that they reject these practices and their ideas because they are female. Nguyen Van Khoan noted that in colonial Vietnam many cults popular with women were not popular with men. This trend that reached its fullest form in the rejection by some mandarins of almost all cultic activities except those devoted to Confucius (Nguyen Van Khoan 1930:110). It is likely, though unproven, that this trend carried over into the revolution, only with different foci of commitment. The rejection of supernatural causality by male party members and veterans also relates back to their socialization. Initiation into both of these institutions involved indoctrination into the party's anti-superstition creed, and once in, members were monitored for their adherence to it, and often sanctioned if they did not support it. As discussed in Chapter 2, Thinh Liet individuals who entered the party without military experience usually entered through the Youth Association. Here they would have regularly received 'education' (*giao duc*) on party ideology. They would have then been expected to serve as exemplars for the community and vigorously supported and propagated official ideology. The latter activities were essential because without them they would not be accepted into the party. Youth Association members were often distinguished by their zeal. By the time they entered the party, normally in their late twenties, they would have been socialized into official ideology for many years. Many who entered the party in the late 1940s and early 1950s did not go through the Youth Association, but their zeal and commitment to official ideology were equally strong.

Thinh Liet residents who entered the party through the military were similarly socialized. From its inception in 1940s, the People's Army and the Communist Party were tightly linked and party ideology dominated military life. In most cases this related to directly military matters, but the anti-superstition creed was also propagated, notably with regard to rejection of the idea of fate. This was of particular importance in the military because cadres wanted soldiers to believe that life or death, or success or failure on the battlefield, had nothing to do with fate. Whatever happened was simply the result of the hard work, planning, and discipline. The rejection of fate had a particular potency for the soldiers as most of them faced death and suffering on a massive scale. Subjection to such violence and misery can lead to questions regarding their cause or meaning. Yet, as one former soldier noted, even if he felt that there was something like fate at work in the death or injuring of his comrades, he would never have dared to mention it publically while he was in the army. Most veterans recall that during their time in the military they tended to interpret death and suffering as a result of chance (*may rui*, or 'good fortune (*may*), bad fortune (*rui*)'), an arbitrary secular phenomenon, and not fate. Others also comment that during war time, when their lives were constantly in danger, they simply did not have the time to think about such matters.

In contemporary Thinh Liet those with party and/or military backgrounds tend to reiterate the official position: there is no such thing as fate or other forms of supernatural causality, they are but superstitions. One former lieutenant who served for more than ten years and worked his way up the ranks from private summed up this position best when he commented that such ideas are 'backward' (*lac hau*). These people tend to mobilize material causal explanations, though explanations based upon secular chance, which do not involve the workings of a god or deity, are also common. Differences between the different groups often produce different interpretations of the same event. To give one example, on the evening of 10 April 1971, Nguyen Tien Dat of Giap Tu was driving a truck along the Ho Chi Minh Trail, moving supplies south for the North Vietnamese war effort. As they were driving along, American aircraft attacked their convoy. Dat pulled the truck off to the roadside and he a companion riding with him raced off to take cover in a bunker there. Once inside, Dat realized that if a bomb struck their bunker, both men would likely die and no one would be able to take the supplies to the soldiers. He therefore decided that he and his companion should split up so he left the bunker and took cover in another nearby. Not long after, an American aircraft released its bombs over their section of the trail. One struck Dat's bunker directly, killing him, while his companion emerged from the air strike unscathed. Different members of the family each had their own explanations for his death. His brother, a party member from a farming family who was active for many years in the local administration, saw his death as nothing more than bad luck (*rui*). His opinion was shared by a number of his male relations, several of whom had also served in the military. Dat's mother and sister-in-law saw the matter differently. To his mother, her son had died as a result of his fate. He was a good person, deprived of his life in his early twenties, thus his fate had been to die young. For his sister-in-law, multiple forces were involved. On the one hand, it had been his fate to die young, but it had also been bad luck for him to have been the one to leave the safe bunker and move to the other. Her convictions regarding the existence of fate had been recently reconfirmed when her husband, who rejected the idea of fate, had become extremely ill but, after a long convalescence, regained his health. 'It was,' she commented, 'not his fate to die.'

While such general sociological differences exist in contemporary Thinh Liet, it should again be noted that there are exceptions, and that attitudes change. Many people, both male and female, have shown an increasing interest in having their own or their child's horoscope calculated (*xem tu vi*) in order to learn their fate as determined by the time and date of birth. Some women, notably elderly women who are active Buddhists, oppose the idea of fate. Thinh Liet has also seen a growth in the number of male spirit priests from two or three in the 1980s to over a dozen now, including a former army doctor. Some men, including former officials, have constructed new spirit shrines (*dien*) in their family compounds. These changes among former advocates of official ideology have been the most interesting. A female former vice-president of the commune has become active in spirit mediumship. A former head of the commune's party cell who held other high ranking administrative positions is now the commune's most skilled spirit priest. Another former party member and land reform cadre is regarded as one of the most skilled manufacturers of votive paper objects, a family tradition he secretly returned to in 1977. Both men were expelled from the party. A number of war veterans have also changed their ideas regarding fate. One long standing party member who had fought the French and occupied several important administrative positions commented, 'For me, all deaths occur as a result of fate, and fate influences our lives.' Many veterans note that as they look back on the war, they often struggle to make sense of why some died and others did not. As they reflect on this, some have begun to wonder whether their survival was the result of fate or some other supernatural or divine force. A number of other men who were enthusiastic revolutionaries in their youth have turned toward the supernatural and softened their opposition as they have aged (This will be fully discussed with regard to funerals in the next chapter). All of these changes illustrate the dynamic character of residents' attitudes toward the supernatural.

Defining Religion and Superstition

When investigating the category of superstition in Thinh Liet life, it is clear that the party and state have exercised a dominant role in defining what a superstition is. In doing so, they have also attempted to define what constitutes a legitimate religious practice (*tin nguong*). In social life, Vietnamese generally do not employ the word most commonly translated as 'religion' (*ton giao*) to describe their own ideas and practices. This word is generally only used for religion as a general category, or to describe institutionally complex religions, such as Buddhism, Christianity, or Islam. To describe their own practices, people employ the term *tin nguong*. The importance of this term is evident in the fact that the Vietnamese government has always described the freedom of religion in its constitutions as *tu do tin nguong* (*tu do* means freedom) and not *tu do ton giao*. The word's semantics, however, are complex as they involve ideas of faith, belief, or doctrine, combined with the actual practices that invoke those ideas. Toan Anh in his two volume set *Tin Nguong Viet Nam* notes in his definition of tin nguong that, 'Here I would like to speak of religion, especially of the revered beliefs of the Vietnamese with regard to the shapeless forces that control the sacred aspects of human life. Speaking of these revered beliefs also implies speaking about propitiation, about the performance of rites derived from religion (*ton giao*)' (Toan Anh 1969:11). From the 1940s onward the government encouraged cadres to protect and nurture the tin nguong of the people. The use of this term brought with it a strong sense of prestige and legitimacy, while superstition implied stigma.

In contemporary Thinh Liet, people offer diverse ideas about what falls under the rubric of tin nguong and what is a superstition. Regarding the latter, strong opponents of superstitions hold to the official line and argue that any practice that involves supernatural causality is a superstition. Such critics tend to invoke specific cases, such as the woman severely burned in the healing rite, the vague declarations of diviners that people immediately apply to the particulars of their lives, or the burgeoning but sometimes ineffective rites of spirit priests, as examples of superstitions. These cases are usually followed with comments that superstitions waste resources, have no empirical effect, add to people's worries (*them lo*), often harm people, and are nothing more than sophisticated shake downs. While some people are sympathetic to this approach, many others are more ambivalent or uncertain. A common response to the question of what constitutes a tin nguong is that 'ancestor worship is a legitimate religious practice of the people' (*cung to tien la tin nguong dan toc*). One former officer commented that only ancestor worship is legitimate, but others offer more expansive definitions that include rites conducted at shrines or even spirit mediumship. Of particular interest here is that the worship of Ba Mau, the female spirit central to spirit mediumship, is now argued by some to represent the true core of Vietnamese tin nguong that was displaced with the sinicization of Vietnamese society. The use of votive paper objects is another interesting case. The party designated these as superstitious for over three decades, but many people now regularly use them and regard them as legitimate paraphernalia for propitiating ancestors. One producer of the items even claimed that their production was a 'meritorious occupation' (*nghe cong duc*) because it enabled people to properly attend to their family and religious responsibilities. All of these definitions acknowledge supernatural agents and ways of interacting with them as part of tin nguong, but their content varies. The government has also recently started to include communal house rites under the rubric of tin nguong. This further muddied the definitional waters, but it also showed the term's changing, politically influenced, and often contradictory semantics. One older man commented that 'the freedom of religion is not the freedom of superstitions' (*tu do tin nguong khong phai la tu do me tin*), but given this ambiguity, it is difficult for many to say just how they are different.

Conclusion

Contemporary Thinh Liet society remains divided over the existence of supernatural entities and forces, and whether people should perform rituals that engage them. Many men oppose practices they regard as superstitious, yet they will just as willingly perform rites at their family ancestral altars, in their lineage halls, at Buddhist temples, and in the village communal house. Women, on the whole, are less concerned about the legitimate religious practice versus superstition issue, and readily engage the supernatural in diverse ways. Perhaps the comment of the previously mentioned party member and French war veteran best summed up the sense of compulsion and ambivalent attitudes felt by many. As he stated, 'As long as I have ancestors, there will be an incense urn on the altar. And as long as I have a family, I will perform rites at the shrine (*dien*).' The party's position was beset by an internal contradiction in that despite the fact that they preached an atheistic creed, they still allowed for the worship of ancestors and national heroes. The doors to the supernatural were never completely closed. For many people, even though the party said that there were no spirits, official ideology never could account for all of life's vicissitudes, thus many people kept looking back to earlier causal notions and systems of explanation to help them make sense and take control of their lives. Many also felt that if they truly abandoned the ancestors or the supernatural, misfortune would come to them. It is this final point, the feeling of obligation to the spirits of the dead and how they should be fulfilled, that will provide the focus of the next chapter.

CHAPTER FOUR

Reconstructing Funerary Ritual

Funerary ritual provides one of the most fruitful arenas of social action for functional analysis. Early scholars such as Durkheim and Radcliffe-Brown recognized that the death of an individual, beyond simply representing a loss for family and loved ones, also represents a potential threat to the social order. As a result, funerary rites frequently publically foreground and display ideas considered salient to the maintenance of the social order. As Maurice Bloch and Jonathan Parry commented, 'What would seem to be revitalized in funerary practices is that which is culturally conceived to be the most essential to the reproduction of the social order' (Bloch and Parry 1982:7). Funerary rites in a country such as Vietnam that is firmly within the Confucian cultural sphere would also seem to be fruitful ground for functionalist analysis. The *Analects* of Confucius are replete with references to the importance of proper mourning behavior. Confucius himself asked, 'What can I find worthy of note in a man who is ... lacking in sorrow when in mourning?' (Confucius 1979:71). Later, Vietnamese scholars and officials took their lead from such Chinese scholars as Chu Hsi and published extremely detailed instructions on the proper organization of funeral rites. The logic behind these instructions was that the proper performance of sanctioned ritual, as Laurel Kendall has stated of pre-modern Korea, 'fostered the morality and well-being of the people' (Kendall 1994:166), while also legitimating the hierarchical relationships that structured the social order. Pre-revolutionary scholars and officials, one can fairly argue, were themselves committed functionalists who endeavored to create through funerary ritual a unity of morality and values among the people.

When revolutionary authorities began their cultural reforms they embraced a similar attitude toward funerary ritual. In the reforms they implemented, they wanted funeral practices to retain their functional character, but they wanted to change them so they only displayed and reproduced those values championed by the revolution. The imposition of these reforms created problems at the local level because many of the values and ideas articulated in the new rites clashed with local ideas regarding the proper conduct of funeral rites. Indeed, many Thinh Liet residents felt that the reforms violated basic moral obligations they had to fulfill, and therefore continued to try to conduct rituals as they deemed appropriate. This chapter's purpose is to examine Thinh Liet funeral rites in order to disentangle the web of ideas and values mobilized, invoked, and debated within them. Party reforms have enjoyed mixed success in Thinh Liet as some still structure certain aspects of contemporary rites, while others have been rejected. Indeed, a comprehensive survey of contemporary funerary practices reveals that Thinh Liet residents often do not agree on how to conduct these practices, and the ways in which they debate their proper organization and structure involves ideas that preceded the revolution and those derived from official ideology. The analysis that follows will examine these ideas, as well as the social actors articulating them, in order to demonstrate the diverse and competing ideas residents have regarding why they conduct funerary rites and also the appropriate ways to conduct them.

Creating the Socialist Funeral

Mortuary practices were always a focus of intense official scrutiny in pre-revolutionary Vietnam because they constituted a forum for the public expression of filial piety (*hieu*), the ideological core of the hierarchical monarchic state. Filial piety received extensive ideological emphasis as a result of the logical assumption that if a child was obedient to his parent, he would similarly be obedient to his king and other superiors in social life, and would therefore maintain the status quo. As Yu Tzu stated in *The Analects*, 'It is rare for a man whose character is such that he is good as a son and obedient as a young man to have the inclination to transgress against his superiors; it is unheard of for one who has no such inclination to be inclined to start a rebellion' (Book 1:2).[1] The expression of filial piety was a lifelong process, but funerary rites represented its quintessence because it involved one of the most basic responsibilities of a child: putting the soul of a dead parent to its final rest in an appropriate fashion. Accordingly, the government's Ministry of Rites and independent scholars published detailed instructions on the proper organization of funerals and death anniversary ceremonies, such as Ho Si Tan's 'Book of Family Rites' (*Tho Mai Gia Le*). They also instituted severe sanctions for those who ignored official dictates. Among the ten 'heinous crimes' (*thap ac*) of the sixteenth century Le dynasty legal code were the 'lack of filial piety' (*bat hieu*) and 'disloyalty' (*bat nghia*), offences defined by not showing the proper measure of grief after a close relative's death. Other heinous crimes included treason and harming the emperor (see Nguyen Ngoc Huy and Ta

109

Van Tai 1987:110). Despite the placement of such significance on funerary practices, the government still could not completely control their conduct at the local level, a point evident in the efforts by successive dynasties to reduce the feasting that accompanied funerals at the village level (see Tran Trong Kim 1954:244–246; Woodside 1971:27).

When the Vietnamese Communists attained power, they took it upon themselves to create a new set of funerary rites that accorded with the new ruling ideology.[2] The reformed rites had a number of primary characteristics and objectives. First was an effort to make rites 'simple' (*don gian, gian di*). Cadres regarded the lengthy and detailed schedule of pre-revolutionary funerary rites as a tremendous burden that needed drastic reduction. Second, cadres wanted to eliminate all feudal elements. As officials from Hanoi commented, the feudal regime had defined orthodox funeral practices, thus many aspects within them, such as prolonged mourning periods or the requirement that women lie on the ground to impede the funeral procession, were feudal in nature (Hanoi, Culture and Information Service 1975:33). Third, officials considered pre-revolutionary practices to be both 'wasteful' (*lang phi*) and to provide contexts for ostentatious (*khoe danh, pho truong*) display and status competition. This was particularly true of feasting and its associated exchange relations. The new rites were to be 'economical' (*tiet kiem*) and emphasize unity. Fourth, certain elements of funerary rites involved the propitiation of the deceased's soul or were superstitious in character. The party sought to remove these elements and turn all funeral rites into strictly commemorative acts. Fifth, the reformed rites were to have an 'educational' (*giao duc*) effect on participants. Thus, particularly with the orations, the party wanted the deceased's revolutionary virtues highlighted. Finally, in order to ensure the implementation of these reforms, government officials assumed a number of important roles, such as arranging pallbearers or delivering orations, formerly performed by family or kin. Through these insertions, the party hoped to effectively neutralize the role of family members and make funeral rites a proxy of the state and its ideology.

As discussed in Chapter 2, the party articulated its vision of the new rites in detailed ritual primers written by government officials. The main actors involved in defining this new orthodoxy were the Communist Party, the Ministry of Culture, and occasionally other institutions such as the Ministry of Health. The common pattern for defining the rites was for the party to detail its vision first, and then the government, the Ministry of Culture, and others followed. Given that provinces, districts, and even communes had their own 'Cultural Services' (*ty van hoa*), 'Committees for the Propagation of the New Ways' (*Ban Van Dong Nep Song Moi*), and party mass organizations that sometimes published their own sets of regulations, there was not a universal model that applied to all North Vietnam. Regulations stayed within the boundaries established by the party, but certain provinces, such as Thanh Hoa, often took a harder line than others and tinkered with the smallest details of funerary rites. Hai Hung and Thanh Hoa, for example, endeavoured to eliminate funeral music (Vietnam, Ministry of Culture 1975:72, 104). Thinh Liet officials implemented this reform, but soon had to accommodate themselves to local dissatisfaction and dropped it because such funerals were considered 'excessively sad.' Ha Tay attempted to eliminate the distribution of betel nut during the funeral procession (Vietnam, Ministry of Culture 1975:100). Other cases will be noted below. Despite such variations, it was very clear that the reformed rites took precedence over all preceding practices. As cadres from Hanoi commented, 'The "Book of Family Rites" was popularized the most among the people. The distinctive characteristic of that book is the rites described therein are redundant, burdensome, overly long, unhygienic, superstitious, and wasteful of effort and resources' (Hanoi, Culture and Information Service 1975:33). In the new society, reforms would eliminate all such negative consequences and replace them with a convenient and beneficial set of practices.

A final characteristic of the reformed rites was their effort to establish a new morality and tone for them. Cadres wanted the reformed rites to be 'polite' (*lich su*), solemn, and respectful. As a result, they precisely detailed behaviors to avoid. To give one example, regulations propagated by the 'Committee for Civilized Ways' (*Ban Nep Song Van Minh*) in 1971 instructed bicyclists and motorists to stop and let funeral processions pass, while also commenting, 'Whether a close relation or not, when one participates in a funeral procession one should not wear gaudy clothing, talk loudly while walking, look over women, or flirt. Everyone would agree that such behavior is not polite' (Vietnam, Ministry of Culture 1975:59). Numerous regulations cautioned against laughing in the procession and other faux pas. At a deeper level, regulations also attempted to appropriate local idioms mobilized in the rites and redefine important moral components. For example, the Ministry of Culture in 1972, when justifying the elimination of wasteful feasting in funerals, invoked the folk adage also critical of wastefulness, 'In life my child gave me nothing to eat, in death the rice and meat become an oration for the flies' (*Song thi con chang cho an, chet thi xoi thit lam van te ruoi*) (Vietnam, Ministry of Culture 1975:49). The Nam Ha cultural service invoked another important funeral idiom, the adage 'at death lay all to rest' (*nghia tu la nghia tan*). Thinh Liet residents interpret this adage as an admonition for the living to make peace with those they have had conflicts with before they die, but after a description of a simple, economical funeral that places no burdens on the deceased's family, the officials concluded that the new reforms embodied 'the spirit of friendship between people, exactly as in the adage "at death lay all to rest"' (Vietnam, Ministry of Culture 1975:76).[3] Although the party hoped to redefine these moral idioms and create new rites, many of them conflicted with vital moral principles mobilized in funeral rites. The rest of this chapter will examine in greater detail the reforms, the moral principles with which many of them clashed, and the manner in which those conflicts are being negotiated in contemporary Thinh Liet.

On Being Filial

Death in Thinh Liet commune is seen as a normal and natural part of human life.[4] When the death of an elderly person appears near, word spreads quickly throughout the commune, particularly to visiting anthropologists with an interest in funerary rites, and residents wait for word to set the funeral process in motion. Thinh Liet residents refer to funerals (*dam ma* or more formally *dam tang*) and mortuary rites, such as the death anniversary ceremonies (*gio*) and secondary burials (*boc mau*), as 'works of filial piety' (*viec hieu*), a reference to the public expression of filial piety that occurs in their conduct (by contrast, residents refer to wedding ceremonies, which celebrate life and the formation of a new conjugal union, as 'works of amusement' (*viec hy*)). The rhetoric of filial piety originates in the intensely hierarchical relations that pertain between parents and children. Despite revolutionary efforts to create more egalitarian relations between parents and children (see Chapter 5), parents are still the superiors in their families. When Thinh Liet children are socialized, one of the more common expressions they hear is that they must 'respect order' (*ton ti trat tu*), an admonition for children to know their inferior position in society and do as their superiors, particularly their parents, tell them. The wide gap that exists between parents and children partly results from the fact that even though parents decide to have children, as soon as a child is born it has a 'moral debt' (*on*) to its parents for bringing it into the world. This debt continues to accumulate as the parents devote more time and resources to raising the child (cf. Freedman 1958:88). A person is fully responsible for this parental debt, though in fact it can never be completely repaid. While the parents are alive, recognition and payment of the debt occur through obedience to the parents' wishes, financial support if earning an income, and care for the parents when they are old. Payment of the debt is an expression of filial piety. Indeed, one of the most common parental criticisms of children when they disagree with them or do something against their wishes is that they are 'unfilial' (*bat hieu*). Obligations and debts to parents are a basic part of life. In Thinh Liet commune, filial piety is simply correct behavior. As one resident stated, 'if you don't care for your parents, you're not a good person.' Nevertheless, it reaches its highest virtue when not simply done as the fulfilment of an obligation, but also as an expression of love and affection.

A parent's death provides an immediate test of a child's filial piety that is measured by the type and quality of the parent's funeral. People are very

Plate 1 The Giap Nhi communal house, circa 1991, before the market was moved to a location concealed from the communal house facade.

Plate 2 The Giap Nhi communal house, circa 1998.

Plate 3 The Giap Tu communal house, circa 1991.

Plate 4 The Giap Tu communal house, circa 1998.

Plate 5 A simple ancestral altar with a poster featuring an image of Ho Chi Minh above.

Plate 6 Members of the Women's Buddhist Association chant during funeral rites for a former member.

Plate 7 A Giap Tu man delivers a funeral oration. Next to him are food prestations given by guests at the funeral.

Plate 8 A Giap Nhi funeral procession.

Plate 9 The eldest son at a funeral wearing the "straw hat".

Plate 10 Family members bid farewell at the grave site.

Plate 11 "The Fatherland Remembers Your Sacrifice" certificate and simple altar for family war dead.

Plate 12 Residents toast those killed by the French during the 1947 reconquest of Thinh Liet at the 1992 rites conducted to commemorate their deaths.

Plate 13 The spirit cabinet in the Giap Tu communal house containing the
Ho Chi Minh portrait.

aware of the pressures to hold an appropriate funeral. At one level there is strong psychological pressure to 'be filial with my parents' (*co hieu voi cha me*) and show that they understand their 'filial obligation' (*hieu nghia*). However, funerals are also extremely public events, normally carrying on for a period of three days and involving hundreds of people. Family members recognize that others will closely observe and evaluate the funeral. Residents often invoke the adage 'ridicule funerals, scorn weddings' (*ma che, cuoi trach*) to describe the sometimes intense criticism and commentary that can follow a funeral or wedding. Most residents say that they 'live according to public opinion' (*song theo du luan*), a reference to the fact that they wish to behave in a manner that avoids public criticism. One resident noted that this 'puts many restrictions on the individual,' but the pressure is quite effective, particularly since words of criticism almost always finds their way back to the family. Thus, out of a concern for being described as 'unfilial, irresponsible' (*bat hieu, bat nghia*), family members, usually led by senior kin who have participated in many funerals as well as the eldest son, carefully negotiate the funeral's basic features. Though this sometimes can take on an amusing air, such as an instance in 1992 when the nephew of an elderly woman gleefully refused to line his deceased aunt's casket with a newspaper that featured pictures of politburo members, it is extremely serious business. Family members must decide many important issues, such as what mourning clothes to wear, whether or what kind of prestations to accept, whether to have a feast, and what time to take the casket to the gravesite. Within and between some families, divergent standards exist. At times these ideas originate in party ideology, while others come from the rather amorphous notion of pre-revolutionary traditions. Given the absence of a dominant, paradigmatic model or text that all villagers rely upon, organizing funerals sometimes leads to conflicts or funerals some regard as extremely unfilial.

Mourning Begins

The death of a parent or senior relation begins the individual's transition into a state of mourning. Symbolically, mourning is represented by a headband, called a *tang*, and those in mourning are referred to as 'having *tang*' (*co tang*). Mourning officially begins with the 'distribution of the *tang*' (*phat tang*) ceremony held in the deceased's home. This ceremony usually occurs at a convenient time a few hours after death. Thus, as in the case of the deceased woman discussed above, death occurred around 9:30 am and the distribution ceremony at 1:00 pm. The intervening hours are critical as family members complete all necessary preparations to begin the funeral. The first step is to prepare the body and casket. Dying at home constitutes a good death, thus those who are terminally ill or near death prefer to return home for their final days.[5] Soon after death, family members

113

prepare the corpse. Some clean it with a wet towel, others bind it to prevent the leakage of bodily fluids, but all dress it in an attractive set of clothing. At the same time, male family members procure a wooden casket, often purchasing the nicest casket possible as another show of piety. After the casket is brought into the house, the men place it before the family ancestral altar in the center of the house, with the long sides perpendicular to the altar. The casket does not sit on the ground but rests on supports some two feet off the ground. Male family members then line the bottom of the casket with absorbent material in case bodily fluids leak. Historically residents used tea or puffed rice, but newspapers are the most common item today. A pillow might also be included for the deceased's head. Once these are in place, male family members lay the body in the casket (*nhap quan*). The orientation of the body at this stage is very important as the head must be near the ancestral altar while the bottoms of the feet face toward the door to the outside of the home. After this, a variety of items might be placed in the casket, such as uncooked rice in the mouth, playing cards decorated with warriors, or real or votive money, to help the soul make its transition to the 'other world' (*the gioi khac*). The final act is to close the casket and nail the top in place. Male members again do this, but prior to closing the casket, family members take one last look at the deceased. The atmosphere during the preparations is very sad and women wail throughout. This reaches a pitch when the top is nailed on.

After closing the casket, the family places a small urn with burning incense in it on top of the casket, and a bowl of cooked glutinous rice that has two chopsticks stuck vertically into it with a hard boiled egg held between them. These are accompanied by either seven candles for a man, or nine candles for a woman, placed across the casket's top. The number of candles corresponds with the number of the deceased's 'life spirits' (*via*) – seven for men, nine for women – and symbolizes the deceased's gender. The Vietnamese theory of the body's constitution asserts that every body has one 'soul' (*linh hon*) and either seven or nine life spirits. The life spirits die with the body, but the soul lives on and must be cared for. This informs the next act, the placement of a small table at the foot of the casket near the central door. This table, which some residents call the 'distribution of *tang* altar,' will serve as a temporary altar until the casket is taken to the grave site. Family members place a number of items on it, such as candles, flowers, a drawing or photograph of the deceased (this has replaced the older practice of using a sheet of paper with the deceased's name written in characters), and a large incense urn. During subsequent rites, the living will place incense sticks in this urn after propitiating the deceased's soul. In preparation for the distribution ceremony, family members also place the mourning items that will be distributed.

In pre-revolutionary Vietnam, entrance into the state of mourning could in the rare case have its benefits, such as the allowance for officials to temporarily leave mandarinal service for two years to mourn their fathers, but it primarily entailed the imposition of numerous restrictions. These fell heaviest on those closest to the deceased, and became progressively lighter with genealogical distance. Sons, daughters, and wives were officially in mourning for three years after the death of a father or husband; grandchildren mourned their grandparents for one year; and husbands, in an important exception that reflected the male domination of society, mourned their wives for only nine months. During this period, the mourner could not attend other people's weddings, visit other's homes at the beginning of the new lunar year, and most importantly, could not marry.[6]

Party officials regarded mourning restrictions as feudal and highly objectionable. They recognized that 'mourning ... is a representation of the sentimental (*tinh cam*) relationships that exist between the living and the dead. With mourning ... the fundamental function is to display the sense of loss, sorrow, and remembrance of the living for the dead' (Vietnam, Ministry of Culture 1975:39); however, they also felt that they generated too many restrictions. They therefore introduced a number of modifications to mourning practices. Some of these reforms indicated a certain ambivalence by the party. For example, in some areas party officials mandated the removal of all physical representations of mourning soon after the funeral, while in others they grudgingly allowed people to wear them for as long as they wished, an ambivalence also evident in Thinh Liet. The party was completely certain about other changes though, notably that 'mourning restrictions must not interfere with marriage, military responsibilities, or any other responsibilities of the citizenry' (Vietnam, Ministry of Culture 1975:42). With the 1959 Law of Marriage and Family, the government legally abolished all restrictions on marriage during mourning, though enforcement of this law was difficult at the local level (see Chapter 5).

A more important intervention at the local level was the attempt to dictate which items citizens could legitimately wear to indicate mourning. In pre-revolutionary funerals, a knowledgeable observer could quickly identify the relationships of the participants to the deceased by the clothing they wore. Sons and daughters wore gauzy, roughly made cotton tunics and coarse belts. Sons wore special headgear, such as the eldest son's 'straw hat' (*mu rom*), and carried mourning staffs (*chong gay*). Daughters wore peaked cheesecloth caps (*ao so*). The different colors of the mourning headbands of more distant relations indicated their genealogical distance from the deceased. For example, grandchildren wore gold, and great grandchildren red. Funerary reforms dictated the elimination of these different forms and their replacement with generic attire. Mourning staffs, straw hats, and peaked caps were forbidden. All people were to wear only normal clothing. Participants could still wear mourning headbands as a symbol of the 'sentiment' between them and the deceased (Vietnam, Ministry of Culture 1975:39), but were to wear only a generic white headband. According to the party, the ideal symbol of mourning was a black armband or a piece of black cloth worn on the breast, an obvious borrowing from the French. This became popular in urban areas, and is common among those who work in Hanoi's offices, but was not imposed on the countryside.

These simplified requirements profoundly structured the choices for mourning attire in Thinh Liet from the late 1950s through the mid-1980s. Straw hats, mourning canes, and peaked caps basically disappeared, while *tang* became white. There was resistance, however. The main focus of controversy was the feeling among many residents that the failure to wear appropriate mourning attire indicated a lack of filial piety. And although local officials monitored funerals, some families tried to retain as many of the pre-revolutionary items as possible. Since officials relaxed their control over funerals in the late 1980s, no clear standard of appropriate attire has yet to emerge, as the case of the deceased woman discussed above illustrated. At 1:00 pm, one of her senior male relatives began the distribution of the *tang* ceremony. Assembled in the family compound was a group of some thirty close kin and friends. The man announced the reason for gathering that day, and then gave a brief summary of the deceased's life. Afterwards, he began distributing the mourning attire, declaring that from that point on, all those participating must 'bear the burden of mourning' (*chiu tang*), a reference that mourning officially began after receiving the item. Given that the woman had no son, her son-in-law fulfilled the role of eldest son in the funeral. He received a mourning cane, and wore a course cotton tunic, but instead of a straw hat, he wore one made of paper, a not uncommon occurrence today. Under his tunic he also wore his old uniform from his days as an officer in the People's Army – a common outfit for many former officers at weddings and funerals, though particularly for those serving as officials. His wife and her sisters wore coarse tunics, but no cheesecloth caps. And the vast majority of guests wore white headbands, most of which they brought themselves, as opposed to given by the family as in the past. In other funerals, grandchildren and great grandchildren sometimes wear colored headbands, but this is not universal. The general return to mourning styles has been motivated by a shared sense that doing so indicates filial piety for the deceased. However, exactly what constitutes piety on this point remains open to dispute. Some families pass out nothing but mourning headbands at their family funerals, arguing that they are an adequate representation of their piety. And virtually no one wears a mourning headband very long except some elderly widows with long hair who tie their hair with a piece of black, velvet-like material to symbolize their mourning. Although the rhetoric of mourning attire indicating piety remains, its constituent elements remain undecided.

116

Crossing to the Other World

A second important measure of filial piety in funerals is the conduct of rites dedicated to helping the deceased's soul make a successful transition from the world of the living to the 'other world.' According to local reckonings, funerals generally last three days with death occurring on the first day, burial and feast on the second, and clean up and a small feast for those who could not attend the previous day on the third. Of the three days, the first and second days are the most spiritually dangerous. As noted above, a person's soul survives the body's death. At death, the soul leaves the body and roams the nearby area. The transition out of the body is not necessarily traumatic if the soul is in a familiar place, hence the preference to die at home, but death in a strange place can cause the soul to panic and run off, further complicating the funeral rites. Even though the soul leaves the body at death, it is not yet aware that the body is dead. Thinh Liet residents could not agree on when this realization occurred, though most felt that it occurred after either three or seven days. Nevertheless, when the soul has just been released, it is in a liminal state between being wrapped in a living body and becoming a benevolent family ancestor. In this period, the family runs the risk of the soul becoming a malevolent wandering ghost by either running off or having a ghost invade the incense urn intended for the deceased, thereby depriving it of sustenance and a permanent home. Given these concerns, ritual activities here reach their most complex and careful phase as the living engage the soul and attempt to facilitate its transition to the other world and benevolent ancestorhood.

Most elderly Thinh Liet residents, before they die, inform their children of the type of funeral they want. Some people, such as a Giap Nhat man who died in 1992, describe these rites down to the smallest details, while others only make such simple preparations as purchasing a casket and storing it in their home. These parental requests are extremely important because children are morally obliged to arrange the funeral as requested. To do otherwise is the quintessence of unfilial behavior. There is no single set of rites, however, that people request to facilitate the transition of their soul. Part of the reason for this variation relates back to the campaign against superstitions. Similar to its anti-spiritist agenda in other realms of ritual life, the party banned outright a number of common practices associated with funerals in which the living engaged supernatural forces or entities. These included divination (*boi toan*) or horoscopy (*xem gio*) to determine the best time for particular rites, soul-calling rites (*goi hon*), and most importantly, the burning of votive paper objects to supply essential items to the soul. Although the party asserted that people had the constitutional right to exercise their freedom of religion, they also cracked down on rites performed by Buddhist ritual specialists or spirit priests, the two specialists most commonly recruited to assist the soul in its transition.

117

The party's agenda here reiterated their position that there were no spirits that exercised any influence on the living, thus funeral rites should drop any concern with assisting the soul. In this atmosphere, many families were afraid to publically perform such rites for fear of criticism or punishment by local authorities. Consequently, from the 1950s to the early 1980s, the open performance of temple-based rites and the invitation of ritual specialists to local homes declined severely and interrupted previous patterns of cultural reproduction.

A second reason for the absence of orthodoxy relates to gender-based differences in ritual practice. Rituals in the pre-revolutionary village exhibited a significant gender dimension in that men generally focussed their ritual practices on the communal house while women focussed on the Buddhist temple (see Nguyen Van Khoan 1930:110), though some men were active at the temple as well. In contemporary Thinh Liet, a good number of men still regard Buddhism and Buddhist practices as basically female in nature. The consequences of this at death are that most men either request no ritual specialist at all and have family members conduct the rites, or ask for a spirit priest. If a man asks for the latter, the most common option is to invite a spirit priest to come on the first evening after death to perform 'request for the soul' rites (*le cau hon*). These rites, which install the soul in the altar and then send it off, are performed by the spirit priest before the altar at the foot of the casket. Throughout, the spirit priest reads from a standardized text, generally written in Sino-Vietnamese characters, while family members sit behind him. Another factor informing men's choices is their revolutionary background. Some former revolutionaries take an extreme line and refuse the performance of any rites. One Giap Tu man declared that he did not even want the bowl of glutinous rice and egg used in his funeral because they were 'superstitious.' Such a position is rare. A common position among former revolutionaries is to request a very simple funeral that does not include the participation of a ritual specialist, but does involve the performance of family-led rites. Allowance for such simpler rites generally puts children at ease because they might be more worried about the fate of their father's soul than he. It is interesting to note that in recent years a number of formerly devoted revolutionaries have experienced a change of heart regarding funeral rites. Such was the case of the Giap Tu man mentioned in Chapter 3 who for decades had adamantly opposed the performance of any spirit-related rites. He was concerned that his slow and lingering death would indicate to others that he had committed many immoral acts (*toi*) in his life, thus he asked his wife and her friends from the Buddhist Association to mobilize the supernatural through chanting at his bedside.[7] Such chanting, residents say, removes any demerits the person might have accumulated, and helps the soul leave the body – an action that is constrained by numerous demerits. Other men have also evolved from an anti-ritual stance to one that embraces, if not encourages, the involvement of a ritual specialist. Often this change has occurred as the men have gotten older. It is clear in their cases that the change was motivated by a concern over what will happen to them after death. Some might have been comfortable in their younger years asserting that death represented the end of everything, but such assertions do not seem as compelling as they have aged, and the question of the after life and fate of their soul has required a more compelling answer. Many have therefore turned to systems of meaning and explanation they previously rejected. The implications of this change, particularly for what it has to say about the subjective viability of the secular revolutionary creed, are significant and will be discussed in the conclusion.

Most Thinh Liet women prefer for their funerals the involvement of a Buddhist ritual specialist, such as a monk, nun, or the local Buddhist Association. From the late 1950s through the late 1980s, monks or nuns from local temples found it extremely difficult to participate in local residents' ritual lives. They could not openly visit people's homes, nor were residents willing to go to the temple for funeral rites. For many Thinh Liet residents, however, the obligation to assist the soul of a deceased person in its journey remained one of their most fundamental obligations. The main group that assumed responsibility for fulfilling this obligation in Thinh Liet was the Buddhist Association. This organization, which has never received official approval, was the only unofficial social organization to persist from the 1950s onward.[8] Many of the older women who were its members rejected the party's cultural reforms. Given that they could not assemble for rites at the local temple, their main activity was the night-time performance of the 'request for the soul' rite by chanting at other resident's funerals. The normal pattern for these rites was for the group to be informed of the family's desire for chanting around the time of death, and then the members would covertly assemble at the bereaved family's home. They would then chant through the night, and disperse early in the morning. Given the close quarters in which Thinh Liet residents live, local officials were aware of these activities, but no cases were ever reported of the authorities breaking up a session. This was most likely due to the recognition that such a raid would have constituted an enormous affront to the deceased and their family, while also placing the officials in an uncomfortable position with either their lineage mates, some of whom might have been related to the deceased, or their senior female kin, some of whom might have been chanting. Officials were generally ready to aggressively institute their policies, but there were practical limits.

In recent years, local Buddhist ritual specialists and the Buddhist Association have assumed important roles in local womens' funerals, particularly those who were association members. If a woman receives what might be described as a 'high Buddhist' funeral, a number of long and

119

complicated rites will be performed for her at home on the evening of her death. These will always begin with a 'request for the soul' rite and might also include a rite in which family members symbolically feed and bathe the deceased. They will continue with a variety of rites, depending upon the family, that facilitate the soul's transition. These usually begin late in the evening, normally around 10:00 pm, and involve chanting by either the Buddhist Association, a monk, or nun, that continues for a few hours or until morning. Sometimes the chanting takes place while sitting or in a 'running group' rite (*le chay dan*), in which family members chant while repeatedly circumambulating the casket for some 90 minutes. This chanting again helps erase any demerits the deceased might have accumulated. Whatever rites they follow, the family will be certain to ensure the chanting's success by performing a 'rice porridge offering' rite (*cung chao*) prior to its commencement. In this rite, the host family takes an aluminium tray, places several rice bowls filled with rice porridge on it, lights several incense sticks, and then places it on a table or on the ground outside the house. These bowls are intended for wandering spirits so they can eat their fill and not be tempted to enter the home and disrupt the deceased soul's transition.

A number of points stand out about the chanting. The first is the use of prayer books written in Sino-Vietnamese characters by the monk or nun, while the women in the association read out of prayer books written in *quoc ngu*. The dissemination of *quoc ngu* has allowed people to participate in religious rites in a manner formerly denied to them. In the Giap Tu woman's funeral, neither a monk nor nun was present, but given the use of *quoc ngu* texts, the group could conduct the chanting itself without the involvement of a specialist literate in characters. The second feature is that even though the participants read out of *quoc ngu* texts, few of them can understand the text's meaning because they are transcriptions of the characters' pronunciation and not translations of their meanings. This relates back to a deeper point regarding rites dedicated to assisting the soul in its transition to the other world. When a monk, nun, or religious specialist performs such a rite, the texts they read out describe the journey the soul makes from this world to the other. However, although the specialist is aware of the nature of that journey, most Thinh Liet residents have only a general, and sometimes contradictory, knowledge of it. It is well known that the soul will reach a river that it must cross, and that the soul will encounter numerous difficulties along the way, but it is extremely rare to find anyone who can recite in detail the entire voyage. Many also comment that there is a 'king' (*vua*) who rules over this world, and a few note that there is an official named Vo Lam who, similar to a customs officer, controls passage between the two worlds. Outside of religious specialists, those who know the most about the journey are older men. Thinh Liet residents also do not talk about such entities as the multiple levels of Buddhist hell or other areas where immoral souls are punished, nor is their much of a cultural focus on such ideas as karma or reincarnation as one finds in the Theravada Buddhist countries of Southeast Asia (see Spiro 1970; Tambiah 1970). The issue itself raises interesting questions about the social distribution of knowledge in the pre-revolutionary period and how it was affected by the revolution. An examination of Dumoutier's *Les Rites Funeraires des Annamites* creates the impression that at least in the year 1904, the Vietnamese had extremely sophisticated and complex eschatological concepts (see Dumoutier 1904). In contemporary Thinh Liet, such knowledge is not widely known or shared, raising the question of whether it ever was widely distributed, and if so, if the revolution disrupted its transmission.

The rites of the first night after death instigate the process of moving the deceased's soul to the other world. Throughout this period, the family is not alone in their grief. Virtually from the moment the person dies, the bereaved household is filled with people coming to help out, pay their respects, and/or participate in the various rites. By the time the evening rites begin, most of the guests who come for strictly social reasons have left (see the next section), leaving behind a smaller group of close friends and kin. These people might participate in the evening rites, or they might simply sit outside the house playing cards or talking at the tables set up to receive guests. Many will stay the whole night so the family is not left alone.

After morning comes, the family begins preparations for funeral's next stage, the procession (*dua dam*). The timing of contemporary processions differs from those of the past. First, prior to the revolution, wealthy families sometimes displayed the coffin in their homes for as long as one month in order to assert their status, while the poor normally buried their's within a day or two. In the early 1960s the government ordered the burial of all corpses within a maximum of 48 hours (Vietnam, Ministry of Culture 1979:18). Some areas, such as Ha Tay province to the west of Hanoi, decreed that burial must take place within 24 hours after death (Vietnam, Ministry of Culture 1975:87). The justification for this restriction was the maintenance of public hygiene as the long term display of the coffin posed several health risks, such as the putrefaction of the corpse and the leakage of bodily fluids, but the primary motivation was the elimination of status displays. Contemporary Thinh Liet families have adopted this reform and almost always bury their dead on the day after death. Families have also largely abandoned the pre-revolutionary practice of determining an auspicious hour (*xem gio*) to take the casket out of the house. Instead, most families remove the casket according to convenience, usually making the time of the procession known to visitors the previous day.

The ritual sequence leading up to the casket's removal from the home begins with the final funeral orations. In the case of an elderly person's death, the head of the Elderly Association stands up in front of the guests

121

next to the casket. He prefaces his oration with the comment that all have come to 'share the sadness' (*chia buon*) of the family, and then begins a brief speech in which he describes the deceased's life and accomplishments. Following the speech, the eldest son, who sits before the guests with his siblings, thanks the guests. At this stage, families might add an element of their own choice, such as reading out a poem or a message previously drafted by the deceased. After this, the funeral musicians begin to play, and the children bow several times before the caskets, usually with the daughters visibly crying.

The next step is the removal of the casket from the home. Prior to picking up the casket, family members transfer many of the items from the altar at the foot of the casket to another small palanquin, called a *vong xa* (or 'dead car' in Sino-Vietnamese), that travels in the procession and constitutes a type of mobile, temporary altar. At the appropriate moment, the pallbearers pick up the casket and move it out of the house, again accompanied by loud wailing, particularly by elderly women. The identity, number, and role of the pallbearers is revealing. Prior to the revolution, families rented pallbearers, normally young men, from the village. Families paid these men both food and money, and most opted for ten or twelve pallbearers, but some wealthy families used the occasion to assert their status and hired as many as three dozen pallbearers. Party officials were keenly aware of this status issue and decreed that local cooperatives should provide pallbearers for their members' funerals in order to maintain equality. Cooperatives in Thinh Liet took up this charge, but after their dissolution in the early 1990s, local neighborhood heads (*truong xom*) took over the role and now select the pallbearers. Significantly, Thinh Liet families have uniformly maintained the practice of using only ten or twelve. The practice of carrying the casket has also disappeared. In the 1960s the party, in its push to improve hygienic concerns, ordered the use of a trolley (*xe tang*) pushed by a small number of village men to take the casket to the grave site. Cooperatives received instructions to purchase trolleys for local use, but Thinh Liet's cooperatives did not, obliging residents to carry caskets on their shoulders. Many elderly villagers in Thinh Liet felt this was inappropriate and pooled their money to purchase modest funeral palanquins in the early 1960s. Both Giap Nhi and Giap Tu first purchased wooden palanquins, but Giap Nhi's fell into disrepair and was replaced in the 1980s by a metal trolley purchased with contributions solicited by the Elderly Association. Today, each Thinh Liet village keeps its own trolleys and *vong xa* that are available to all villagers.

Once the pallbearers pick up the casket and place it on the trolley waiting outside, the procession begins its slow journey to the gravesite. Most Thinh Liet processions follow a standard pattern of the women of the Buddhist Association at the front, followed by people holding funeral wreaths, the funeral band, the *vong xa*, the casket, and the great mass of guests who have come to watch the burial. Kin in the procession tend to cluster in the area between the *vong xa* and the casket. In the pre-revolutionary period the behavior of children in the procession was regarded as a critical index of their filial piety and sense of loss. Sons were expected to stand before the casket and push against so it could not move forward (*giat lui*), while daughters and daughters-in-law were to wail and lay on the ground before the casket to impede its progress. Children were also to stand before their mother's casket in the procession, and behind their father's (*cha dua me don*), although there was some variation on this point as Giap Tu residents followed this rule while Giap Nhi residents ignored it and always stood behind the casket. Party officials regarded the former practices as feudal and humiliating, while the latter created inequalities in attitudes toward the parents, thus they attempted to eliminate them. Interestingly, despite the invocation of filial piety, the party succeeded in popularizing these reforms and none of the unsanctioned practices have returned in contemporary Thinh Liet funerals.

The soul travels with the casket to the grave site, and participants show their concern for it throughout. In the front of the procession there are often one or two women carrying baskets full of red and white votive paper ingots. As the procession moves, the women throw the ingots onto the ground, providing a visible trail from the home to the grave site. The soul will use this trail to find its way home after burial. Concern is also shown at the grave site. During the cooperative years, cooperative members dug graves for local families, but male kin presently perform that role. Preparing the grave must be done with great care so the soul can easily move into the grave site. Caution on this point is visible in the fact that before digging begins, those digging place single sticks of incense on all of the surrounding graves to inform their residents of the soul's imminent arrival, and also to ask the guardian spirit of the land to allow the soul to move there. As the procession approaches the graveyard, these rites are performed again to make sure that the other spirits will allow the deceased's soul to enter the grave.

The living say goodbye to the deceased at the grave site. With the deceased's children standing at the grave side, and all of the visitors in a large circle around the grave, the pallbearers slowly lower the casket into the grave. Family members usually place a small number of items on top of the casket, such as a bouquet of flowers and a bowl of rice with an egg and chopsticks. Then, beginning with the eldest son, family members each throw a clump of dirt down onto the casket's lid. This is another moment when wailing reaches great intensity. Once the close family members have thrown dirt onto the casket, all stand back and watch as the men who dug the grave fill it with the remaining dirt. What normally results is an impressive grave mound standing some two to three feet high. Family members then place all of the wreaths against the sides of the mound. In the final act, family members, friends, and others light sticks of incense, hold them between their hands, bow usually three times before the grave, and then stick them into the mound. In these prayers people say goodbye to deceased and wish them well on their journey. Following this, people slowly leave the cemetery to return to their homes and wait for the feast's commencement.

With the casket's burial, the deceased soul takes up residence in the area around the grave. The length of time the soul resides there is not entirely clear as Thinh Liet residents hold contradictory ideas on this point. On the day following burial, most families perform a 'return of the soul rite' (le phuc hon) in which a spirit priest invites the soul of the deceased to return to the home. Performance of this rite, it should be noted, only recently recommenced. As one Giap Nhi man stated, 'ten years ago we wouldn't have dared do this.' In Giap Nhi, the return of the soul is also facilitated by a brief set of rites involving the 'white soul' (hon bach). Families place this woven white cloth object on the top of the casket during the funeral, and leave it on the burial mound. Prior to the return of the soul rite, a group of close kin retrieve it from the mound and bring it back to the temporary altar, thereby bringing the soul along with them. Some Giap Nhi residents hold that the soul is actually in the object, though others are not entirely certain. Giap Tu residents avoid the practice entirely. After the soul returns, it resides in the urn previously placed on the altar at the end of the casket. Families do not immediately place that urn on the main ancestral altar. Instead, they erect a temporary altar, usually nothing more than a table with an attractive cloth on it along with candles, the rice bowl and egg, and other items, on the right hand side of the altar. For the first fifty days after death, families members will propitiate the deceased's soul at that altar, providing it every day with fresh food and water. Technically, the soul resides only in that urn, but as the preparation of the grave discussion indicated, it also seems to reside at the grave site. Some older men explained that residence at different locations was possible because of a type of dual nature of the soul, but this explanation was not widely shared. Instead, most people were comfortable with the idea that the soul could be in two places at one time.

By going through some variation of the rites just described, the living can take control of a potentially dangerous entity, the unattached soul of a dead person, and transform it into a benevolent ancestor. In doing so, they simultaneously realize one of their most important filial obligations, putting the soul of a deceased relation on the path to final peace. The diversity of ritual practice described here does not indicate that residents consider the processes involved here unimportant. To the contrary, throughout the years of revolutionary reform, only a minority of residents abandoned the notion that the deceased's soul needed assistance. To the rest, this obligation remained paramount, and had to be fulfilled through ritual practice. What the diversity does indicate, however, is that Thinh Liet residents could not and still do not agree on how to achieve that goal. In the pre-revolutionary period these differences ramified largely along gender lines, as they also do today, but revolutionary ideology has now become a significant factor for many families in their negotiations for how to properly start the soul's journey to the other world.

The Piety of a Feast

Soon after a person dies, family members place a poster, usually made of colored paper with hand-written letters, on the wall outside their compound. The poster declares the deceased's name, date, time of death, and possibly the date and time of the funeral procession. Also evident on the poster is whether the family's desires to receive prestations. An absence of references to prestations on the sheet indicates that they will accept prestations from their co-residents. In rare cases, the poster will read 'we will not accept funeral prestations' (khong nhan do phung), which means that the family only wants guests to present incense and flowers. It also indicates that they seek to organize a severely scaled down funeral with no public feast. Families who opt for the later option may do so out of a concern that organizing the feast and handling the prestations will be too burdensome, or possibly because they accept the party's position on the limitation of feasting (see below). However, in doing so, a family places itself in two morally compromising positions. First, they risk the charge that they lack filial piety with their parents; and second, that they wish to deny the 'sentimental' (tinh cam) relations that should ideally exist between themselves and other families. In placing themselves in this position, the family risks morally isolating itself in village life.

The size of a funeral feast, like the other elements discussed above, provide another measure of a child's filial piety with the deceased parent. Family ritual life in Thinh Liet is animated by the principle of 'wealth gives birth to ritual form' (phu qui sinh ra le nghia). The idea behind this principle is that the size of a ritual should be determined by the relative wealth of the organizers. For example, an extremely poor family could commemorate the death of a parent with only a hard boiled egg and a bowl of cooked glutinous rice, and that family's commemoration will exhibit the same amount of piety as a wealthy family holding a one hundred tray feast. What the family must determine is what is appropriate or 'just right' (vua) to their situation, and then hope that other villagers agree. Nevertheless, there does exist in Thinh Liet an unstated idea that bigger is better, thus many families feel compelled to organize a large feast in order to avoid public criticism. As one Giap Tu resident commented, 'those people who are afraid of being seen as lacking in piety with their parents will arrange a large funeral.'

125

For those who choose not to organize a large feast, one legitimate argument they can make in support of their decision is that they do so in order to follow the party's dictates to limit the use of resources in ritual activities. Much like its Confucian predecessors, the Vietnamese Communists vigorously opposed the profligate consumption of resources in rituals, particularly the consumption of meat and rice in feasting. Party rhetoric regarded feasting as wasteful (*lang phi*). It uselessly squandered resources and weakened the nation and its 'productive strength' (*suc san xuat*). This was particularly true during the American war years when the government sought to limit the slaughter of pigs. The government's position, as officials from Ninh Binh province illustrated, was that 'if we ... slaughter pigs recklessly it will have an impact upon our fertilizer base, our capacity to develop animal husbandry, and ultimately a direct influence on the lives of our people and soldiers' (Ninh Binh, People's Court 1967:10ff.). All the nation's resources were needed to strengthen the nation and build socialism, thus any wasteful practices had to be eliminated. The government took this position from its inception, but following the formation of the agricultural cooperatives in 1959, the government's ability to control feasting and animal slaughter increased through heightened surveillance, the imposition of an annual quota of pork that cooperative members were obliged to sell to the government, and the requirement that villagers receive official permission to slaughter animals. The government's intense interest in preventing illegal slaughter was evident in the fact that it published its first decree forbidding the slaughter of cows and buffalo in March of 1948, and over the next twenty seven years released no fewer than seventeen other such proclamations. Official concern remained so strong because the policy continuously failed. Cadres complained of the problem of 'feasting going first, the interests of the nation going after' (*an co di truoc, loi nuoc di sau*; see Dinh Thu Cuc 1976:35) as people devoted impressive quantities of resources to feasting. In 1970, Ha Bac province released the following estimation of the resources expended:

> According to our still incomplete statistics, in the year 1970 our province had 12,150 weddings and 8,184 funerals. The average expenditures for each ceremony was approximately 500 dong, 50 kg of rice, 50 kg of meat, and 200 days of labor. Thus, for the province that equaled 10,167,000 dong, 1,016,700 kg of rice, 1,016,700 kg of meat, and 4,066,800 days of labor lost. The amount of money and rice stated is enough to support the population of a district for one year. These activities, as the statistics indicate, have had an extremely negative influence on the finances, property and productive strength of the people. These in turn have interfered with the contemporary task of improving production and building socialism.
>
> (Vietnam, Ministry of Culture 1975:94)[9]

The government could endlessly exhort the citizenry to live frugally and economize (*tiet kiem*) in their daily lives, but many people maintained their own structures of meaning regarding the proper disposal of their resources. In the period from 1954 to 1985, Thinh Liet saw a reduction in its average feast size to an average of 10 trays (60 people), while a large feast consisted of 30 trays (180 people). When government interference in feasting relaxed in the early 1990s, the average feast size increased to approximately 45–50 (270–300 people) trays, a large feast consisted of some 80–90 trays (480–540 people), and the occasional feast exceeded 100 trays.[10] Nevertheless, some families have rejected this trend and refused to organize large feasts. Other individuals, many with party backgrounds, openly criticize the return to large scale feasting for its wastefulness. In each case, the invocation of party ideology provides protection against public criticism. Some residents consider the refusal to hold a feast a legitimate action because it involves adherence to the party's sumptuary restrictions. Their supporters also note that such a refusal is not necessarily unfilial, provided that the family was good to the deceased and others on an everyday basis. Still, there are those who reject such claims and regard the refusal to organize a feast as unfilial, regardless of what the party says. It is certainly not the ideal, but it does not result in the stigmatization of the family, and might actually increases their prestige in official quarters.

Sentiment and the Moral Necessity of Exchange

Although the concern for being seen as lacking in filial piety is strong, Thinh Liet residents are equally concerned that the refusal to hold a large feast will place them in a morally compromised position with their co-villagers. When looked at analytically, Vietnamese funerals mobilize three different strands of social relations. Those between the deceased and his/ her close kin; those between the deceased and their co-residents; and those between the deceased's living descendants and their co-residents. With regard to the obligations that pertain in these three sets of relations, the first set are fulfilled through the acts of filial piety, but the second and third are fulfilled through attendance at the funeral and the giving of a prestation to the deceased's family.

Word of a person's death travels quickly in Thinh Liet. Soon after receiving the news, friends, relatives, and co-residents briefly visit the deceased's home. One reason for the visit is to pay respects to the deceased and comfort the family, but an equally compelling reason is to find out whether the family plans to accept prestations and what time guests can begin arriving at the home. This phase of the funeral, which usually begins an hour or two after the conclusion of the distribution of *tang* ceremony, is called the *phung vieng* phase. When broken down, the compound connotes a visit to the home of the deceased (*vieng*) and the presentation of offerings

127

while there (*phung*). In terms of its mechanics, the *phung vieng* phase is quite simple. At its commencement, a senior male relative, or a representative from the commune's Elderly Association if the deceased was advanced in years, stands next to the altar at the foot of the casket and delivers a brief oration to the guests assembled in the family compound. He gives another precis of the deceased's biography, takes three lit incense sticks, bows before the altar, places the incense sticks into the urn, and then invites other guests to come and do the same. After him, a slow parade of friends, relatives, and co-residents file into the deceased's compound and present themselves before the altar at the foot of the casket. People pay their respects to the deceased in two fashions. First, if the family has decided to accept food prestations, the guests bring with them a tray of food and incense, and perhaps other items such as cash, a bottle of spirits, flowers, or a funeral wreath. In the early 1990s, the standard food prestation was a large tray covered with cooked glutinous rice, upon which was placed a boiled chicken or perhaps a boiled pig's head. When the guest reached the area near the casket, he or she gave the tray to one of the deceased's children or another family member sitting on the side of the casket near the altar. This person gratefully accepted the tray, while another family member, usually sitting a distance away, surreptitiously recorded the name of the giver and the prestation's size. The giver's status was very important. A person of decidedly lower status than the deceased presenting the tray was insulting, thus individuals of equal or greater status presented the trays. After they had given the tray to the family, the guests performed a set of ritual obeisances before the altar. Pre-revolutionary customs prescribed an elaborate set of kowtows for individuals paying respects to the dead, but revolutionary reforms attempted to eliminate them and replace them with three short but respectful bows of the head while clasping three sticks of lit incense between the palms. In contemporary Thinh Liet, no single standard of obeisance exists, even for people of a similar generation or relation to the deceased. Some guests perform a set of three bows (*vai*) and three prostrations (*le*), others perform a short set of three bows, and others sometimes kneel on the reed mat placed before the altar and repeatedly prostrate themselves. The single feature they all share is that prior to the obeisance, they light three sticks of incense which they clasp between their palms throughout. Once they have finished, they place the incense into the urn on the altar and the process repeats itself. In situations where a group with many members presents a tray, genealogically senior members pay their respects before the junior members. Like the placement of the corpse into the casket, the performance of the obeisances is often accompanied by loud wailing by woman. By performing these obeisances, individuals simultaneously show their concern and respect for the deceased, help the deceased's soul on its journey to the other world, and show others that the deceased was important to them.

Although the mechanics of the *phung vieng* phase are quite simple, it is in fact rich in moral significance. At the simplest level, a visit to a family that has lost a loved one and the gift of a prestation are part of the process of 'dividing' or 'sharing the sadness' (*chia buon*) that animates the immediate post-mortem period. Before guests deliver trays of prestations to the family and perform the obeisance, they declare to the family that they have come to 'share your sadness' (*chia buon*). The cultural idea behind this statement is that by visiting a family in mourning, the visitor takes away part of that family's sadness. Families therefore hope that many guests will come to the home in the days before burial. A big funeral, as residents frequently comment, is a good funeral. One Giap Tu man said of a funeral in his home that the people coming to share his sadness made him feel 'lighter' (*nhe hon*). The strength of the sadness sharing is also increased by the inclusion of a prestation. The party had sought to limit prestations to incense, candles, and wreaths of flowers, but Thinh Liet residents never accepted such a stripped down funeral. They agreed with the party that they should continue to share the sadness of mourning families, but food and other items were a necessary part of appropriately showing one's concern and respects.

The giving of a prestation also reproduces a second type of moral relationship, known as a 'sentimental' or *tinh cam* relationship. Thinh Liet residents describe the ideal moral world of their villages in terms of the 'spirit of the village' (*tinh lang*). The main idea behind this ethic is that the village constitutes a moral and affective unity in which villagers should be ready to assist each other in their times of need, not simply out of obligation, but out ties of affect, sympathy, and compassion. In mundane moments, the realization of this ethic entails common courtesies, mutual respect, a willingness to compromise, and assistance if requested. For example, tremendous importance is placed on everyday forms of greeting between co-residents. When two people meet out on the local paths, an expectation exists that the younger person will greet the elder, usually with the salutation *chao* combined with an appropriate kinship term, and perhaps a polite particle afterwards. Following this, the older person will *chao* the younger person, and if they stop to talk, the two, beginning with the younger person, will ask about the other and their family's health, etc. Thinh Liet residents say that those who do not greet others in fact disdain (*khinh*) them, thus the oft-quoted adage, 'a word of greeting is greater than a tray at a feast' (*loi chao cao hon mam co*). Although such activities as greetings modulate the everyday realization of the spirit of the village, it reaches its quintessence with the death of a villager. This tendency is most clearly visible in the frequently repeated 'at death lay all to rest' adage. Residents recognize that conflict is a normal part of life in a village's tight quarters, thus many people fail to live up to the spirit of the village's requirements. However, even if one has experienced bitter conflict with

129

another, when that person passes away, one is morally enjoined to forget past acrimony and assist the deceased's family. Ideally, all village families will have at least one member attend a co-villager's funeral, but given the large population today, this does not occur in practice. Also, in contemporary Thinh Liet, the obligation to attend a family's funeral still largely ramifies within each individual village, but given the extent of intermarriage between the villages, as well as relationships formed through working in the cooperatives, administration, and other places, most funerals have guests from all villages.

Living in accordance with the spirit of the village also entails that one will have many sentimental relations in one's life. This idealization finds perfect expression in the commonly voiced adage, 'Vietnam is a poor country, but very rich in sentiment' (*Viet Nam la nuoc ngheo ma rat giau tinh cam*). Of all the non-kin-based moral relationships in Vietnamese society, sentimental relationships are among the most prized. The reason for this importance links back to the hierarchical nature of Vietnamese society. People constantly encounter hierarchy in their lives. Some is easy to deal with, such as that between people of roughly similar ages, but other kinds are more burdensome, such as differences between rich and poor, and those who exercise authority and those who do not. According to the spirit of the village, such differences should be minimized in social life. The minimization of hierarchy, and the assertion of a rough form of equality, reaches its highest form in sentimental relationships. To create these relationships, one must engage in numerous activities. The greetings, compromise, and cooperation discussed above are salient, as are invitations to one's own weddings and attendance at others'. The most important action is the rendering of assistance to a family in time of need, particularly by visiting the home of an ill person, and by attending and giving prestations at another's funerals. Those who have many sentimental relationships are regarded as virtuous in village life. Such individuals are said to 'live with sentiment' (*song tinh cam*), to be 'rich in sentiment' (*giau tinh cam*), and importantly, to 'live virtuously' (*song dao duc*). In their lives, they are held to value equality and solidarity over hierarchy and distance.

Thinh Liet residents comment that attendance at another's funeral, or a visit during illness, shows one's sentiment with that family, but it also creates a debt between the parties. The semantics of this debt merit detailed explanation. Vietnamese has two words commonly translated as 'debt': *on* and *no*. The latter term carries with it the connotation of a potentially amoral transaction. Thus, if one borrows money, one has a *no* to the giver. *On* carries with it the connotation of a powerful, morally-charged relationship between giver and receiver. For example, as mentioned before, children have a limitless *on* to their parents, and when one comes to another's funeral, the deceased's family has an *on* with the guest. Numerous metaphors further distinguish the two. A *no* is considered 'lighter' (*nhe hon*).

An *on* is 'deep' (*sau*) and a 'heavy responsibility' (*nghia nang*). A *no* also ends, while an *on* 'is remembered forever' (*nho mai*). One does not openly display one's *on*. Instead one 'stores it in one's belly' (*de trong long*) until an appropriate time comes to repay it. In a way, however, a person can never completely repay an *on*. One should ideally always maintain an attitude of conscientiousness and solicitousness toward those with whom one has an *on*, even in everyday life. This is particularly true of children with their parents, but also with non-kin as well. This enduring quality of *on* can be seen in the fact an *on* is often passed down through the generations. Thus, if one man's father had such a debt to another man, it passes down to his son. An *on*, now matter how far back in time, should always be remembered. Semantically, *on* is best rendered as a 'moral debt,' while *no* is simply a debt.

The repayment of a moral debt occurs in two fashions. At the simplest level, one can partially repay this debt through displays of sentiment, such as visits to a sick person, assistance in time of need, or attendance at a wedding or funeral. But again, that which most compellingly repays the debt is a prestation at a funeral. Thinh Liet residents, it should be noted, show a certain ambivalence on this point. When asked about the repayment of a moral debt, the common response is that 'repaying a moral debt through sentiment is more prized than a material repayment' (*tra on bang tinh cam la qui hon bang vat chat*). This gives the impression that material items are unimportant, but such statements mask the fact that people do expect a prestation. The existence of this expectation is evident in the form of the verb 'to give' employed when giving a prestation. During the *phung vieng* phase, families 'present' (*bieu*) their trays, rather than simple 'give' (*cho*). To 'present' the tray again binds the giver and receiver in a moral relationship. As a common adage states, 'that which is presented creates worry, that which is given creates debt' (*cua bieu la cua lo, cua cho la cua no*), a reference to the moral obligation to reciprocate that 'presenting' creates.

The gift of a prestation at a funeral simultaneously achieves two goals. First, it helps repay a moral debt between guest and host; and second, it reproduces the sentimental relationship between the parties. People like to use the metaphor, 'if you go, you have to come back' (*co di, phai co lai*), and the return of a prestation fulfills this moral obligation. More practically, the regular exchange of prestations establishes enduring exchange relations between families. Residents' exchange relations ramify along many lines. The primary axis is always based on kinship, either affinal or consanguineal, followed by those between neighbors and other co-residents. Beyond these axes, relations can form from any number of means of affiliation, such as friendship; studying, working, or serving in the military together; co-membership in social groups, such as the Buddhist Association; or other things. Although many relations are formed through

131

the actions of individuals, the moral debt is often conceptualized as belonging to the entire family and, as mentioned above, passes down between generations. This diachronic aspect, and the fact that it seems that almost all villagers are somehow related, mean that most families have expansive exchange networks that are mobilized in funerals (and also weddings, see Chapter 5). To not keep that relationship alive means that the family has committed a major moral transgression, the failure to repay a moral debt. This requirement to repay places significant moral pressure on people, pressure that increases with the intimacy of the relationship. To keep their relationships alive, and to maintain their positive moral status, families must help out and give prestations whenever the situation demands. To do otherwise is not only a failure to maintain a sentimental relationship with the family, it also implies that one has sworn off one's moral debt.

The question remains of what size prestation adequately repays the moral debt and reproduces the sentimental relationship. As noted above, when a family receives a prestation, one family member immediately records the size and nature of the gift in a ledger. In funerals, families are extremely careful about recording exactly what they have received. The purpose of the ledger is to provide a written record of past prestations so families can accurately repay their debts at others' funerals in the future.[11] However, the figure in the ledger constitutes only a minimum standard as local politesse also encourages people to add just a small amount more to their return prestations (an obvious source of inflationary pressure). For example, if one received a tray with two kilograms of glutinous rice and one boiled chicken at a family funeral, one might reciprocate with the same items plus a bouquet of flowers or a small amount of cash; although a return prestation of the exact same size would not invite derision. The trick in giving a return prestation is to give one that is 'just right' (*vua*) in size. Giving one that is excessively large opens one up to charges of attempting to 'buy sentiment' (*mua tinh cam*), while giving one that is too small can create the idea that one does not respect the other family or value that relationship. This standard is flexible though. If in the time since the last exchange a family has fallen on hard times, a small prestation or none at all will be acceptable. Thinh Liet residents like to state that they are ready to 'show sympathy with the situation' (*thong cam hoan canh*) of the struggling.

One Giap Nhi resident commented that 'sentiment makes a large funeral' (*tinh cam tao dam ma dong*). Those families and individuals who have many sentimental relationships will always have many guests at their funerals. The benefit of having a wide exchange network is that when tragedy strikes one's home, many guests come and their prestations can be used to hold a large feast. The presentation of a food tray indicates that the guest will attend the feast, likely accompanied by other family members.

But by giving a gift of food and also money, people effectively pay for themselves at the feast. As a result, organizing a funeral is generally not a large financial burden. Death usually mobilizes a wide range of kin and friends who will donate their time and labor to help the family clean their home, prepare the feast items, and clean up afterward. And the gifts of food, spirits, and money are generally enough to cover most funeral costs. Sentiment, in effect, brings villagers together and helps those who have experienced a loss put on the best funeral possible and publically restate the 'spirit of the village.'

Vietnamese describe the system of exchange that takes place at weddings and funerals as 'exchanging debts through eating and drinking' (*an uong tra no mieng nhau*). Its existence dates back to the pre-revolutionary period (see Dumoutier 1904), but revolutionary reforms attempted to eliminate it. The reasons they sought to eliminate the system were many, such as their desire to simplify all ritual practices, its reputed wastefulness, as well as its capacity to provide venues for ostentatious display. Despite this rhetoric, official efforts also served a more subtle agenda to transform the mechanism for the reproduction of sentimental relations. Officials recognized that reforms needed to 'respond to the worthy psychological and sentimental demands of the masses' (Vietnam, Ministry of Culture 1975:31). All funeral reforms had to 'respect the problem of "at death lay all to rest"; thus funerals must candidly display feelings of sentiment and compassion' (Vietnam, Ministry of Culture 1975:32). Nevertheless, the party also wanted to 'construct for the masses a new "socialist sentiment" (*tinh cam xa hoi chu nghia*) in their social relations' (Son La, Cultural Service 1975:45; see also Do Huy 1978). Officials also spoke of 'revolutionary sentiment' (*tinh cam cach mang*). This new sentiment was to be concordant with socialist ideology and take precedence in social life. Officials in Ha Tay commented, 'We must place socialist ethics and sentiment above the problem of customs' (Ha Tay, Cultural Service 1967:27). Importantly, the new sentiment was not to be reproduced through exchange relations, but instead through mere sociality. All one needed to do was show up at another's wedding or funeral, and that was adequate. As one set of regulations noted with regard to prestations in wedding ceremonies, 'if they don't give anything then that's fine' (Vietnam, Ministry of Culture 1975:34). For villagers in the new socialist society, 'that which is most prized,' noted one official source, 'is the presence of one's face' (Son La, Cultural Service 1975:24).

From the late 1950s onward, local officials exerted significant pressure on Thinh Liet residents to eliminate the practice of exchanging food items at weddings and funerals. The previously mentioned obligations to sell pork to the government and the restrictions on slaughter helped to constrain exchange practices, but they never disappeared. Several factors allowed the system to continue. First was the allocation of five percent of cooperative land to local farmers so they could grow crops needed to raise pigs. As discussed in Chapter 1, cadres were frustrated by the fact that cooperators worked harder on the five percent land than the regular cooperative lands. Thinh Liet residents exhibited a similar devotion to their five percent land, frequently using its proceeds to raise more pigs than needed to fulfill their pork quota and slaughtering them for consumption at feasts. A second factor was inconsistent enforcement of government dictates by local officials. The Thinh Liet administration split into two main camps on this issue. On one side was a group of officials, headed by a series of secretaries of the commune's party cell, who attempted to vigorously restrict exchange relations and enforce slaughter regulations. Their efforts were undercut by several high-ranking officials in the agricultural cooperatives who, though still party members, tacitly tolerated illicit slaughter. Their normal tactic was to require cooperators to request permission to slaughter one animal for a feast, but then turn a blind eye when they slaughtered several. The motivation of these officials to allow illegal slaughter captures the same reasoning for the return to large scale feasting that has occurred in Thinh Liet since the early 1990s. These men, who residents generally consider to live with a great deal of sentiment, saw the exchange of prestations as vital for the reproduction of sentimental relations. Although they recognized that large scale feasting and animal slaughter was impossible under the prevailing political conditions, hence the drop of average feast size to some thirty trays per feast, their total elimination would entail a violation of the moral integuments of local society. Some measure of feasting and exchange needed to be maintained in order to allow villagers to express their sentiment to those who had lost loved ones. As feasting and exchange continue to grow in contemporary Thinh Liet, the moral necessity of exchange and sentimental relations remain powerful motivations for local residents.[12]

A Buffalo Leaves His Skin, A Person Leaves His Reputation

Thinh Liet residents frequently say that funerals give you the true measure of an individual and their family. As they state, 'When a buffalo dies it leaves behind its skin, when a person dies he leaves behind his reputation' (*Trau chet de da, nguoi chet de tieng*). This adage refers to the fact that death and the ritual response to it set in motion an evaluative process in which other villagers, often through their actions more than their words, publically express their opinions on the moral worth of the deceased and his or her family. A large funeral is considered both psychologically and aesthetically pleasing. A large turnout helps to lighten the host family's sadness and also creates a warm and supportive environment for those in need. A large turn-out has another consequence in that it indicates that other residents view the deceased and its family in morally positive terms. At a general level, one can fairly state those who live with much sentiment, and are the most conscientious about living according to the spirit of the village, have the largest turnouts at their funerals. For example, one of the largest funerals in the early 1990s was of a Giap Nhat man who was recognized as an extremely pious Buddhist, as well as a good villager who regularly assisted others and gave gifts at funerals. He had played a critical role in the construction of Tam Phap Temple before World War II, and then had served as a moderating influence on the administration as it implemented the cultural reforms. When he died, hundreds of villagers from all three Thinh Liet villages presented funeral wreaths, food trays, and labor to his family. Guests at the funeral also frequently commented on what a good man he was and how he had lived with much sentiment. The only exception to the principle of high moral standing producing a large funeral is the case of high-ranking official's death or an individual whose children occupy important administrative positions or political offices. The three largest funerals of the 1980s were held for the mother of the chairman of the agricultural cooperative, arguably the most powerful man in the commune at that time, and the parents of a group of brothers who held important party positions in Hanoi. These funerals featured hundreds of guests, with the latter pair counting over 1,000 guests each. The three deceased residents were all esteemed individuals, but their children's positions made their funerals significantly larger.

While moral rectitude and living by the spirit of the village can increase a funeral's size, disrespect for co-residents and other moral transgressions cause the opposite. Although few admit it of themselves, many residents comment that the first few hours after a person's death have an extra measure of tension in the deceased's home as they worry about the number of people who will come and the statement that will make about their moral worth. If the family has a history of conflicts or immoral behavior, this tension will increase the fear that few will turn up. One of the most infamous instances of the display of disrespect and its negative consequences was the case of a Giap Nhi farmer. One day, in a fit of rage of unknown origin, the farmer walked up and down the brick path that runs through the middle of the village, yelling curses and insults at his co-villagers. He berated them for their worthlessness and addressed them by the extremely insulting term *chung may*, a term reserved for addressing groups of small children or hated adversaries. After an hour's tirade the farmer desisted, but afterwards apologized to no one. A few weeks later, his daughter-in-law died of illness, but given the enmity created by his insulting and disrespectful words, the family received the cruelest social rebuff of all as villagers avoided the funeral and only a handful of close kin attended. The turn-out was so small that the family had to perform the mortifying act of forcing kin to remove their mourning headbands to serve as pallbearers – a task that non-kin should always perform. This incident has become a paradigmatic example that many Giap Nhi residents use to illustrate the importance of respect and sentiment in village life, as well as the moral evaluation of the deceased and their family that occurs during funerals.

Memorializing the Dead

While funeral practices served to reproduce moral relationships among the living and the dead, funeral orations (*dieu van*) have historically served to publically reiterate the deceased's moral worth. In delivering an oration, the speaker is obliged to not only list the life and accomplishments of the deceased, but also to highlight their virtuous acts and qualities. With the advent of the revolution, cadres retained the practice of using funeral orations to declare the deceased's moral worth, but they wanted that moral worth measured in revolutionary terms and for the funeral to be a lesson for the living. As regulations from Nam Ha province noted, 'During the funeral ceremonies, the biography of the deceased's activities must be recounted. Bring out the deceased's virtues and good thoughts so the family can remember them, study them, and follow their example' (Vietnam, Ministry of Culture 1975:77). Virtues worthy of praise included the deceased's achievements as a war hero, committed revolutionary, or enthusiastic participant in the construction of socialism.

To achieve this goal, the party decreed that a member of the collective deliver a funeral oration. In Thinh Liet this responsibility fell on the secretaries of the party's mass organizations, though most frequently on the secretary of the Elderly Association due to the elderly's natural attrition. Officials appropriated the role of delivering the first funeral oration before taking the casket to the grave site, a task previously carried out by kin. In some cases, other officials delivered additional orations after the first secretary, and once these were completed the family could deliver its own. The secretary of the Elderly Association still delivers the first oration in contemporary funerals. Thinh Liet residents have never openly resisted the insertion of officials into this role, but one focus of controversy has been the orations' contents. Government regulations mandated the mention of officially sanctioned qualities in orations, but local officials received permission to develop the oration's text themselves. Thinh Liet officials developed a generic oration to deliver at all funerals. Residents never liked this because, as one former official stated, it asserted that all residents were alike, which in fact they were not. The generic oration erased each individual's unique accomplishments. Furthermore, not all people really deserved an official oration. 'You have to do something if you want an oration' (*co cong moi co dieu van*), he declared. Officials used the generic oration for several years, although in some cases they apparently did not. In 1984 they abandoned it. At present, official orations still include any military or revolutionary accomplishments of the deceased, but instead of a generic oration, the speaker closely follows the deceased's life and experiences.

While orations constituted one mechanism for commemorating the deceased, the party also assumed control over a more enduring commemorative form, the disposition of graves and cemeteries. Graves and grave sites were important forums for the assertion social status in pre-revolutionary Vietnam. At the most obvious level, wealthy families often constructed imposing mausolea or headstones to mark the graves of their dead, but more subtly, they sometimes hired geomancers (*thay dia ly*) to determine the most auspicious burial site and then bought that plot. The land of colonial Thinh Liet had several scattered plots that wealthy Hanoi families had purchased to bury their dead. The experience of poor families was often the opposite. They did not hire geomancers. Instead they buried their dead in convenient or uncultivated sections of land, or even in areas along local roadsides. They also frequently lacked the resources to leave a headstone or other object to mark the grave, thus many disappeared over time. The party sought to eliminate these distinctions by asserting control over cemeteries and headstone styles. At the national level, the government decreed that all villages demarcate a distant section of village land that would serve as a common cemetery (Vietnam, Ministry of Culture 1979:35). In Thinh Liet, the communal administration did not designate a single cemetery for the entire commune but instead allowed villages to retain their own. Government solicitousness regarding the sensitivities involving cemeteries was evident when, on the several occasions when Thinh Liet cemeteries were moved to accommodate construction projects, the caskets and skeletons of the previous sites were exhumed and reburied by government workers in the new cemeteries. Thinh Liet did not follow a government request to demarcate a section in the local cemeteries to commemorate war dead or others who had performed meritorious acts for the country or the people (Vietnam, Ministry of Culture 1975:103). As local officials commented, most of the local war dead were buried where they died, and not enough of their bodies returned to create a special section (see also Chapter 6).

Inside the cemeteries, the government mandated the burial of all caskets according to convenience and forbid the practice of geomancy. On each count, Thinh Liet residents followed official regulations. They also implemented government directives that forbid the construction of large mausolea and demanded the use of simple headstones. Thinh Liet headstones, however, often did not live up to the government request that they record the deceased's name, date of birth, date of death, and possibly their rank in the military, government or party. Instead, they often recorded only the name and date of death, though the year of birth was sometimes included. The trend toward a common burial place and simple

137

commemoration remains dominant in contemporary Thinh Liet. Families still bury their dead in the village cemeteries, and there has been no large-scale resurgence of geomancy or the purchase of symbolically auspicious grave plots. Virtually all families select the first and secondary burial plots according to convenience without consulting a geomancer, a trend that might be facilitated by the fact that Thinh Liet no longer has a living geomancer.[13]

Although most families still use the small, unimposing grave stones the party advocated, and no mausolea have been constructed, a trend has emerged in which some families and lineages invest moderate to substantial sums of money into either headstones or common plots marked with cement walls. Families bury the urns containing the bones of numerous family members after the secondary burial at these sites. These sites also serve an important ritual role in that they always include a small altar-type area where family members perform ancestral rites. The justification for building these structures is that they provide another expression of the living's filial piety as an attractive grave area is pleasing to the dead. This same logic has informed the construction of a wall around the Giap Nhi cemetery along with a large altar next to the entrance. Under pressure from residents, the administration and cooperative contributed several million dong to finance the project, which makes the Giap Nhi cemetery the grandest in the commune. Like the move to more elaborate grave sites, it is undeniable that there is a element of status competition involved in the cemetery renovations as many Giap Nhi residents want to have the grandest cemetery, but this impulse is secondary to the desire to provide properly for the dead. At present, official directives still heavily influence the geography of cemeteries, the selection of burial sites, and their adornments. Some larger graves have been constructed, but there is no uniform movement in the direction of geomancy or the elaborate tombs of the colonial period.

Death Anniversaries and Secondary Burials

The passing of the third day marks the end of the first phase of a three year period in which the living must carry out an extensive set of rites to ensure that the deceased's soul becomes a benevolent family ancestor. The first five to seven weeks after death represent an important time for the family. During this period, families keep the independent altar dedicated to the dead on the right side of the main ancestral altar, perform brief propitiations there, and bring to it every day fresh offerings of rice, water, hard-boiled eggs, and other foods. On the seventh day after death, families hold propitiatory rites and a small feast in their home. The next major ritual event occurs either on the 35th, 49th, or 50th day after death, depending on the family's wishes, when families organize a 'raising the soul' (*cau sieu* or *sieu hon*) ceremony that will raise the soul into the other world. The form this rite takes again tends to split along gender lines. Local men will likely have this rite conducted by a spirit priest in the home, while women will generally have it performed by a monk or nun at a Buddhist temple. The preference for this rite among Thinh Liet women reveals an interesting problem that some women feel they face. Ancestral cults in Vietnam are patrilineally based, and male ancestors occupy pride of place in them. One potential problem women can face is that the living will forget to care for their souls over time as most family-based rites propitiate no more than three ascendent generations, and many patrilineage rites do not mention women's names. However, if a woman has a raising the soul rite performed for her at a Buddhist temple, her soul will permanently reside there. Whenever offerings are presented in the temple, her soul will receive a portion, thereby sustaining her. Thinh Liet residents comment that if your soul is installed in a temple, your soul will be able to 'eat of the Buddha's good fortune' (*an may cua Phat*). For women, this rite at the Buddhist temple gives the living confidence that the deceased's soul will not be forgotten.

At the conclusion of the raising the soul rite, family members have a small meal at their home, take down the independent altar, and then transfer the deceased's urn to the main ancestral altar. This transfer marks the deceased's closer integration with other family ancestors, yet the soul still remains outside the main realm of family ancestors. This exclusion ends at 100 days when families perform a final rite in which they take ashes from the deceased's urn and mix them with those in the main urn on the altar. From that point on, the deceased's soul is fully integrated with other family ancestors and will be worshipped communally with them on such important days as the first and fifteenth of every month, and the series of *Tet* holidays. In the 1960s and 1970s, some provinces, such as Ha Bac, Ha Noi, and Ha Tay, sought to end the performance of all of these rites (Vietnam, Ministry of Culture 1975:86, 91). Similar pressures existed in Thinh Liet, but officials never interfered with their quiet conduct in homes.

Another area of official intervention in family commemorative rites was the attempt to modify the next major event in the cycle of post-mortem ritual obligations, the death anniversary ceremony (*gio*). Family members must perform commemorative ceremonies for all deceased family members, usually up to at a minimum the third ascendent generation, on the anniversary of their deaths. Although this is an annual responsibility, the ceremonies performed one and three years after death are the most important and are marked by large feasts organized on each occasion. The feast on the former occasion is large because it provides an occasion for those unable to attend the funeral to pay their respects, while the latter occasion is large because it coincides with the conclusion of all major post-mortem rites. Death anniversaries are normally conducted in the home of the eldest son and divide into two main segments. The first consists of rites to propitiate the deceased's soul and usually involves only the deceased's children, their spouses and children, and perhaps a small number of close kin or friends. This segment serves the united purposes of providing a context for the children to demonstrate their moral debt and filial piety for their parent, while also allowing them to deliver to the deceased's soul a variety of important items, such as food, money, and clothing. Prior to the rites' commencement, family members clean the altar and place numerous plates of food and fruits on it. In Thinh Liet, siblings share the ceremony's expenses, although there is an expectation that either the eldest son or the wealthiest siblings will contribute the most. When the altar is ready, the eldest son begins the propitiation of the soul and invites the spirit back. Once he has finished, other family members follow. When the propitiation has concluded, family members will burn any paper money, clothing, or other items they presented. The second segment, the feast, then begins and a larger group of friends, relatives, and neighbors attend.

Official modifications of death anniversaries took numerous forms. At the most surprising level, regulations promulgated in January of 1975 by the Communist Party's executive committee commented that 'it is not obligatory' to organize the ceremonies (Hanoi, Cultural and Information Service 1975:4), an assertion that would have been unthinkable prior to the revolution. Evidence does not indicate, however, that the government ever took steps to enforce this at the local level. Instead, officials attempted to alter different parts within them. Similar to the appropriation of the funeral oration, cadres endeavoured to bring out elements in the ceremonies that could serve an 'educational' function. Thus, at that point of the ceremonies where the living recalled the dead, the Ministry of Culture encouraged people to 'recall again the deceased's virtuous qualities and honorable traditions' (Vietnam, Ministry of Culture 1975:50). Thanh Hoa province stated it more directly when their regulations declared that such orations should specifically include an accounting of industrious labor or participation in the resistance, 'in order to develop the educational awareness of children and grandchildren' (Vietnam, Ministry of Culture 1975:104). Afterwards, the Ministry of Culture wanted families to visit the deceased's grave, and while in the cemetery, to recall the sacrifices of fallen comrades. The regulations declared:

> Everyone has the responsibility to protect and care for the cemeteries for revolutionary martyrs (*liet si*) in the cities and communes; remember and display your moral debt to the heroic martyrs who have performed meritorious service to the revolution. Teach young people to protect these cemeteries and to study the exemplary revolutionary traditions that the revolutionary heroes have left behind, especially the heroes of the people, outstanding personages, party leaders, communist soldiers, and all the

revolutionary heroes who sacrificed their lives for the party and the people.

(Vietnam, Ministry of Culture 1975:50)

Official intrusions on this point elicited little response in Thinh Liet, largely because the commune did not have a cemetery for war dead nor did officials monitor local ceremonies. Today, families do visit the grave, but no one specifically attempts to educate young people on revolutionary virtues in a death anniversary oration, though a history of involvement in the resistance or local administration can receive honorable mention.

One reform that was successful in Thinh Liet was the attempt to decenter the use of the lunar calendar in death anniversary ceremonies. In pre-revolutionary times, families recorded the death date according to the lunar calendar and all future death anniversary ceremonies had to be conducted on that date to be effective. Ministry of Culture regulations stipulated that all Vietnamese were to 'calculate the date of death according to the solar calendar' (Vietnam, Ministry of Culture 1975:50). In an unexpected turn of events, the diminution of the lunar calendar has occurred in Thinh Liet, although not in the fashion outlined by the party. Most families now record the deceased's death date according to the lunar calendar, but do not rigidly adhere to that date for the conduct of the death anniversary. The most common pattern is for families to conduct a small death anniversary ceremony on the lunar calendar death date, and then wait for a more convenient date to arrange a larger ceremony that many family members will attend. The most common example of this pattern is when the lunar calendar death date falls on a weekday. Families will hold a small ceremony on that day but wait until the following Sunday, normally a day off, to conduct the larger ceremony. Ironically, this trend supports the party's agenda to prevent death anniversaries from having any effect on 'production, work, or study' (Vietnam, Ministry of Culture 1975:41). Families prefer to hold the full rite according to the lunar calendar, but few are concerned about destroying its efficacy.

The reforms that received the greatest opposition from Thinh Liet residents were the attempts to simultaneously secularize the rites, reduce the extent of non-family participation, and eliminate feasting. The party recognized that families would still perform commemorative rites, but instead of involving any interaction with the soul, they wanted the rites to be strictly commemorative. The reformed rite was to 'remember the person who has passed away' and not 'lead to making offerings or worship' (Vietnam, Ministry of Culture 1975:50). They were also to preclude the involvement of superstitious practices, notably the burning of votive paper offerings.[14] The party also wanted the rites to include only family members. The Ministry of Culture instructed officials to keep them 'in the "realm of the family" (*pham vi gia dinh*) and avoid inviting numerous friends and neighbors from near and far' (Vietnam, Ministry of Culture 1975:50). Finally, all rites were to be simple, economical, and avoid 'wasteful eating and drinking' (*an uong lang phi*). Party regulations from 1975 declared that the ceremonies 'must be simple, frugal, and must be rid of the practices of profligate feasting and inviting guests in order "exchange debts through eating" (*tra no mieng*)' (Hanoi, Cultural and Information Service 1975:4).

The effort to reduce death anniversary feasts was met with significant dissatisfaction in Thinh Liet. Like other elements in the mourning process, organizing the death anniversary ceremony is part of the continuing process of children repaying their moral debt to their parent, thus efforts to change the ceremonies created the possibility for unfilial behavior. The agenda to end its obligatory character was also completely rejected by local residents. As one Giap Tu resident commented, 'not organizing a death anniversary ceremony is equivalent to forgetting the person who gave birth to you.' Another resident stated more concisely, 'no death anniversary means you have no filial piety.' Although the size of death anniversary feasts and numbers of guests did decrease, families never renounced the responsibility to present offerings and propitiate ancestral souls. One dynamic that likely exercised a conservative effect on death anniversaries reforms was that fact any conflict among family members in the organization of the death anniversary is itself considered unfilial. Contemporary death anniversaries have again become large and ritually complex affairs involving the participation of many family members, friends, and neighbors. Many families set out large sets of offerings for the dead, burn votive paper objects, and then have feasts with usually some sixty to ninety guests in the case of the recently deceased. The object of these ceremonies is to properly display one's respect, affection and moral debt to the deceased, while also ensuring that its soul is content and properly cared for. And as the switch toward holding feasts on Sundays showed, the affective and commemorative aspect plays the dominant role in contemporary death anniversary ceremonies.

The final stage of the post-mortem ritual obligations occurs approximately three years after death when people perform a secondary burial ceremony (*boc mo*) for the deceased. When a corpse is first buried, the casket is placed in the 'fresh' (*tuoi*) section of the cemetery with other recently buried caskets. During these first three years, the family carries out the multiple commemorative rites discussed above, but their mortuary obligations have yet to finish. The final act requires them to disinter the deceased's casket, clean and remove the bones, and place them in a smaller urn (*tieu*) for reburial in the 'dry' (*kho*) section of the cemetery. Although the party showed an extreme interest in other details of mortuary rites, secondary burial instructions were relatively undeveloped in the majority of national and local ordinances. Thanh Hoa province went so far as to ban it, but Ha Bac province was the only other province to mention it, and there only discouraged its practice (Vietnam, Ministry of Culture 1975:

104 and 91). Government health regulations published in December 1964 acknowledged its practice, but only sought to ensure that its conduct minimized the threat to public hygiene. In 1971 the government, at the instigation of the Ministry of Health, tightened regulations regarding secondary burials in order to control hygienic problems. They introduced a new schedule, in which a person who died of non-contagious disease could be disinterred after receiving permission from local health authorities, yet all secondary burials were to be conducted between October and April (Vietnam, Ministry of Culture 1979:37ff.). Later on, the Ministry of Culture sought in 1978 to eliminate all superstitious, backward, or wasteful aspects of the practice (Vietnam, Ministry of Culture 1979:29). In Thinh Liet, the rhetoric of maintaining hygiene and eliminating waste and superstitions was prominent, but residents continued to perform their secondary burials without seeking official permission.

Thinh Liet residents employ a number of different terms to describe secondary burials, such as *boc mo*, *boc ma*, *cai mau*, *sang cat*, or *cai tang*, and also a number of cleansing metaphors such as 'changing the clothes' (*thay quan ao*), 'washing and bathing' (*tam rua*), or 'cleaning up' (*don dep*). All consider the secondary burial the last time to see the deceased. Secondary burials usually begin very early in the morning before the sun begins to rise. During the 1960s and 1970s, residents did not check for an auspicious time to begin the rite, but most families do now, and might also take in other considerations that influence auspiciousness, such as the zodiacal year of the eldest son, to make sure no problems exist. Darkness is imperative for the rite because the deceased's bones should not receive direct exposure to sunlight. Like funerals, the rites begin with the participants placing incense sticks on surrounding graves and asking the dead and the guardian spirit of the land for permission to dig up the grave. Unlike funerals, usually only twenty or thirty close kin and friends attend. Sons or other close male kin dig up the earth, open the casket, and retrieve and clean the bones. People acknowledge that handling the bones can be a somewhat unpleasant job, either because the casket is filled with muddy water and the person must fish around in the water for the bones (as often happens in Thinh Liet's cemeteries because they are out among the rice fields), or because there is still 'meat' on the bones. Some residents comment that you really have to love the deceased to do it. All families hope that when the casket is opened it is completely dry and the bones lay there black and orderly. The color of the bones is important. As one man commented, 'the blacker the better.' Residents call such a casket *ket*, which indicates the body's proper decomposition.

One major aspect of the rite is the purification and exact accounting for all of the bones. If the casket is dry or filled with water, those retrieving the bones will first pour several liters of rice spirits into the casket. Many residents feel that this helps decontaminate the water and bones. They next

143

retrieve every bone from the casket, searching through all of the dirt on the bottom of the casket if it is dry, or fishing around in the water, to make sure that they leave none. An incomplete transferral of the bones is extremely bad form. It also complicates the soul's goal of finding peace. In order to prevent such mishaps, many families today bury their dead with nylon socks placed on the hands and feet to keep these easily lost bones together. Once all of the bones are out of the casket, male members place them on a large tray and clean them by rubbing them down with rice spirits. After this, they begin the intricate process of placing the bones into the urn. Properly carrying out this task is considered something of an art, thus many Thinh Liet lineages have one or two senior men who help their lineage mates. Placement begins with the assorted small bones of the hands and feet placed on the bottom, and long bones such as the femurs, fibia, and tibula laid on top of these. Next, the spinal vertebrae are placed together down the center of the casket between the long bones, and then the skull, with the clavicles and ribs placed below it, sits on top near the head of the urn. Sometimes families place a cloth in the bottom of the urn before the bones. This is then pulled over the bones at the end, leaving only the skull exposed. Family members then place the top on the urn and move it to the final burial spot. Before they lay the urn in the grave, patrilineal relations of the deceased light incense sticks and propitiate other senior patrilineal relations at their graves. The urn is then placed in the grave, covered, and the participants disperse.

Once the urn is in the ground, the family returns to their home for a small feast of perhaps ten to twenty trays, a marked increase over the very small feasts of perhaps three or four trays in the 1960s and 1970s. Among the guests are lineage mates, good friends, and neighbors. Unlike funerals, there is no expectation for guests to contribute money or food, although some guests in rare cases do bring a small amount. Residents also feel no pressure for a large turnout as the size it is in no way related to the deceased's or the family's moral worth. All told, secondary burial feasts constitute a pleasant and somewhat celebratory occasion for the living to meet together, eat, and remember the deceased. Indeed, it is an occasion for sociality that many residents consider to be one of the most positive aspects of contemporary practices. At its conclusion, the family has discharged all of their mortuary obligations to the deceased. If all was performed correctly, the deceased's soul has left its dangerous liminal state where it could have become a malevolent ghost and has definitively become a benevolent family ancestor.

Revolution and the Egalitarianization of Funerals

According to official ideology, the ideal revolutionary funeral arrangement was one in which the deceased's family's only responsibilities were the placement of the corpse in the casket, the donning of the mourning headbands, and the receiving of kin and co-residents when they came to pay their respects at the house (Vietnam, Ministry of Culture 1975:103). As a result of the party's bans on feasting, exchange, and supernatural rites, families did not have to concern themselves with food preparation, the receiving and recording of food prestations, or ceremonies dedicated to contacting or soothing the deceased's soul. Families also did not have to worry about obtaining a casket, digging the grave, or arranging for pallbearers as the cooperative took care of those. To the party, this was the proper arrangement. As the Committee for the Establishment of the New Ways and the Cultured Family in Thanh Hoa province declared, 'This method helps alleviate some of the wasteful demands imposed on the family. It also has a deep meaning in that when the person was alive he gave himself to improving the collective. When he has left this life it should be the collective which takes care of everything for him. This is the true way of realizing the slogan "All for one and one for all"' (Vietnam, Ministry of Culture 1975:103). In funerals, the individual and the collective were united, but unlike the divisive social organization of the pre-revolutionary period, citizens of revolutionary society were ideally united as equals.

In an ironic twist, many Thinh Liet residents feel that revolutionary reforms did make funerary ceremonies more egalitarian. The manifestations of this are numerous. To begin with, many of the most obvious mechanisms for status display have been eliminated. Coffin styles have become standardized; all families bury their dead within 48 hours and wealthy families do not display the casket for long periods; all families use ten to twelve pallbearers; no one rents wailers for their funerals; no one employs geomancers to purchase auspicious plots nor builds enormous mausolea; and families have not returned to the practice of placing elaborate paper houses (*nha tang*) on the top of caskets when taking them to the grave site. This decorative element, which was popular among wealthy families, was burned after burial to provide a home for the deceased in the other world, but was outlawed for its status and superstitious associations. The symbolic abasements of funeral rites have also disappeared. Sons do not push back the casket during the funeral procession, nor do daughters or daughters-in-law lay on the ground to impede the casket's progress.

At a more significant level, contemporary funerals are more inclusive than their predecessors. Despite the sometimes controversial elements within the reforms, officials still hoped that they would retain a spirit of sentiment and mutual assistance within them. One set of regulations noted, 'funerals ... are the expression of sentimental relations between the living and the dead. In funerals ... the most important factor is the sincere expression of compassion and remembrance of the living toward the deceased, and the consolation and conscientious assistance of the deceased's family' (Vietnam, Ministry of Culture 1975:39). The revolutionary transformation of Thinh Liet society allowed for a fuller realization of the latter segment of this exhortation. One elderly man from Giap Nhi summed up the revolutionary changes with the concise comment, 'during the war and revolution, we were poor, but everyone was poor.' This shared poverty, and the shared experience of living through the land reform, collectivization, and later the American War, broke down many barriers that had separated people in local society, and created a measure of unity among them. Granted, those years do have a definite nostalgic cast in many accounts, there were still conflicts and disagreements, and the commune's increase in population has also likely increased the number of guests at funerals to some extent, but there probably is some truth in the assertion that revolutionary reforms helped produce an expansion of sentimental relations between co-villagers and greater participation in others' funerals. While poor people would rarely attend funerals of their wealthy co-villagers in the pre-revolutionary period, and vice versa, people from all different strata from local society today attend each others funerals. It is not uncommon for a family to have almost 500 hundred people participate in a funeral, while a pre-revolutionary funeral would likely only reach 200 guests. Other innovations, such as the emergence of public funds organized by lineages or other groups to help defray funeral costs, the public purchase of funeral trolleys, and the appropriation of the pallbearer-appointment role by the neighborhood chiefs, all point to greater public involvement in funerals and highlight the sense of community and shared moral responsibility they bring out. Although the party had attempted to eliminate exchange, the main mechanism for reproducing sentimental relations, other reforms did open up society so that sentiment could be more freely constructed. This is not to say that status competition is completely absent from funerals. The choice of feast items, such as choosing chicken over pounded pork roll, is one way to make such assertions, but status competition in funerals is markedly attenuated when compared to weddings. In a sense, revolutionary reforms allowed for a closer realization of the moral expectations of the spirit of the village than before.

The consequences of revolutionary funeral reforms in Thinh Liet have thus been contradictory. On the one hand, numerous reforms violated local residents conceptions of moral rectitude and therefore failed. The party could not eliminate pre-revolutionary mourning attire, rites dedicated to assisting the deceased's soul, feasting, death anniversary ceremonies, or exchange relations. Each of these mobilized basic moral obligations that the living had toward the deceased or to each other, and many people were unwilling to abandon those relations. Much of this is not surprising, particularly in the light of the last chapter's discussion on the moral salience of ancestral rites. However, other reforms were acceptable, and even allowed for an expansion of moral relations between co-villagers. It is on this point that one can return to Bloch and Parry's earlier claim that 'what would seem to be revitalized in funerary practices is that which is culturally conceived to be the most essential to the reproduction of the social order.' Thinh Liet funerary practices revitalize moral relationships. However, there is not one single set of relationships that is revitalized, but multiple relations that link the living with the living, the living with the dead, and even the living with the state. Perhaps most importantly, although the reproduction of these moral relationships occurs in the rites, complete agreement on which moral relationships are most important to reproduce and maintain, and the what is the most appropriate way to do this, still does not exist. People bring multiple, diverse, and even conflicting answers to these questions. The ideas they bring forth, whether endorsed by the party or not, constitute the broader fabric of ideas and meanings mobilized when residents set about putting their loved ones to rest.

CHAPTER FIVE

How to Marry?

The Consequences of the Campaign to
Reform Marriage and Weddings

Thinh Liet residents are fond of stating that marriage and weddings are 'a work of the family' (*viec gia dinh*). The implication of this statement is that the process of forming a conjugal relation and finalizing it in a marriage rite is the responsibility of the family. While this statement is to a certain extent true, it obscures the fact that over the past fifty years the Vietnamese state has significantly meddled with and transformed the 'work' of the family in marriage and weddings. This chapter's purpose is to examine contemporary controversies regarding marriage and weddings in order to demonstrate the manner in which ideas and practices introduced in the revolutionary reforms have become sources of both change and dispute in Thinh Liet social life. When officials launched their reform campaign, their over-arching aim was to create a voluntary and egalitarian marital regime. In doing so they attempted to abolish certain practices, such as underage or arranged marriage, and transform others, such as the composition of wedding guest lists, the range of potential marriage partners, and the nature and meaning of marriage payments. As will be shown, the results of these reforms have been mixed, and in some respects unexpected, but they have nevertheless been controversial. Consequently, that which constitutes the proper limits and nature of the 'work' of the family in Thinh Liet remains open to dispute and disagreement.

Reforming Marriage and Weddings

The reform of marriage and weddings was a centerpiece of the socialist state's agenda to eliminate feudal elements from Vietnamese society. Pre-revolutionary social life had featured countless feudal attitudes, such as those captured in the adages 'respect men, despise women' (*trong nam, khinh nu*) or 'one man is something, ten women are nothing' (*nhat nam viet huu, thap nu viet vo* – a reference to the desirability of sons), yet one set of practices that had played a vital role in reproducing feudal relations was marriage because of the marked disparities it created between men and women in conjugal relationships. Men could take multiple wives, remarry without stigma if their wives died, beat them, and easily divorce them. Wives could not ask for a divorce, were expected to show obedience to their husbands, and remain 'faithful' (*chung thuy*) to them.[1] In the short term this meant not having sexual relations with other men, but in the long term meant not remarrying if widowed. A wife was also expected to endure harassment by her mother-in-law or sisters-in-law. One adage summed up the pre-revolutionary marriage structure as 'the husband is the lord, the wife the subject' (*chong chua vo toi*). Feudal relations also existed between parents and children, particularly in the practice of parents arranging their childrens' marriages. Young people could not freely court nor marry voluntarily. In a limited survey of marriages conducted in Thinh Liet, nearly 100 percent of the pre-1940 marriages were arranged.[2] Thinh Liet residents who went through the experience of arranged marriage recall the sense of worry, concern, and perhaps fear they felt on their wedding day as they were about to marry an individual they often did not know at all. Many couples also married at extremely young ages, frequently in their early teens, although Thinh Liet couples seem to have married somewhat later, at an average age of 21.5 years for men and 20 years for women.

The revolutionary state desired to eliminate the feudal marriage regime and replace it with 'a free and progressive marital regime' (Vietnam, Government Gazette 1960:54). The first legislative indications of the establishment of the new regime were the passage of Decree 97 of 25 May 1950 and Decree 159 of 17 November 1950. The system received full formalization with the passage of the Law of Marriage and Family by the National Assembly in December 1959.[3] This law enshrined a number of new principles, including the granting of the right to divorce to women, the outlawing of polygamy through the establishment of the 'one wife, one husband' (*mot vo, mot chong*) principle, the allowance for widows to remarry, the abolition of arranged marriage, and the establishment of a minimum marriage age (eighteen for women, twenty for men).[4] Through the marital reforms the state hoped to help establish 'male-female equality' (*nam nu binh dang*) while also improving the rights of children. The state hoped the new regime would produce 'happy, democratic, and harmonious families, in which all members were united, loved each other, and helped each other in a progressive manner' (Vietnam, Government Gazette 1960:54).

The party realized that if it was to succeed in propagating the new regime, it needed more complete control over weddings and marriages. To achieve this end, it employed two main strategies. First, as outlined in the marriage law, the state attempted to make itself the exclusive authority empowered to legitimize a newly formed conjugal union. The marriage law stated that 'All marriages must receive official approval from the relevant administrative authorities from either the groom's or bride's place of residence and be recorded in the marital register. *All forms of marital rites uniformly have no validity from a legal perspective*' (Vietnam, Government Gazette 1960:54; emphasis added). In a move to place all marriages under greater official scrutiny, the government from 1954 onward required all citizens to register their marriage (*dang ky ket hon*) at their local People's Committee. Thinh Liet officials instructed residents to register their marriage before their wedding ceremony, making the couple officially married first. Despite this new formality, most Thinh Liet residents did not consider the registration to confer true conjugal status. Those who have registered but never held a wedding ceremony are still referred to as 'not yet married' (*chua cuoi*). Some residents have never even bothered to register.

The party's more significant strategy was to take control over wedding ceremonies. Prior to the revolution, the formation of a new conjugal union commenced with a series of meetings and exchanges between the two families and concluded with a wedding ceremony that featured feasts at the bride and groom's homes and the symbolically significant 'retrieve the bride' procession (*don dau*) in which the groom, accompanied by his kin and friends, walked to the bride's home and then brought her back to his. This latter rite definitively marked the new union as at each home the bride and groom conducted rites to ask their ancestors for permission to marry, and then after returning to the groom's home, senior kin gave speeches recognizing the new marriage. Official reforms sought to wrest control over these rites from families and place them under the control of local officials. This agenda reached its zenith in Thinh Liet during the mid-1950s when the local administration, under the Youth Association's leadership, organized a series of 'collective wedding' ceremonies (*cuoi tap the*). These rites constituted a significant rupture with Thinh Liet's past. Most obviously, they involved the marriage of several couples in one ceremony. However, they were also conducted in village communal houses instead of the participants' homes; they involved no premarital exchanges to gradually formalize the union; there was no procession; they had no ancestral rites; they transpired in a one or two hour period in one evening, instead of several days; their guest lists were determined by the Youth Association, who invited expansively; guests could only bring small gifts; there were no feasts at the bride and groom's homes, only a small party with tea, cigarettes, biscuits, and officially approved (though not always unofficially appreciated) musical performances at the communal house afterwards; and perhaps most significantly, the symbolically crucial first wedding speech that publically acknowledged the new union was delivered by the secretary of the Youth Association, who was then followed by the participants' senior male kin.[5]

Initially, there was some enthusiasm in Thinh Liet for the new rites. Many who were young then like to recite Lenin's comment that 'revolution is a holiday for the masses' and were caught up in the spirit of the times. But, as time went on, enthusiasm waned, largely because people began to object to the official appropriation of roles they felt should or must be performed by family members. The collective communal house wedding lasted only a few years, yet even had a modified procession before its abandonment. The rites then returned to the participants' homes and over the following decades families re-inserted ancestral rites, re-appropriated the issuance of invitations, re-invigorated exchange relations between families, organized feasts, returned to a multi-day schedule, and reserved for senior male kin the role of delivering the first speeches. By the 1980s Thinh Liet residents did not even feel it necessary to invite local officials to their weddings. The re-appropriation of wedding rites by families is a relatively uncontroversial part of Thinh Liet's history. I have never encountered even a local official who argues that the state should exercise exclusive authority on this point. However, despite this failure, there are aspects of contemporary ideas and debates regarding weddings and marriage that demonstrate that the reform campaign continues to have an impact.

To Court or to Arrange?

The elimination of arranged marriage was a key component in the Vietnamese government's effort to create a new marital regime. Generally referred to in official sources as 'forced marriage' (*cuong ep ket hon*), cadres asserted that arranged marriage produced a number of negative social consequences. It provided parents with arbitrary reasons for preventing the marriages their children desired, such as horoscopic inauspiciousness or inadequate brideprice. It often stuck children into socially desirable but unhappy marriages. And the Minister of Justice, Vu Dinh Hoe, even declared during the National Assembly debate on the marriage law that arranged marriage adversely affected the education of children as well as public order and morality (QH #39). General sentiments ran in favor of the new regime, but its implementation proved problematic almost from the beginning. Daniel Goodkind reports that in one northern province from 1958 to 1962, the proportion of parent-arranged marriages only fell from over 60 percent to under 20 percent (Goodkind 1995:345). In Thinh Liet, the percentage of arranged marriage fell to approximately 42 percent in the period from 1954–60, but still constituted some 20 percent of marriages from 1961–69. Phi Ha and Thanh Binh report that in a 1958 survey of 228 weddings, nineteen involved under-age marriages with several contracted between children eleven and twelve years of age (Phi Ha and Thanh Binh 1960:6), a strong indication of parental arrangement. As state control slowly increased over the years, these numbers declined further.

'Forced marriage' remains highly stigmatized in contemporary Thinh Liet. The favored adage employed for describing the old practice is, 'The parents say where and the children sit there' (*bo me dat dau, con ngoi day*), generally accompanied by a disclaimer that people no longer do such things. The limited survey I conducted, as shown in Figure 5.1, has shown a steady decline in arranged marriage since 1954. Of the 382 cases of marriage that took place after 1954 for which I had data, only fifty were arranged, and forty four of these occurred before 1970. Six cases occurred after, but five of those came from the family of one particularly spirited elderly woman who said that there was no way imaginable she would have allowed her children to find their own marriage partners. Arranged marriages, as Figure 5.2 shows, have also tended to be village endogamous.

When asked about how their relationships developed, Thinh Liet residents almost universally employed the courtship metaphor of 'coming to understand each other' (*tim hieu nhau*). This metaphor's origins are difficult to date. Not included in the marriage law, it began to feature prominently in official documents from the early 1960s onward. 'Coming to understand each other' involves a number of different ideas. At one level, it refers to an evaluation of a couple's compatibility and the viability of their marriage prospects. Those who court and marry have 'come to

Figure 5.1: Percentage of Arranged Marriages

	Arranged	*Non-Arranged*
Period:		
pre-1954:	81.9%	18.1%
1954–60:	41.7%	58.3%
61–69:	20%	80%
70–79:	2.75%	97.25%
80-present:	1.82%	98.18%

Figure 5.2: Relationship Between Arranged Marriage and Village Endogamy

	Arranged and Endogamous	*Arranged and Non-Endogamous*
Period:		
pre-1954:	94%	6%
1954–60:	56.5%	43.5%
61–69:	83.3%	16.7%
70–79:	100%	0
80-present:	100%	0

Figure 5.3: Percentage of Village Endogamy for All Marriages

	Endogamous	Non-Endogamous
Period:		
pre-1954:	78.7%	21.3%
1954–60:	66.7%	33.3%
61–69:	45%	55%
70–79:	46.8%	53.2%
80-present:	43.6%	56.4%

understand each other.' Those who court but do not marry are said to have partially 'come to understand each other.' Full understanding presumes the recognition of a viable and desired marriage. The central idea behind the metaphor is romantic love (*tinh yeu*). When establishing the voluntary marital regime, the party foregrounded love (*tinh yeu*) as a necessary component of every new marriage. A 1962 government pamphlet *Struggle Against Bad Practices and Corrupt Customs, Reform Old Habits and Build the New Ways* declared that the aim of the marital system was to 'build happiness on the foundation of love (*tinh yeu*) and mutual help' (Vietnam, Government 1962:14). Official pronouncements resonate with local understandings of the relationship between love and marriage. Couples say that to marry, a couple should love each other (*yeu nhau*). Circulating in this discourse are ideas that there is but one person in life one can truly love and marry. Many people will claim that their spouse is that person, but this idea is also seen in popular stories of unrequited love, such as the high status woman whose parents forbid her to marry the low status man, or in comments by the unhappily married that it was their 'fate' to not marry the one they truly loved. This singular nature and experience of love is particularly focused on women as a good woman should love only one man in her life. This ideal is best exemplified in Vietnam's greatest epic poem, *The Tale of Kieu*, in which the heroine, a woman named Kieu, endures multiple torments and indignities at the hands of men, yet never loses her feelings for her first love. In the relatively enclosed world of contemporary Thinh Liet, courtship between young people is a relatively obvious and commented upon activity. Young women are careful not to be seen courting too many young men for fear of developing a negative reputation.

Despite the stigmatization of forced or arranged marriages, neither official nor unofficial attitudes sanctioned the complete removal of parental involvement in finalizing a marriage. A 1961 government pamphlet declared,

Those marriages built on the foundation of mutual understanding and passionate love will bring young people immeasurable happiness. Saying that, however, does not mean that children need not come to an agreement with their parents on their marriage. On the contrary, they should and perhaps must reach a consensus with their parents or others before marrying. Still, the final decision is their's.

(Phi Ha and Thanh Binh 1961:14)

Thinh Liet residents echo similar sentiments when they comment that, despite the arranged marriage ban, marriage is still a 'work of the family.' Barring unforeseen events, such as an extra-marital pregnancy, most Thinh Liet courtships last approximately one year and during that time a woman's suitor regularly visits her home. Initially he will visit briefly to become acquainted with her family, but later he may begin to take meals and spend time with them. The prospective bride also pays visits to the suitor's family. Throughout this period, the parents on both sides evaluate their potential in-laws. Beyond polite behavior, factors they look for are a reputation for family 'orderliness' (co ne nep), which is to say that the family is not driven with discord and is conscientious in its public and private affairs; no history of mental illness; no history of scandal among family women; and a roughly comparable social status. If everything is satisfactory, parents make their intentions clear by using intimate forms of address, such as calling them 'niece' or 'nephew' (chau), or by issuing invitations to regularly come to the home or participate in family rituals. If there are problems, some parents might take their child aside and give them their frank opinion of the match. Others might address the prospective spouse with formal and distant terms of address, such as 'older brother' (anh) or 'older sister' (chi). Still others might turn the person away and tell them to never visit again, a not unknown occurrence, or inform the child that if they do marry, they will no longer be considered part of the family. Young people often take such threats to heart and some prospective marriages are terminated by parental dissatisfaction. Nevertheless, parents generally do make an honest effort to accommodate the children's desires.

A second area for parental involvement in marriage is in 'introducing' (gioi thieu) a child to a potential spouse. Thanh Binh commented that,

Parents making introductions for their children with the purpose of marriage is not something that is forbidden. In practice, there have been many instances in which parents arranged introductions, both sides were satisfied, and they became happily and lovingly married husbands and wives. However, if the parents make the introduction and the children are not satisfied, they may still completely refuse.

(Phi Ha and Thanh Binh 1961:14)

154

The practice of introductions illuminates a counter-current in Thinh Liet marital discourse. While people champion romantic love as a prerequisite for marriage, the more basic factor of compatibility or suitability for marriage sometimes receives greater consideration. Parents are often perceived as sound judges of this issue, thus children sometimes defer to their parents in choosing a spouse. This was most evident during the war years against France and the United States. During this period, young, unmarried soldiers sometimes returned home on leave for one to two weeks. Before they arrived, a soldier's parents would have surveyed the surrounding possibilities and initiated discussions with another family about a potential marriage between their daughter and the soldier. If the other family agreed, the families arranged an introduction between the pair after the soldier returned. And if after meeting the couple was amenable, they hastily organized a wedding. Dozens of such marriages occurred in Thinh Liet during the war years. Colloquially, Thinh Liet residents refer to arranged marriage with the neutral phrase, 'my parents arranged it' (*bo me sap xep*), rather than the strong, official term 'forced' marriage (*cuong ep*). Despite parental involvement in marriages contracted after an introduction, such marriages do not fall in the 'arranged' marriage category because the children had the right of refusal. People instead refer to them as marriages resulting from an 'introduction,' but as many cases show, these couple often had little knowledge of each other before marriage.

The question of whether the absence of courtship and romantic love presents a long-term problem for these couples reveals a second cross-current in Thinh Liet marital discourse. Although romantic love is important for the initial stages of marriage, that which holds a marriage together over the long term is *tinh nghia*, roughly translated as a 'feeling of responsibility.' Tinh nghia grows between a man and a woman over time. Initially weak, it strengthens as a husband and wife share their lives together, particularly the experience of raising children. Tinh yeu can be a fleeting, transitory emotion, but that on which the strongest marriages rest is tinh nghia. Couples who marry through introduction, therefore, are equally capable of building tinh nghia between them.

One final area of ambiguity regarding arranged marriage relates to the 'marriage squeeze' on Vietnamese women. Demographers have demonstrated how the large number of male deaths in warfare and the significant migration of men in the ten years after the 1975 reunification produced an insufficient number of marriage partners for women of marriageable age from the late 1970s through the 1980s (Goodkind 1995:347–9). Many women of this cohort often married later in their lives, never married at all, or married a less than ideal partner. In Thinh Liet society, marriages of the latter variety were noteworthy because parents usually arranged them. Two of the most undesirable marriage partners are men with some form of physical deformity or mental retardation. Historically, such men would

155

likely go through life never marrying. The surplus of 'women lacking husbands' (*phu nu e chong*) from the marriage squeeze, however, made such men potential spouses, and many of them in Thinh Liet married in the 1980s. The women involved married to avoid a life 'without family' (*vo gia dinh*), a reference to never marrying and having children. Unlike marriages by introduction, which manifest a quality of interest or desire in the marriage partner, these marriages were completely practical, an occurrence that one man described as an 'accommodation to the circumstances' (*phu hop voi hoan canh*). The parents chose the partner, and the daughter married that man, without any understanding or evaluation. Thinh Liet residents describe such marriages as parentally arranged marriages (*bo me sap xep*), and think that such women's lives are difficult. The existence of such marriages, as well as marriages through introduction, indicate that contemporary Thinh Liet marital practice is more complicated than official ideology admits.

Who Can You Marry?

The growth of courtship and the decline of arranged marriage illustrate one area where parental control over a child's marriage prospects has decreased. Although people still invoke the 'marriage is a work of the family' adage, contemporary Thinh Liet marriages have become more of a negotiation between children and parents. The latter may express their dissatisfaction over a potential marriage partner, and take steps to discourage a union, but few parents will take the step to disown the child or refuse to participate in wedding ceremonies. When evaluating a potential marriage partner for a child, parents take into account the characteristics mentioned above, but their considerations are also guided by kinship and other status related concerns. With the exception of some kin relations, contemporary Thinh Liet society lacks distinct social groups between which marriage is prohibited or discouraged. In the pre-revolutionary period, a preference for status endogamy (*mon dang ho doi*) differentiated local society into distinct sets of hierarchically-ordered affines (e.g. Goody 1973:19ff.). Commoner families tended to marry among themselves, usually within the same village (*lay cung lang*), while the children of elite families tended to marry into other elite families from outside the village or commune. Few marriages occurred between the two groups, and those that did fit local customs that allowed hypergamy (women marrying up) but prohibited hypogamy (women marrying down). Vietnamese cadres recognized the same insight as Jack Goody when they commented,

> At base, the preference for status endogamy (*mon dang ho doi*) both protects feudal power and influence, and differentiates according to occupation, disdaining labor. How can the child of a poor

family, dressed in rags, exhausted from trading, marry the child of
a mandarin, no matter how much they love each other?

(Thanh Hoa, Cultural Service 1975:6)

After war, revolution, and collectivization, these categories changed.
Among the most desirable marriage partners for young women during
the war years were young men who had been wounded and discharged
from the military. They would never die on the battlefield. During the years
of collectivization, other sets of desirable spouses were those with links to
the party or administration, or those employed in the distribution of food
stuffs at local cooperatives. This was particularly true of young women
working in cooperative stores who could obtain the choicest bits.
Stigmatized categories also emerged. People avoided marriage with the
children of landlords. The children of families who did not enter the
cooperatives also encountered many difficulties. They were often accused
of lacking patriotism and the spirit to build socialism. The government
denied them and the landlords a number of important advantages, such as
party membership; access to the best jobs, such as factory work; university
education; and the best health care. Local families therefore regarded such
marriages as politically dangerous or simply a dead end. These categories,
however, no longer exist. A preference for status endogamy remains, and
one can suspect that this will lead to differentiation into categories of rich
and poor, but it is too early to say. Nevertheless, people still criticize
hypogamous marriages, as evident in marriages when the wife's father is of
higher status than the husband's. People scathingly refer to the husband as
'the wife.'

One area that can become a focus of sometimes bitter inter-generational
dispute is the question of marriage between people of the same patrilineage
(*lay cung ho noi*). Pre-revolutionary customs uniformly forbid such
marriages, regardless of how distant the relation. Another prohibition
forbid marriage between people within five degrees (*nam doi*) of either
agnatic or cognatic relation. The Law of Marriage and Family challenged
these principles by reducing the range of prohibited marriages to the latter
five degree category. Thus, beyond obvious exclusions such as marriage
between siblings or parents and children, Vietnamese could not legally
marry second cousins but could marry third cousins or beyond, regardless
of lineage affiliation. The law also allowed for marriage between anyone
within five degrees (*nam doi*) of relation if it accorded with 'local customs'
and received the approval of the local administration. In practice, Thinh
Liet officials interpreted the law as prohibiting marriage between people of
the same or different patrilineage within five degrees of kinship, but
allowing for marriage between anyone of six or more degrees of relation.
This has led to open conflicts over who people can legitimately marry. The
most renowned dispute occurred in Giap Tu in the late 1970s. Two distantly

157

related people of a Nguyen lineage went off to study at a university in Vinh Phu province. While there, they fell in love and decided to marry. After completing university and returning to the village, the couple broached the topic of their marriage with their parents. Both sides firmly opposed the union. The couple was 'of the same patrilineage' (*cung ho noi*), thus 'customs did not permit it' (*phong tuc khong cho*). Such relations were like 'brothers and sisters of the same home' and allowing the marriage would have been 'impolite to the ancestors.' The father even predicted that their marriage would produce a life of hardship for them. The couple approached their marriage from an entirely different perspective. The single factor that determined the viability of their marriage was whether it fulfilled the necessary legal requirements. As one of their lineage members commented, 'young people grow up with the law from the beginning,' thus they value it over local customs. Given that their relationship fell beyond the stipulated five degrees, the couple sought and received the local administration's approval to marry. The families held a wedding ceremony, but it was significantly reduced in size because the parents did not deem it appropriate to openly celebrate such a union nor did other villagers wish to attend. After marriage, the couple found that their marriage made it extremely difficult to remain in the village. They later moved to southern Vietnam where they remain. Other marriages within the same patrilineage have occurred, though they remain rare and apparently do not receive the same measure of censure. In many cases, young and old disagree on this issue with the former asserting the primacy of customs and the latter the legal requirements for marriage.

How Much For Your Daughter?

Brides in rural northern Vietnam settle virilocally after marriage. Given the social importance of patrilineages and the family ancestral cult, daughters receive less public valuation than sons because of the latter's importance in maintaining cultic rites. 'Daughters are the children of others' (*con gai la con cua nguoi ta*), a reference to their leaving the natal home at marriage, is often one of the first proverbs a researcher learns when investigating the Vietnamese family. Prior to the 1950s, several sets of gifts given by the groom's family to the bride's preceded the finalization of a marriage (see Malarney 1998). Each of these increasingly formalized the union. Historically, the most important of these transactions was the brideprice (*thach cuoi*) given by the groom's family just prior to the wedding.[6] Determination of the brideprice was the result of long and often delicate negotiations between both families. It generally took the form of a range of standardized items, such as quantities of areca nuts, live pigs, cooked pork, glutinous rice, tea, and possibly gold, money, and cloth (cf. Toan Anh 1968:340–343). The brideprice served several purposes. First, as in southern China (Ebrey 1991:4), Vietnamese brides received little in the way of dowry. Upon leaving her natal household, the bride received a small trousseau from her family and close kin, such as gold, jewelry or cloth, called the *hoi mon*. Items from the brideprice helped to provide the bride with clothing and jewelry for the wedding, and then perhaps a small part of the brideprice returned with the bride to the groom's home where it would serve, along with the *hoi mon*, as an independent fund for the bride. Second, brideprice items, such as the areca nuts and tea, accompanied invitations to the wedding banquet given by the bride's family (see below). Third, the brideprice provisioned the premarital distribution of food items to the bride's kin and a small banquet at her home on the wedding morning. The groom's kin usually delivered the brideprice a day or so before the wedding ceremony. After receiving it, the bride's family divided it into separate trays (*mam*). One of these they placed on the altar of the bride's lineage hall and the others they presented to important kin, such as the bride's lineage chief, and her maternal and paternal grandparents. On the wedding morning, the family consumed the remainder of the brideprice items in a modest feast for close kin and a small number of family friends. Responsibility for the bride's feast, therefore, fell largely upon the groom's family.

The practice of demanding brideprice brought with it a number of difficulties. Some families, when negotiating, made absurdly high demands. Toan Anh records a folk song in which a daughter of a wealthy family laments her family's demands which include one hundred pieces of jade, twenty-eight stars from the heavens, a tobacco pipe made of silver, a lime-pot made of gold, ten baskets of white glutinous rice, ten baskets of glutinous rice with fruit, 80,000 cows and buffaloes, 70,000 goats and pigs, nine casks of liquor, and ninety widowed bats (Toan Anh 1968:341–342). Such demands were obviously an exaggeration, yet brideprice negotiations had the potential to become bitter and divisive. Brideprice could become a major financial burden on the groom's family. In cases where the bride's family was wealthier and sympathetic to the union, they might secretly give assistance, but more often the groom's family incurred debts to cover the costs. If relations between the two sides became extremely unpleasant, the bride's side might make their demands so great that the groom's side could not meet them, thereby forcing an end to the relationship.

Revolutionary policies completely opposed the payment of brideprice and the marriage law specifically forbid 'demanding items for marriage' (Vietnam, Government Gazette 1960:54). Although cadres said little about the other prestations, they portrayed brideprice as parents selling their children (*ban con*) to the highest bidder. The feudal system 'treated women as a commodity to be bought and sold at the right price' (Ha Tay, Cultural Service 1970:13). Moreover, under the collective economy, the demanding of brideprice usually forced families to purchase items from the

159

black market (Hanoi, Cultural and Information Service 1975:32). Linked to the prohibition of brideprice was a ban on the payment of a 'marriage fee' (*cheo*) demanded by the authorities in the bride's village to finalize a marriage. Sometimes these levies were quite heavy, such as Giap Nhi's demand for bricks for village roads or Giap Tu's requirement of money plus labor. Most villages also required men from other villages to pay more than village males. Each of these practices fell into the 'bad customs' and 'backward' categories as they encouraged the practice of 'buying wives, selling husbands' (*mua dau, ban re*) (Vietnam, Government 1962:14).

Official regulations targeted both practices for elimination. The ban on the marriage fee succeeded from the beginning, and it has not reappeared in Thinh Liet. The success of the brideprice ban has been more ambiguous. Cadres easily enforced the ban during the reform campaign's initial years, but as families gradually regained control over weddings, brideprice re-emerged, though in an unexpected manner. At an ideological level, most Thinh Liet residents have internalized the official position on brideprice payments. When asked whether brideprice has re-emerged, residents almost universally respond that families no longer demand it. The common follow-up comment is that demanding and accepting brideprice, just as the party declared, equals selling one's daughter. One Giap Tu resident confidently declared, 'Brides' families no longer accept brideprice payments.' Moments later, he noted that 'accepting money is selling one's child. A few things are accepted though, in order to provide a fund for the bride.' The foregrounding of money and the admission that families do accept some articles illustrates a common contradiction regarding contemporary marriage payments. In the time leading up to a wedding, the bride and groom's families still negotiate the different sets of prestations that the groom will deliver to the bride's home. Contemporary residents have dropped the pre-engagement ceremony (*dam ngo*) and the gifts it had involved, but still perform the engagement ceremony (*an hoi*) (now held at least several months but sometimes as long as a year before the wedding), accept calendrical prestations from the groom, and receive brideprice from his family. These prestations take different forms. Engagement prestations will include several cartons of cigarettes, several bottles of liquor, tea, areca nuts, betel leaves, molasses-flavored glutinous rice cakes (*banh com*), perhaps money, and other items the bride's family requests. Acceptance of the items confers 'engaged' (*dinh hon*) status on the couple, or, as colloquially noted, they have become 'a husband and wife who have yet to marry' (*vo chong chua cuoi*). The calendrical prestations, the most important of which is given at the lunar New Year, will often include such items as fruits, cooked glutinous rice, and boiled chicken. The brideprice items generally include cartons of cigarettes, tea, biscuits, perhaps rice and pork, and rarely money or gold. As in the pre-revolutionary period, the negotiations for these items are delicate and potentially divisive,

160

although there were no cases of weddings cancelled due to insufficient marriage payments. Still, families have definite ideas about the appropriate size prestation for a family of their status and will bargain hard to get it. The amount of pork, gold, or money given is not as significant as before, yet the quantities of cigarettes, tea, and biscuits given at the engagement or in the brideprice remain large. One reason for maintaining these, residents argue, is because they are essential for distribution as engagement announcements and wedding invitations. And the reason for maintaining the calendrical prestations is because they are vital for the groom to register his respect for the bride's family. Despite the formal similarities to pre-revolutionary practices, most Thinh Liet residents do not regard contemporary prestations, and particularly the brideprice given just before the wedding, as equivalent to selling a daughter. A few assert that the contemporary practice of giving gifts just before the wedding is a scaled-down version of its predecessor, and therefore employ the term thach cuoi, but the more common opinion is that none of the prestations buy anything. In a sense, the payments remain, but their purpose has been transferred away from directly profiting the family to helping it fulfill its obligations to other families. They are also described as simple expressions of good feeling and 'sentiment' between families. Instead of falling into the stigmatized category of brideprice, today's prestations are instead part of an effort to provide the best possible wedding for all involved parties. No children are sold, only new families and positive affinal relations established.

Is a Bride Equal To A Groom?

The reconfiguration of the semantics of marriage payments links with a broader transformation of the bride's position in marriage and weddings. Confucian-inspired adages, useful for articulating male-centered elite ideology, in some cases obscure Vietnamese social reality. The position of women in the Vietnamese family is a case in point as Vietnamese families are more similar to those of Southeast Asia than China. Women engage in production, are responsible for the family finances, and often have a voice in important family decisions such as the children's education or building a new home. The position of women in the home has earned them the appellation of 'general of the interior' (*noi tuong*). Luong has demonstrated that despite the predominance of patrilineal kinship relations, matrilineal relations were also important in Vietnamese villages (see Luong 1989). And although a woman leaves her home after marriage, she and her husband must return to her home for important family rituals, such as death anniversaries. In the days leading up to the Lunar New Year celebration, she and her husband must also return to her natal home to give gifts to her parents and propitiate her family ancestors. Despite the spoken preference

161

for sons, many older Vietnamese comment that daughters are more loyal and reliable for taking care of parents in their old age, thus at least one daughter is ideal. Time spent in a Vietnamese home reveals that once one strips away the Confucian-veneer, Vietnamese women are very powerful. Publically, however, Vietnamese women are still at a decided disadvantage to men.

Pre-revolutionary wedding ceremonies reproduced distinctions between the bride and groom. The first measure of distinction was the larger size of the groom's wedding feast. Each family held a feast on the wedding morning. For a commoner family, the bride's feast might include some ten trays of food or sixty guests. This feast was primarily a family affair, thus invitations were only issued to family members, close kin, and perhaps a few friends. Overall, the mood at the bride's home was modestly festive. Unlike a grinning American bride, Vietnamese brides often wear sad, pensive, and perhaps slightly frightened expressions on their wedding day, the consequence of leaving the comfort of their natal home and moving in with potentially troublesome in-laws. Indeed, a common expression for someone crying heavily is 'crying like a woman on her wedding day' (*khoc nhu co gai ngay di lay chong*). The size and mood of the groom's feast were quite different. A man taking a wife was an occasion for celebration, thus levity and good humor characterized his feast. It was also larger. Unlike the family-focus of the bride's, the groom's family invited more guests on a more socially expansive basis. Kin and close friends still constituted the main base, but a wider range of friends, neighbors, and associates also attended. In total, an average groom's feast was generally approximately three times larger with 30 trays.

The relationship between host and guest at the different feasts also differed. Responsibility for provisioning the bride's feast fell upon the groom's family through the brideprice. Guests invited to the feast bore no responsibility for providing any prestation or payment to attend the feast, although those close to the bride might voluntarily bring a small gift. Guests who attended the groom's feast were obliged to give the groom's family a small prestation, called a *mung* prestation. Mung is the word for happy, a reference to the indigenous classification of weddings as 'work of amusement' (*viec hy*). Prior to the revolution, mung usually took the form of food items, such as rice, tea, or eggs, or as is standard today, money.[7] The prestations were not directly intended to help families defray the cost of the wedding ceremonies or feast, a point evident in the fact that a poetic couplet (*cau doi*) composed for the couple was an equally prized mung gift. Grooms' families issued invitations to kin and those whose wedding feasts they had previously attended. The evening before the wedding, those individuals who had received invitations visited the groom's home to declare their intention to attend the feast, present the mung gift, and state how many family members would attend. The size of the mung was a delicate matter. Local standards existed regarding an appropriate sized gift, and families were expected to present that amount. In the 1940s, for example, a common mung gift was one kilogram of rice. Or, if a family had received a large gift previously, they were obliged to return that amount, if not slightly more. An inappropriately-sized gift could lead to a rupture in social relations. Families in Thinh Liet often recorded the size of mung gifts in a ledger so they could reciprocate the appropriate amount in the future. Unlike the bride's side, non-kin guests of the groom belonged to the category of those with whom one 'exchanged debts through eating and drinking.'

The difference between feast size and exchange relations asserted the relative inequality that existed between the bride and groom on their wedding day. A young man taking a bride was an occasion for a public celebration that involved a large feast and the groom's family's broader network of social relations. A woman taking a husband was a modest, family-centered celebration. Revolutionary ideology never directly declared the equality of the bride and groom in wedding ceremonies, but a combination of policies has indirectly produced a marked attenuation of the distinctions between them. As discussed previously, families encountered great difficulties organizing feasts during the years of the reform campaign. The government sought to eliminate all feasts because they were wasteful and weakened the nation's 'productive strength.' These restrictions, combined with the general poverty of the period, the ban on brideprice, and a ban on mung prestations, generated a number of organizational difficulties. In Thinh Liet, wedding feasts for grooms averaged ten to fifteen trays during this period, while the brides' feasts were only a few trays. Restrictions on feasting gradually loosened in the late 1980s and by the early 1990s an average wedding feast in a groom's home had risen to some 45 to 50 trays, but at the same time the size of the bride's feast also increased and families began celebrating a daughter's marriage in a roughly comparable manner. Beginning around 1975, brides' families began receiving mung prestations on the night before the wedding. The cessation of large-scale brideprice payments had created a problem in provisioning the bride's feast, but this deficit is now covered by mung gifts. The standard mung gift, usually around 10,000 to 20,000 dong, is given for both feasts. Brides' families also invite a larger number of guests on a more socially-expansive basis. Like the groom's, they engage in 'exchanging debts through eating and drinking' in wedding feasts. Accordingly, the average total number of trays for the bride's feast has increased to the point where a contemporary bride's feasts is closer in size to the groom's. One January 1992 wedding, for example, featured a feast of 55 trays at the groom's home and one of 40 trays at the bride's. Other feasts in this period differed by only 5 trays. Such cases are particularly evident when the bride's father is an important individual who needs to invite many guests.

Families are still careful, however, to make sure that the size of the bride's feast does not exceed the groom's.

Beyond relatively similar feast sizes and exchange relations for the bride's and groom's families, one final measure of the improved position of the bride is the increase in the average trousseau size. In addition to gold, many brides now receive such items as clothing, mosquito nets, household implements, or even bicycles. Unlike previously, these gifts originate in the family and are not part of the brideprice. Luong comments that Son Duong village in Vinh Phu province has seen a similar improvement in the bride's status in local wedding ceremonies. Gifts to the bride have increased, a new wedding-eve reception for the bride has emerged, and feasts have grown larger. An elderly Son Duong villager commented that 'parents complain to no avail' about the many new financial demands that marrying a daughter now imposes, but all the same, 'If the parents scold the daughter, she will just smile ear to ear, and the parents will have to pay quietly' (Luong 1993:279). Thinh Liet parents do not complain about the increased demands placed upon them. Many instead view the changes as a positive innovation and welcome the idea that the marriages of both sons and daughters are worthy of celebration. Nevertheless, though many might not openly acknowledge it as such, the marriage of a son is still slightly more significant.

Who To Invite? And How Many Trays Is Appropriate?

The imposition of the collective wedding ceremony transformed the distribution of wedding invitations. Families did not invite widely in the colonial period, nor did invitations often pass between families of different status. The expansive issuance of invitations by the Youth Association ended the exclusivity of former wedding practices and attempted to replace it with a generic, egalitarian social relation between all guests. Families regained control over the issuance of invitations in the early 1960s, though the effects of the new invitation practices were not immediately evident due to the retention of small weddings caused by the reluctance of people to congregate in large numbers in case of an air strike during the war, as well as the resource scarcity of the late 1970s. When the economic situation began to ease in the mid-1980s, families began inviting larger numbers of people on a more socially expansive basis, leading to a general expansion of 'exchanging debts through eating and drinking' networks in the commune.

Thinh Liet residents account for the retention of expansive invitations and the growth of exchange networks in a number of different fashions. Prominent among them are the consequences of revolutionary policies, warfare, and poverty. The most frequent explanation one encounters, which echoes one put forth regarding funerals, is that the land reform broke down many status distinctions in local society, as well as the mechanisms for reproducing those distinctions, and replaced them with a more egalitarian social order. A decade of shared hardship during the American war, followed by an almost universally shared level of poverty under the collective economy, created a measure of unity and commonality previously absent in local life. Although social distinctions still existed, particularly with regard to the politically ostracized, they were comparatively fewer during this period, and a rough and imperfect egalitarianism emerged. With fewer obstructions, this argument goes, families interacted with and extended invitations to a more socially expansive set of people. A second explanation relates to the reproduction of sentimental relations in weddings. As in funerals, exchange in weddings reproduces sentimental relations. Many residents argue that revolutionary policies, both ritual and economic, allowed for the sentimental element of wedding ceremonies to grow. One 92 year old Giap Tu man who had participated in many rituals before the revolution and witnessed the reforms commented that, 'poor people live with sentiment, with greater equality.' Revolutionary changes produced a wider range of sentimental relations for families, relations which they now mobilize and reproduce through exchange. Families also prize the presence of many people at weddings. One commonly held opinion is that a wedding cannot be fun unless there are many happy participants. Older residents recall that the small, reformed ceremonies 'weren't fun,' and more pointedly, 'were without sentiment' (*vo tinh cam*). A large number of guests increases the sentimental element and indicates to others that the family has many sentimental relations. People who live without sentiment, also described as people who 'live without virtue' (*song khong co dao duc*), are shunned socially, creating difficulties for them in assembling guests for their weddings, just as with their funerals. A large feast shows the family's esteem and that it lives with sentiment. Given these considerations, many families invite widely to show their good qualities and increase the wedding's celebratory nature. Through the imposition of revolutionary policies, this argument runs, weddings have become affairs that bring villagers together in sentiment instead of restating differences between them.

Most Thinh Liet residents agree that revolutionary reforms have opened the way for an expansion of the sentiment element in weddings, and that the increase in average wedding feast size from 30 to 45–50 trays supports this point. However, other changes have also been involved. At a simple level, population increases have in many cases increased the number of kin for families. All kin must be invited, which pushes the numbers up, though people also note that the number of non-kin guests has also expanded. More importantly, advocates of the sentiment expansion argument also recognize that since the early 1990s there has been a less positive aspect to these transformations as the expansion of sentiment has also been accompanied by changes in weddings that derive from increased display and status competition. On this point, it is relevant to readdress the uneven changes in Thinh Liet's economy over the past decade. At the end of the 1980s, Thinh Liet was a relatively poor community in absolute terms, though it was better off than some other surrounding communities. Since the introduction of economic reforms, some families have prospered tremendously, while the situation of others has remained constant or, in many cases, worsened. The former's success is easily visible in their clothes, new homes, televisions, video players, and motorcycles. The latter often live in run-down houses, struggle to get enough to eat, and some, such as elderly widows without children, must take the meager amount of public assistance the People's Committee can offer. Many former veterans struggle too. Members of these two groups often have different occupations. Many of the former engage in business or larger-scale commercial activities, while the latter are usually confined to handicrafts, agriculture, or petty trading. As the poor tell it, the wealthy, though particularly those with links to officialdom, also benefit from corrupt activities, such as the receipt of prized land plots in the agricultural land redistribution of the early 1990s (see Malarney 1997). Since my first visit in 1991, the emergence of these differences has become increasingly evident, and some of the poor feel that the wealthier make no effort to conceal their better position, particularly in their wedding ceremonies.

The problem of display and status competition manifests itself in weddings in a number of ways. Perhaps the most obvious measure is feast size. The size and quality of local feasts is a common topic of conversation, if not withering critique. The commonly quoted adage, 'ridicule funerals, reproach weddings' captures the sometimes vicious spirit of this practice. Whenever families hold a feast, the number of trays served spreads quickly throughout the village. For the ethnographer, the ability of people to accurately recall feast size is remarkable. The feasts that generate the most discussion are the largest ones, such as that held for the son of the Giap Nhi agricultural cooperative chairman in 1993, which featured some 130 trays (780 guests). This was the largest feast in Thinh Liet history, its size almost tripling the village average of 45 to 50 trays, and far exceeding the previously record of some 90 trays. Local reactions to the feast varied. Some argued that the size was appropriate because the chairman had to nurture his many contacts with people in the commune, district, and city of Hanoi. Others noted that although the size was rather excessive, the family only served modest food items, thus it was not egregiously so. Another strand of opinion, common among those who continued to adhere to the revolutionary doctrines of ritual simplicity, was that the feast was a serious waste of resources, excessively large, and completely dedicated to conspicuous consumption and status assertion. Most poor residents agreed with the latter two criticisms. In any case, what was plain was that the feast had completely captivated the local population, and many would not have at all minded having the ability to organize such a feast. Indeed, one trend evident in Thinh Liet life is withering criticism of other feasts for their garishness, but an undeniable impulse to organize the largest one possible for one's own family members. 'You will only do it once,' the justification goes.

A second measure of status assertion in weddings is the choice of food and drink items at the feast. Prior to the revolution, local practices generally restricted feast items to 'six bowls, six plates' (*sau bat, sau dia*), a combination of six plates of pork-based dishes and six bowls of vegetable or fruit dishes, including green bananas, cabbage, and kohlrabi (*su hao*). These were often accompanied by *quoc lui*, a contraband form of distilled rice spirits. During the 1960s and 1970s, Thinh Liet families maintained a simplified feast menu dominated by boiled pork and vegetables. This menu remained popular until the mid-1980s. In recent years, feast items have changed noticeably, often in the direction of including items with increasing status value. In the late 1980s and early 1990s, the most prestigious feast items were *gio* and *cha*, two types of pounded pork roll. Although individuals with the necessary skills can produce them themselves, most families purchased them commercially at a price greater than that of raw pork. After pork roll became commonplace, families turned toward the more expensive boiled chicken. In this case, chickens were boiled whole and their parts distributed on trays, with the most prestigious bits, such as the head, gizzard, and tail, given to high status guests. One Giap Nhi man inadvertently illustrated the importance of chicken as the essential feast item when he declared, 'Chicken meat is the most prized feast item. Without chicken, it is not a large feast.' The average contemporary feast of 45 to 50 trays now usually includes approximately one hundred kilograms of pork (2 kilograms/tray) accompanied by around thirty chickens, although those trying to make a greater statement might include more chickens. The choice of alcoholic drinks has undergone a similar transformation. Feasts into the early 1990s almost exclusively featured distilled rice spirits. In mid-1992, a small number of families began serving a locally produced grape wine, which subsequently became more widespread. By late 1993, Vietnamese beer replaced wine as the most desirable alcoholic drink. Rice spirits remain the most commonly consumed alcoholic beverage at feasts, but when the trays are laid out with the food items for the guests, five or six cans of beer might also be placed there. On average, a tray for six people cost 45,000–50,000 dong, but the cost of trays at a small number of weddings in the early 1990s exceeded 90,000 dong.

As evident in the criticism of the chairman's son's wedding feast, some Thinh Liet residents have become quite critical of the expansion in feast size and the increased elaborateness of wedding ceremonies. A less visible

167

source of criticism is the current heightened sensitivity regarding issuing invitations. Historically, wedding invitations divided into two main categories. Those guests invited to either 'eat salty' (*an man*) or 'eat sweet' (*an ngot*). 'Eat salty' is a general reference to eating cooked foods, usually meat, almost always prepared with salty fish sauce. The difference between the two categories was that an 'eat salty' invitation entitled the guest to eat at the feast, while an 'eat sweet' invitation entailed participation in the procession to retrieve the bride and the convocation at the groom's home afterwards, where guests snacked on tea, fruits, biscuits, and seeds. Many families admit to difficulties in distinguishing between salty and sweet guests. 'The demands of the times,' one older Giap Tu man commented, 'have increased feast size. Now you have to invite many people, at least thirty trays, or you will make people angry.' Families feel pressured to invite large numbers of guests or risk generating ill will among others. Families must first invite those whose feasts they have attended, as well as close kin and lineage mates, but beyond those it becomes difficult. At the extreme, some assert that one must invite every village household, a practical impossibility never realized, but pressure does exist to at least invite almost all families in one's neighborhood.

The most stringent criticisms of contemporary practices focus on issues of economy and authenticity. The expansion of exchange relations has placed an increased economic burden on residents, sometimes making it difficult to attend feasts, particularly for the poor. When the 'wedding season' (*mua cuoi*) arrives during the cool, slack period between the second harvest in the tenth month and the end of the first lunar month, families often receive numerous invitations, many clustered on the same astrologically auspicious days that are again popular for weddings.[8] Over the season, they might receive fifteen or more invitations. One elderly man with many friends and relations received five invitations for one day alone in January 1992. Given the expectation of a standard per capita mung gift of 20,000 dong for close relations and 10,000 dong for more distant relations, feast attendance can become a significant financial burden because most families are reluctant to decline an invitation for fear of damaging their social relations. Families must also make difficult decisions about who will attend which feast. In the elderly man's case, he attended the feast of a patrilineage mate, and sent four of his children to the others. One elderly Giap Tu woman ironically summarized the present situation when she noted, 'In the past it was hard to get an invitation ... Now it's hard because you get too many.' Another point of frustration is that fact that a recognizable economy has emerged in wedding feasts in that the more guests invited, the greater the possibility of realizing a profit. Local gossip often identifies certain families regarded as having organized their weddings with this goal in mind. They are said to 'do business through weddings' (*kinh doanh qua dam cuoi*). Those who organize extravagant wedding feasts 'put on airs' (*choi troi*). At a more critical level, they are also said to 'buy sentiment.' Like with funerals, families must organize a wedding that is 'just right' (*vua*) to avoid criticism.

All of these comments reveal the ambivalence many residents feel about contemporary weddings. Many welcome the expansion of sentimental relations in wedding practices that they attribute to revolutionary changes, but they also feel that the sentimental element is slowly disappearing and being replaced by the pursuit of money and status. Thinh Liet residents recognize the competitiveness that exists between co-villagers. This is part of the 'eat jealousy, live hatred' (*ghen an, ghet o*) spirit that residents reluctantly admit plays a powerful role in local life. And with all the rhetoric of sentiment and equality aside, people acknowledge that they 'follow each other' (*theo nhau*), so if one family hosts a 45 tray feast, their neighbor will try to hold at least a 45 tray feast. As local wealth and incomes have increased, their presence in wedding festivities has begun to accentuate distinctions between villagers, particularly the rich and poor. Poor families complain that the wealthy no longer show much concern for them, nor are they sensitive to their situation. This has produced some resentment and a reluctance by the poor to interact with the wealthy, a tension increasingly played out in determining guest lists. Contemporary weddings, therefore, are very contradictory. On the one side they mobilize the sentiment and good feeling that many present as the ideal characterization of their community, but wrapped up with this is a strong measure of status competition, divisiveness, and ambivalence about the direction of contemporary changes.

Conclusion

A cursory look at weddings in contemporary Thinh Liet might create the impression that, with a few small modifications, today's weddings are much the same as they were fifty years ago. Wedding ceremonies are preceded by a set of meetings and exchanges between the bride and groom's families; the main focal points of the ceremonies are the bride and groom's homes; the essential ritual act is the propitiation of the ancestors of both homes to seek their permission for the union; the legitimacy of the union is conferred through the propitiation of patrilineal ancestors and speeches given by senior male kin on both sides at the groom's home; local families mark their participation in the festivities through gifts to the families; and feasts are a vital component of the celebrations. The analysis presented in this chapter has demonstrated that beyond these formal similarities, much has in fact changed in Thinh Liet marriages and weddings. Arranged marriage has largely disappeared, the range of potential affines has expanded, the meaning of marriage payments has changed, and the network of marriage related exchanges has grown. Other changes have also occurred that are

169

worthy of note. Polygamy has generally been eliminated, and in those cases when it occurs (almost always without the wife's knowledge), is usually condemned. One Giap Nhat man had no sons and some people encouraged him to take a second wife, but he did not because he felt it would 'destroy sentiment' (*mat tinh cam*) within his family. Both men and women also criticize the idea of the 'family chief' (*gia truong*), a pre-revolutionary practice in which the husband made all of the family decisions and expected their wives to do all of the housework. Official ideology was extremely critical of this notion and men who practice it today often hear about it from others. The average age of marriage has also increased. On average, Thinh Liet residents marry at an age of 26.1 for men and 23.4 for women, an increase from 21.5 for men and 20 for women prior to 1954. All of these changes point to the significant impact of the wedding and marriage reform campaign, but as was also shown, Thinh Liet residents also disagree about many elements of the campaign and their consequences.

One important question that remains is whether the changes that have occurred in marriage and weddings indicate an improvement in women's status. Many scholars investigating revolutionary changes in China have concluded that, despite revolutionary policies, women's status still remains far below that of men (see Croll 1981; Wolf 1985), and marriage and wedding practices remain an important mechanism for maintaining these differences (see Lavely 1991; Watson 1991:351). With regard to revolutionary changes in marriage and weddings in Vietnam, it is fair to conclude that they have produced improvements in the status of women in Thinh Liet. The manifestations of this are many, though there are ambiguities. With the abandonment of arranged marriage, women can now choose their own marriage partners, although a woman who openly courts too many men will develop a negative reputation, while a man who does the same will not. People have also abandoned the practice of searching for signs of the bride's virginity on her wedding night, such as bloodied sheets, and have also stopped the practice of presenting the bride's family with a boiled pig's head with an ear cut off if it appeared she was not a virgin. Older Thinh Liet residents often claim that all young people now have premarital sex, but such assertions are probably exaggerated as well as difficult to prove empirically. Some women divorce their husbands. In cases where the woman's husband was abusive, an alcoholic, or a philanderer, she will likely receive public support for her decision. Nevertheless, it is usually difficult for such women to find another marriage partner unless she marries either another divorcee or a widower. The majority of women choose to remain in a difficult marriage, despite the difficulties. If a woman becomes a widow, pressure exists for her to remain 'faithful' to her late husband, but if her husband died before they had children, she can return to her natal household and remarry without stigma. If she has children, significant pressure will exist for her to remain with her in-laws. Perhaps the most significant changes have been the growth in the bride's feast size, the increase in the average trousseau, the decrease in brideprice, and the emergence of mung collection at the bride's home. Unlike the pre-revolutionary situation in which the groom's family subsidized the bride's feast, and also organized a larger feast for themselves, greater parity has emerged and brides' families now 'exchange debts through eating and drinking' in weddings. The marriage of a daughter is also as much a cause for celebration as that of a son, although the son's marriage does receive slightly greater emphasis. Brides still tend to settle virilocally, and many young brides will comment that life with a new mother-in-law and sisters-in-law is rarely easy, yet the changes of the past several decades have improved their situation vis-a-vis marriage and weddings. Nevertheless, although revolutionary policies have improved some aspects of Thinh Liet women's lives, women still tend to have lower rates of literacy, finish school earlier, shoulder a significant part of family labor responsibilities, and have limited access to public office and influence. Thus, significant constraints remain.

CHAPTER SIX

Commemorating War Dead in Thinh Liet Commune

The experience of revolution in Thinh Liet commune was never far removed from the realities of warfare. Seventeen months after the establishment of the first revolutionary administration in August 1945, Thinh Liet lost thirty seven of its fathers and sons when French colonial troops reconquered the commune on the morning of 7 February 1947. Over the next forty years, well over one hundred Thinh Liet soldiers and an almost equal number of civilians died in the wars against the French, Americans, Chinese, and Khmer. For the anthropologist in the field, the consequences of war are omnipresent. Strolls around the commune are often punctuated with comments about which buildings or fields were bombed by the Americans and how many died. On the walls of many homes one finds framed 'The Fatherland Remembers Your Sacrifice' (*To Quoc Ghi Cong*) certificates given by the government to record the death of a soldier killed in battle. And in general conversation, older residents often refer back to the war years. The dominant narrative of this period portrays it as a golden age in which the small Vietnamese nation united to defeat their wealthier and more powerful adversaries. People acknowledge that those years were extremely difficult. Crops yields were low, food was scarce, villagers were dying, and death and fear were always just around the corner in the possibility of another air strike or news of a loved one's death. Still, this nostalgic image prevails, particularly as a criticism of the perceived lack of unity and camaraderie in contemporary life.

This chapter examines two linked questions that have profoundly informed social life since war began: what are dead soldiers and how should they be dealt with? That dead soldiers feature prominently in Thinh Liet life is evident in the monuments, certificates, and rituals dedicated to them. However, as the analysis presented here will demonstrate, dead soldiers are different things and have different meanings for different social actors, and these meanings and assumptions compel different ritual responses. Since the outbreak of the French war in 1946, the government has made a tremendous effort to ennoble those who gave their lives in battle, both through the articulation of new categories of heroic action and sacrifice, and the creation of commemorative ceremonies and monuments. However, lingering in the background of these innovations was a central ambiguity: the dead soldier was to be commemorated, but as the government officially advanced a policy of atheism, it either denied or simply ignored the question of whether the dead soldier's soul existed and lived on. For the families who lost loved ones, dead soldiers' souls did exist, and therefore needed ritual attention to put them to rest. This chapter will examine the diverse ontologies and ideas associated with war dead and the way in which, despite the general acceptance of government efforts to ennoble war death, different assumptions about them have produced different, though ultimately complementary, ritual practices.

Creating the Revolutionary Martyr

The Vietnamese Communists began their struggle against colonial occupation in the 1930s and from the beginning death in the service of the cause was a real if not likely possibility. Early on, the party articulated a new social category to mark those who died serving the revolution, the revolutionary martyr (*liet si*). The word *liet si* predated the revolution and generally indicated a person who performed a noble deed, but the Communists over time reworked its semantics to exclusively indicate those who died carrying out revolutionary duties. Thus, the soldier who died in battle was a *liet si*, yet thousands of Vietnamese soldiers who died from accidents or disease while serving along the Ho Chi Minh Trail during the American War were classified as 'war dead' (*tu si*) and the large numbers of North Vietnamese civilians killed in American bombing raids were 'victims of war' (*nan nhan chien tranh*). Revolutionary martyrs constituted an exclusive group.

The state reserved for itself the right to determine who was classified as a revolutionary martyr. In order to earn this appellation, the individual had to be recognized as having 'sacrificed' (*hi sinh*) his or her life for the revolution. In the socialist state, one of the greatest virtues was the transcendence of self-interest and the selfless devotion to the collectivity. As General Secretary Le Duan declared, 'The revolutionary differs from the non-revolutionary in that he knows to forget himself for the service of the collectivity, for the common interest. Before all else he always thinks of the revolution and the collectivity. He always knows to place the interests of the fatherland, the interests of the collectivity, above the interests of the individual' (Vietnam, Institute of Philosophy 1973:275). 'To relentlessly think of one's self, of one's family,' the General Secretary declared on another occasion, 'is inadequate, selfish' (Vietnam, Institute of Philosophy 1973:272). The greatest virtue was earned by sacrificing (*hi sinh*) one's life for the revolution (Like *liet si, hi sinh* was another case of the state restricting a pre-existing word's semantics to revolutionary activity). Party ideologues provided precise definitions of what constituted sacrifice. 'Thus sacrifice is to sacrifice what, sacrifice for whom? It is to sacrifice one's being, it is to sacrifice to serve the country, the people, the revolution' (Vietnam, Institute of Philosophy 1973:275). Sacrifice was also the test of true revolutionary mettle and integrity. 'Without the virtuous willingness for sacrifice,' Le Duan argued, 'one is not an authentic revolutionary. If you want to realize the revolutionary ideal, but will not dare to sacrifice yourself, then you are only speaking empty words' (Vietnam, Institute of Philosophy 1973:275).

The revolutionary elaboration of 'sacrifice' has had important linguistic consequences that continue to distinguish and ennoble those who had died advancing the revolution or fighting the enemy. The verb 'to die' takes multiple forms in Vietnamese with each particular form providing important social information about the deceased. Common people, for example, are generally said to *mat*, 'to be lost' or *bi chet*, to 'suffer death.' Elderly people *qua doi* or 'pass from life.' The emperor in pre-revolutionary times would *bang ha* or 'pass far below.' The death of Ho Chi Minh and others are often described in obituaries with the poetic and respectful expression *tu tran*, 'to leave this world.' Against these, revolutionaries and soldiers killed fighting against the enemy were sacrificed. One interesting point regarding the utilization of *hi sinh* is that unlike the subtle emphasis of difference between the *qua doi* of everyday people and the *bang ha* of the emperor, the expression *hi sinh* applies to all who have fallen for the cause, regardless of rank or position. In everyday conversations today one regularly hears people using *hi sinh* to mark those who fell for the revolution. The honor that both *hi sinh* and *liet si* can bring are evident in the cases of individuals acknowledged to have sacrificed their lives, but later denied the martyr classification. Such was the tragic case of Nguyen Ton Duyen, the party official from Giap Tu who was wrongfully executed during the land reform. After the Correction of Errors, party officials admitted that Duyen's death had been a mistake. They granted that he had sacrificed himself for the revolution, but they would not allow him to be classified as a martyr, despite his family's protestations. The honor and nobility that inheres in being a martyr is poignantly evident in the fact that Duyen's family, to this day, is still trying to have the decision reversed.

After a martyr's death, the state made significant efforts to maintain the nobility and exclusivity of those who sacrificed their lives for the revolution. At an ideological level, the government glorified their deaths and argued that their lives and deaths should become examples for all to follow. Ho Chi Minh declared when discussing the deaths of a number of party members killed or executed by the French that, 'The blood of the martyrs has made the revolutionary flag dazzlingly red. Their courageous sacrifice has prepared the earth of our nation to bloom into a flower of independence and result in our freedom. Our people must eternally record and remember the meritorious efforts of the martyrs. We must constantly study their courageous spirit to transcend all difficulties and tribulations, and realize the revolutionary work that they have passed on to us' (Vietnam, Institute of Philosophy 1973:275). The government also made material commitments to the martyrs' families. When a family had one of its members leave for the military, it became what was referred to as a 'policy family' (*gia dinh chinh sach*), a category created after 1954. Policy families received a number of different forms of government assistance. At the time of the land reform, they received priority treatment in the distribution of land.[1] During the American war, government officials recognized that a child serving in the military represented the loss of a high quality laborer for the family, thus they received increased food rations provided by the local agricultural cooperative. For many families, the policy family designation ended when their son or husband returned home from the war. The loss of a member transformed a regular policy family into a special policy family category, the 'martyr's family' (*gia dinh liet si*). The dispensations they received in the years before the 1986 introduction of the Renovation policy were substantial. They included preferential admissions to hospitals for members of their families; priority status for entering schools and universities for their children; easier access to government jobs; easier admission to the Communist Party; and a stipend for wives, children, or parents (see also Pike 1986:315). In Thinh Liet they included greater rice allotments than other families; easier work in the agricultural cooperatives; and priority for the most prized work assignments, notably the lucrative fishing brigades. When agricultural land was redistributed to the farmers in 1991–92, the martyrs' families also received the most productive and convenient pieces of land. A former official in Thinh Liet's administration summed up the policy families' situation with the statement, 'whatever they do, it's always easier.'

Commemorating Revolutionary Martyrs

Although the ideological and material commitments to the martyrs constituted an important part of social discourse associated with them, the state also committed itself to the public celebration of their lives and commemoration of their deaths. As early as 1947, when the government designated 27 July as 'War Invalids and Martyrs Day' (*Ngay Thuong Binh Liet Si*), the government began publically commemorating war dead. This holiday, irregularly organized in the late 1950s and early 1960s, became an annual occurrence starting in 1967 (Pike 1986:318). On this day, government officials held ceremonies in which they mourned the fallen soldiers and expressed their gratitude, with both speeches and possibly small gifts, to the martyrs' families and to all those who had served. The memories of the war dead's singular contributions were also kept alive through the creation of exclusive ceremonies or the delineation of special areas for war dead in local cemeteries. If a martyr's corpse was returned, it was to be buried in this cemetery and, in keeping with the revolutionary campaign to simplify funeral rites, a small headstone that recorded the deceased's name, rank and death date placed on it. Government regulations mandated that these cemeteries should not be neglected or divorced from everyday social life. As discussed in Chapter 4, officials wanted people to protect and care for these cemeteries and display their awareness of the martyrs' sacrifices. In some localities, the young were to be taken out to the cemeteries so they could appreciate the martyrs' sacrifices and learn to care for the cemeteries (Ninh Binh, Cultural Service 1968:64). In other localities, such as Nam Ha province, officials decreed that when a young couple married, the ceremony was to conclude with their placing a bouquet of flowers on the war dead monument. Through this act, the couple could express their debt and appreciation to those who had given their lives for the nation and revolution (Vietnam, Ministry of Culture 1979:24). Given that few corpses of Thinh Liet's war dead ever returned to the commune for burial, no special cemetery was ever established nor were commemorative visits to their graves ever held.

After the American War's commencement, the most important commemorative rite conducted by state officials was the official memorial service for war dead (*le truy dieu*). This short and simple ceremony, which took place in the deceased's native community, was the product of delicate planning. The organization of an official memorial service began when military authorities sent official word of the soldier's death to the People's Committee of the soldier's commune. Official confirmation was required because the ceremony could only be performed for those declared by the military to be martyrs. The person in charge of the ceremony was the Social Policy Officer (*Pho Ban Chinh Sach Xa*).[2] This senior administrative post was created during the American War with the exclusive responsibility of assisting policy families. After learning of a soldier's death, the Social Policy Officer usually did not immediately inform the family. To help ease the shock of the news, which, even if expected, had a terrible finality to it, the People's Committee allowed friends or kin to tell the family that word had arrived and the Social Policy Officer would be coming to inform them. After giving the family some time to grieve and prepare themselves for the visit, the Social Policy Officer went to make the official announcement and then arranged a date and time for the official memorial ceremony.

The government's memorial ceremony, like regular funerary ceremonies, took place in the fallen soldier's home. In Thinh Liet, the ceremony was generally held at two o'clock in the afternoon and lasted for one hour.

Unlike a regular funeral in which mourning attire was worn, the family and their guests dressed in normal clothing. The official presence at the ceremony was extensive. The communal administration was represented by the President of the People's Committee, the Village Militia Commander, and the Social Policy Officer. The agricultural cooperative was represented by the chairman. The party was represented by the secretary of the commune's party cell, the secretary of the residential cell in which the family resided, and at least one person from each of the party's mass organizations. On some occasions every member of the executive committee of the administration and the party cell attended. Beyond the official personnel, the ceremony was also heavily attended by kin, friends, and co-villagers.

The Social Policy Officer presided over the official ceremony and brought a bouquet of white flowers with him. White is a mourning color in Vietnam and this type of flower, called *hoa hue*, is commonly featured in funerary ceremonies. When the delegation of officials arrived at the late soldier's home, they placed the flowers on an altar constructed for the dead soldier. After one minute of silence, the policy officer began a eulogy of the fallen soldier. The purpose of his visit, as he stated, was to officially commemorate both the person and the sacrifice of the soldier. The soldier had selflessly sacrificed his life (*hi sinh*) so the war effort could succeed. The nobility of the soldier's death was reiterated in the standardized statement the policy officer then read. The post-1969 text of the official's speech read:

> In our people's glorious revolutionary effort against the Americans to rescue the nation, Comrade (the soldier's full name) has with his comrades in arms raised up the spirit of struggle, surpassed all difficulties and hardships to carry out the responsibilities of his unit, and sacrificed his life on (day, month, year)
>
> The cadres and soldiers of the unit are infinitely sorrowful and proud to have had a person united in will, a comrade in arms, who has offered up (*cong hien*) his life in the struggle for an independent and free country; who swore to never stop raising up the will to fight and the strength to eliminate the enemy; and who brought forth all his spirit and strength to carry on to victory in the war of national salvation against the Americans and to fulfill all the responsibilities that the party, government, and the people gave him.
>
> Dear family members:
>
> Comrade (soldier's name) has left us. The Fatherland and people have lost a loyal and faithful child. His unit has lost a person united in will, a comrade in arms. His family has lost a loved one. All of the cadres and soldiers of the unit respectfully send their

wishes and ask to share the sadness (*chia buon*) with the family. They hope that the family will turn its grief into activity for the revolution, strengthen their hatred for the American enemy and their lackeys, and with the rest of the people and soldiers firmly resolve to realize the sacred words from President Ho's will, 'Resolve to completely defeat the American enemy,' to protect the North, liberate the South, and unite the Fatherland.

By organizing the ceremony, the government gave thanks to the family for that sacrifice. Official sensitivities to the situation were evident in their declaration that they wanted to 'share the sadness' (*chia buon*) of the grieving. The family's grief was evident during the ceremony. Even though the memorial service often occurred some time after the soldier's death, people wept openly throughout.

Following his speech, the policy officer delivered three items to the soldier's family that formalized the state's recognition of the soldier's sacrifice. The family first received a government issued 'Death Announcement' (*Giay Bao Tu*). This began with the statement, 'We Very Regretfully Declare and Confirm' (*Chung Toi Rat Thuong Tiec Bao Tin Va Chung Nhan*), and was followed by the soldier's name, rank, and unit. The form also noted if the soldier had been 'sacrificed.' Other important information included the date of death, place of death, place of burial, and, if it were the case, confirmation that certified the soldier was a revolutionary martyr. Although these categories were helpful, the information on them was sometimes extremely vague. In some cases they noted only that the soldier had died in the south in the struggle against the Americans and that his unit had buried his body near the front. Still, this certificate was necessary for future interactions with the government bureaucracy. The family also received a certificate, approximately twelve by fifteen inches, upon which was inscribed in large red lettering, *To Quoc Ghi Cong*, literally rendered as 'The Country of the Ancestors Records Your Work,' but perhaps more accurately rendered as 'The Fatherland Remembers Your Sacrifice.' This certificate recorded the slain soldier's name, natal commune, and death date. It was issued for every martyr and definitively marked the deceased's assumption of that status by its placement in large black letters of the words 'revolutionary martyr' before the deceased's name. It also stated that the soldier had sacrificed his life during the war and included an inscription along the bottom that read, 'Eternally remember the moral debt (*on*) to the revolutionary martyrs who have sacrificed their lives for a bright future for the people' (*Doi Doi Nho On Cac Liet Si Da Hy Sinh Cho Tuong Lai Tuoi Sang Cua Dan Toc*). The final item given to the family by the policy officer was a sum of money amounting to approximately one hundred and fifty dollars. This sum was a one time form of immediate assistance given to the family. In delivering these three items, the government marked its gratitude to the family for the sacrifice their family member had made. At the ceremony's conclusion, a family member stood up and thanked the officials.

The Vietnamese state went to great lengths to ensure that its claims regarding the glory and nobility of suffering and dying for the cause were compelling. Not only did it glorify those who suffered and died in public discourse, it also created a range of new public ceremonies that expressed the honor and nobility of those actions. For many Thinh Liet residents, these ideas and ceremonies were compelling. Some describe dying for the country as an 'honor' (*vinh du*).[3] Similar to the official's speech, some relatives of those killed in battle employ the verb *cong hien*, which means to give something up to something greater than oneself, to describe their family's sacrifice. Their relations had given up their lives to ensure Vietnam's independence and freedom, or as one veteran stated, 'to bring back happiness and comfort to the people.' People also appreciated the commemorative rite, a fact evident in its continued performance even in the 1990s when official confirmation of those long dead was received. These ideas and attitudes remain prominent in local life, and a discourse publicly critical of them has not emerged, though some might privately entertain critical notions.[4]

War Death and Wandering Souls

An examination of official commemorative rites for war dead reveals a basic point. From the state's perspective the war dead were dead. They had a living past, but their relevance to and existence in the present was defined by an immutable biography that had received final form with their death. The dead soldier was an object of commemoration and remembrance, but its objectiveness did not extend beyond that, and human interactions were not to extend beyond that either. In short, it had no other existence. For the dead soldiers' living relatives, their dead relations had a different ontology. Their bodies were dead, but their souls lived on, and similar to all other deaths, the living were obligated to perform the ritual acts needed to put that soul rest and send it to the other world. In the case of war dead, this obligation was particularly important because of the dangers that war death presented. As previously discussed, Vietnamese have very strong notions regarding what constitutes a good death. Being advanced in years, having many surviving children, dying a quick, painless death, and dying at home, all constitute a favorable end. With a good death, the soul of the living is gently released from its temporary, corporeal form and can easily pass into its ultimate form as a non-corporeal but benevolent ancestor. One's children will ensure that a proper funeral is performed and then they will care for the deceased's soul through offerings in ancestral rites.

Death on the battlefield was the quintessential bad death. Young, often childless people died painful, violent deaths, usually hundreds of miles from home. The corpses of many remained intact to be buried by their

179

comrades, but, as the author Bao Ninh describes in his novel of the American conflict, *The Sorrow of War*, others 'had been totally vaporised, or blasted into such small pieces that their remains had long been liquidised into mud' (Bao Ninh 1991:21). War death was a bad death because it created the possibility that the living would be unable to transform the deceased's soul into a benevolent ancestor. Instead, it could become a wandering, malevolent ghost (*con ma*). The possibility of becoming a wandering ghost derived from a number of different sources. As discussed in Chapter 4, the task of helping the soul to the 'other world' is easier if the person died in the familiar surroundings of their home, but the death of a soldier in a distant, strange location increased the likelihood that the soul would run off and could not be coaxed back and sent on its way. Many soldiers never received proper burial rites, making it difficult to bring their soul back. Others were theoretically barred from ever making the transition because a corpse that is missing parts or otherwise incomplete is doomed to forever roam the earth and never cross to the other world. Other souls were considered angry for having their lives quickly and violently taken from them, others because they had died young. At a more mundane level, family ancestral cult practices dictate that offerings to care for the ancestors' souls in the other world can only be made by those genealogically junior to the deceased. Those who die good deaths have their descendants to care for them and essentially placate them to keep them benevolent in the afterlife. Those who die young are often without such sustenance, so they angrily roam the earth looking for any food or care they can find.[5]

The deaths of young soldiers on the battlefield posed serious dangers as their prematurely terminated lives created an army of wandering souls. Soldiers died young and heirless, their corpses shattered and incomplete, their souls and deaths unmarked and neglected, their passage to the other world obstructed. They were left stranded on the earth with no one to nourish them, their only course being to become malevolent, wandering souls that opportunistically invade other people's homes in order to gain the sustenance and succor they are denied. For Thinh Liet families, this reality was paramount. Families therefore needed to appropriately honor and care for the deceased soldiers' souls so they were not condemned to wandering the earth. However, the ritual corpus of pre-revolutionary Vietnam and the official ceremonies sponsored by the state were largely inadequate for coping with these concerns. As a result, Thinh Liet residents developed a set of innovatory ceremonies during the American War to cope with the problems that war death presented.

Family Commemoration of War Dead

When a soldier was killed, his unit was responsible for reporting the cause of death and burying the corpse. Military units usually had soldiers attached to them in charge of the war dead. After they had discharged their duties, the family was then informed of the soldier's passing. Official confirmation of a soldier's death was notoriously slow in coming, sometimes taking years to arrive. To give one example, on 10 April 1971, the previously mentioned Nguyen Tien Dat of Giap Tu died in an American air strike on the Ho Chi Minh Trail, yet his family did not receive official notification until 7 May 1974. Delays in notification were frequently due to the poor quality of communications within and between military units, and with the rear areas. Some Vietnamese speculate that the party deliberately delayed notification in order keep morale high in the rear areas.[6] Soldiers were keenly aware of the possibility of death as well as the delays in notification. In order to spare their families unnecessary anguish, many who served together made arrangements between themselves for the survivors to either write a letter or pay a visit to the deceased's family to inform them of the date, location, and possibly the circumstances of the soldier's death. Through this informal system of notification a great number of families first learned of a son's or husband's death. The information provided by the deceased's comrade helped ease many of the proximate causes of distress inflicted by their loved one's death. Knowledge of the exact date of death helped families organize a proper death anniversary ceremony for the deceased. Many people held that this ceremony was only effective if performed on the true date of death. Families therefore wanted to know the exact date so they could properly fulfill their ritual obligations. In cases when the death date was unknown, families would usually select the day the soldier left, a choice that reflected pre-revolutionary practices (see Toan Anh 1969:62–63). Information regarding the location of death was also valued. Unlike the policy of the American military which attempted to transport home the corpses of all its dead soldiers, the soldiers of the People's Army were basically buried where they fell. Few were transported back to their natal villages for burial. Although they could not act on it immediately, many families wanted to know the location of death in the hopes that at some future point they could retrieve the corpse and give it a proper burial. Finally, the mere knowledge of the soldier's death allowed the family to immediately conduct some form of funerary rites for the deceased and ward off the possibility of it becoming a wandering soul. Prompt notification by the deceased's comrades helped to slightly alleviate a small measure of the anguish and suffering caused by a young soldier's death.

The death of a young soldier in battle involved other complications in the performance of funerary rites for him. Conventional Vietnamese funerary rites, including the simplified reformed rites propagated by the party after 1954, function under two guiding assumptions. First, that the deceased will generally have surviving children; and second, that the deceased's corpse will be physically present when the funeral is held. A wide range of activities evident at funerals, from the distinctive mourning attire and acts of ritual obeisance that children perform for their parents, to the presentation of food prestations and public feasts that accompany funerals, are all linked to these two assumptions. If either condition is not fulfilled, changes are needed in the rites' structure. The death of a childless individual presents fewer problems than an absent corpse as a regular funeral can still be held. The ceremony features its requisite feast and the transportation of the corpse from the home to the grave. The only difference will be that the parents or other senior kinfolk do not propitiate the lost child, nor do they accompany the casket to the gravesite. A funeral without a corpse demands a completely different ceremony. Unlike funerals in which the corpse is present, kin and co-villagers do not present money, food prestations, or funeral wreaths to the deceased's family. There is also no feast. Nor is there any type of symbolic casket that is carried to the grave. Unlike regular funerals, in which sociality is at a premium and families exchange gifts and debts, funerals in which the corpse is absent are radically simplified.

The deaths of soldiers during the American War necessitated the performance of thousands of funerary rites in which the deceased's corpse was absent. As noted above, in Thinh Liet commune virtually no corpses were returned. One common form these rites took was a private ceremony arranged by families and known as a *le tu niem* or *le tuong niem*. This ceremony, which can be glossed as a 'remembrance of the dead' ceremony, was organizationally distinct from the regular funeral held under normal circumstances. The defining characteristic of the 'remembrance of the dead' ceremony was its modest, familial nature. Funerals mobilized people and resources throughout the village. The remembrance ceremony was a family affair that only a restricted number of family and close kin attended. Funerals also adhered to the lengthy and complex set of rites that began immediately after death. The remembrance ceremony was a simple affair that only lasted a few hours. It was also generally held several days after a family learned of their loved one's death whereas normal funerary activities began immediately after death. Both events, however, were united in their objective of giving succor to the deceased's soul and helping it make its transition to the other world.

When the news of a soldier's death initially arrived, the first task was to set up a funeral altar to commemorate the deceased. These altars were always set up in the home of the deceased's parents and arranged in the same manner as those of non-war dead. A table was set in the main room of the home on the right hand side of the family's ancestral altar. The centerpiece of the altar was a framed photograph or drawing of the deceased. In some cases with deceased soldiers, the family would place a portrait of the deceased in military uniform. Directly before the portrait an urn for incense sticks was placed, and then on either side of the portrait were a number of other items, such as candles, flowers, and perhaps a small oil lamp to light incense. If the family had been notified within one hundred days of the soldier's death, they would set a small bowl of glutinous rice upon which a hard-boiled egg held between two chopsticks, pushed straight down into the bowl, was resting, possibly along with other food items as well. These were meant to feed the deceased's soul for the first one hundred days after death. It was not set up if death had occurred earlier. The completed altar would always have a clear area before it that would provide the main location for the performance of all ritual activities.

News that a native son had been killed in the war spread quickly. The ubiquitous kinship ties shared between co-villagers facilitated this transmission, but a sense of shared experience, perhaps even commiseration, in the face of war and its consequences produced a heightened sense of togetherness that was accentuated when a local villager was killed. Almost all families had or knew someone serving in the military, and everyone knew that next time the loss might be their's. The news of death therefore disseminated rapidly, and village families were quick to demonstrate their sympathy for the aggrieved family. Just as they would in a normal village funeral, kin and co-villagers went to the house of the deceased to express their condolences and 'share the sadness' of the grieving. They carried incense with them, and upon entering the deceased's home they would light three incense sticks, say a brief prayer, and place them in the incense urn on the altar. Their visit gave public expression to their sympathy. It simultaneously helped the grieving cope with their loss and provided a testament to the dignity and esteem of the deceased and his death. What was most remarkable about these visits was their singularly affective nature. Virtually every village family would send at least one representative to visit the deceased soldier's family to express their condolences. Many sent more. When they arrived, however, they brought no gifts. They were not reciprocating former debts incurred during their own family funerals, nor were they sealing a future obligation with a material prestation. These visits fell beyond the purview of 'exchanging debts through eating and drinking' that characterized all other funerary practices. What characterized them instead was an unmistakable sense of the tragedy of a life lost, and the common desire to help others cope with an event that could or did happen to them. With their visits, families asserted their care and concern simply through the act of being there, not through any material items that would form the basis of an exchange relation.

Village families continued to pay visits to the deceased's family for several days after the news first arrived. During this time the home was full with people but the family's sobbing was still audible in neighboring homes. At about the same time as the number of visitors began to tail off, the family performed the 'remembrance of the dead' ceremony. The remembrance ceremony was always organized in the home of the deceased's family. All immediate family members who could attend were present, as well as a small number of other close relations. The ceremony usually took place in the daytime. Prior to its conduct, family members would go through the normal preparations that preceded family rituals such as cleaning the house and family altar, and purchasing any ritual items, such as incense, they would use in the ceremony. They would also prepare a nice set of clothes for the event. Family members only wore normal clothing during the ceremony. The elaborate mourning attire of regular funerals, such as the gauzy white tunics and peaked cheesecloth caps, were absent. The only standard funeral attire visible at the ceremony were the white mourning headbands worn by those junior to the deceased.

All of the rites in the remembrance ceremony were carried out before the altar constructed for the deceased. Similar to other funerary rites, the purpose of the ceremony was to propitiate the soul of the deceased so it could rest in peace in the other world. The ceremony began with the entire family assembled on the floor in front of the deceased's altar to say prayers (*khan*) for the deceased's soul. Straw mats had been laid on the floor and the senior members of the family were seated in the front of the group, with the mother and father placed in the most prized positions nearest the altar. The task of inviting the deceased's soul back to the home was given to a senior male, usually an uncle or great uncle, from the deceased's patriline. Standing before the altar, the man repeated the invocations to bring the soul home. Once these invocations were completed, and the soul successfully installed in the home, the family members individually performed a brief reverence of the spirit. Clasping three incense sticks in their hands, each person would stand and kowtow before the altar one, three, or five times. These prayers and obeisances were somewhat non-specific in nature yet they were dedicated to ensuring the general well-being of the soul in the other world. When their prayers concluded, each person placed their incense sticks in the urn.

The ceremony's second phase involved the direct propitiation of the soul (*cung*). Apart from the simple act of assisting the soul make its transition to the other world, the remembrance ceremony was also dedicated to providing specific items, such as food, clothing, or money, that the deceased could use in the other world. Prior to the ceremony, family members placed paper votive objects that symbolized the clothing or money on the altar along with an array of food items.[7] After saying the initial prayers, one person assumed responsibility for propitiating the deceased's soul with the objective of delivering these items to the deceased in the other world. A spirit priest assumed this role in some households, but since the revolution endeavored to eliminate all rites performed by spirit priests and placed them under official surveillance, some families instead chose a younger sibling of the deceased. The choice of a younger sibling was linked to the prohibition against genealogically senior family members propitiating their juniors. The propitiant kneeled on the floor before the altar and said prayers to entreat the deceased's soul to accept the assembled items. The food items were transmitted through the smoke from the incense burning on the altar. To deliver the money or clothing, the paper items were taken outside into the family compound where they were covertly burned, their substance traveling to the other world through the smoke. Although considered 'superstitious' and prohibited by the party, many families still burned these items. When these rites concluded, the deceased's soul had been provisioned for life in the other world. It had also been installed in the family altar and would thenceforth always be propitiated there.

The prayers and offerings to the deceased's soul usually did not exceed one hour. The remembrance ceremony then concluded with the family members and guests sharing the food from the altar in a commemorative meal. The foods eaten were simple meat and vegetable dishes, a selection partially due to wartime scarcity. At the rites' conclusion, family members took the dishes from the altar, placed them on trays with other dishes, and then the assembled group ate the dishes together, usually sitting on the mats laid out on the floor before the altar. This private, family meal was the only occasion that involved the consumption of food in commemorating a soldier's death. Unlike the sometimes grand feasts of funerals, the remembrance ceremony had only a simple meal. As such, there was neither the public sociality that came with feasts nor the giving of prestations that preceded them. War death engendered a simpler and humbler form of commemoration. Village families still came to the aggrieved family's home to express their sympathy and share their sadness, yet the commemoration of war dead and the assisting of their souls in their migration to the other world were largely family affairs family.

The Commemorative Project Today

The reunification of Vietnam in 1975 did not mark the end of official efforts to commemorate war dead. Soon after the war was over, the government began commissioning the construction of monuments for war dead (*dai liet si*) in localities across Vietnam. These monuments are now visible in nearly every commune and district in the lowlands. Often tall spires adorned with a red or gold star at their apex, and the words 'The Fatherland Remembers Your Sacrifice' or 'Eternally Remember the Moral Debt to the Martyrs' written across the base, these monuments provide continued public testimony to those who gave their lives for the country.[8] The largest monument for war dead, completed in 1995, now sits directly across from Ho Chi Minh's mausoleum in Hanoi's Ba Dinh Square. These monuments are still the focus of official commemoration on War Invalids and Martyrs Day. In nearly all communes, the administration organizes a

185

ceremony for the local war dead. In Thinh Liet's rites, led by the President of the Commune's People's Committee and the Social Policy Officer, the party and administration reiterate their thanks and appreciation to those who have fought and sacrificed themselves, and restate the glory and nobility of what they have done. When the speeches are completed, the families of war dead receive a small gift, such as sugar, condensed milk, sweet biscuits, flowers, or fruit. Many families today receive a small amount of money. These ceremonies are always well attended. Families still take pride in and are appreciative of the government's efforts to recognize and ennoble the contributions of the fallen. The War Invalids and Martyrs Day has also become a second occasion for most families to organize a modest commemorative ceremony and family meal. In Thinh Liet, families return home after the ceremony for a gathering of approximately ten to twenty people. Here they perform a simple propitiation of the dead soldier's soul and then share a communal meal. The propitiation generally takes the form of lighting incense sticks, bowing, and placing the incense in an urn on the altar. This act is significant as few if any people light incense sticks at the war memorial. The act of commemoration and remembrance at the memorial is clear, yet it has not become a site to tend to the needs of the dead soldiers' souls.

The main commemorative ceremony for families remains the soldier's death anniversary. Up until the mid-1980s, wartime scarcities and government regulations prohibiting large-scale death anniversary ceremonies restricted their size (see Chapter 4). Over the past decade, families have begun to organize ever larger ceremonies. Today, an average death anniversary ceremony will feature a communal meal for fifty to sixty people. It begins with rites dedicated to caring for the dead soldier's soul. These are similar to those performed during the commemoration of the dead ceremony. The ceremony is always conducted before the ancestral altar in the deceased's parents' home, the soul is invited back and propitiated, and perhaps some votive paper items, such as money or clothes, are burned for the soul's use in the other world. The main participants are also close family members. If the soldier was survived by his widow, she will participate in these rites at her parents-in-law's home. Almost all widows of war dead in Thinh Liet commune never remarry and remain in their husband's parent's home, particularly if they have children. Remarrying is considered an act of infidelity to the late husband. Despite the social importance of patrilineages in Vietnamese villages, they have assumed no ritual role in commemorating war dead. The rites remain firmly with the husband's immediate family. Once the rites conclude, a communal meal is held for the guests. These usually include friends, neighbors, and relatives who are invited to the ceremony.

Other methods of commemorating and caring for the souls of war dead also exist in Thinh Liet. A number of Thinh Liet families have installed the souls of dead soldiers in the local Buddhist temple. The virtue of installing the soul in the temple is that it receives care and sustenance from all ceremonies conducted there. Such souls 'eat of the Buddha's good fortune' and will not be left uncared for if there are no more family members to conduct rites. A nun at the temple claims that several dozen families have done this, though the figures are disputed by some local residents and impossible to verify. Families who perform this rite will later conduct a ceremony at the temple on every death anniversary and will also participate in ceremonies for dead souls at the temple in the first two weeks of the seventh lunar month.[9]

The most remarkable form of commemoration to emerge in Thinh Liet was the dedication of an altar to war dead in the Giap Tu communal house (see Chapter 7). This communal house had been heavily damaged during the battle with French soldiers in February 1947, producing a great deal of later conflict over which spirits inhabited the communal house. When the communal house was refurbished in the late 1980s, local men decided it was appropriate for villagers to pay respects to local war dead there. This movement reached its zenith on the 11th of the 1st lunar month in 1992, the 45th lunar year anniversary of the aforementioned battle, when local villagers conducted a ceremony to propitiate the souls of eleven local guerrillas who had died that day. The ceremony featured trays of offerings as well as a moving eulogy by the son of one of those killed. The organizers, mostly older men, hoped the ceremony would become an annual event, but resistance mounted, particularly among older women. They felt that while villagers should propitiate war dead, the communal house was not the appropriate venue. As a result, the ceremony was never organized on a large-scale again. In early 1996, the altar for war dead in the communal house was rededicated to the guardian spirit of the land on which the communal house sits. For a short period afterwards, some villagers continued to pay their respects to the war dead in the communal house, particularly on the battle's anniversary, but public rituals stopped. In 1997, the village succeeded in raising enough money to construct a monument dedicated to the village's war dead. This monument, which records the name of every Giap Tu soldier who died in battle, as well as the names of a number of 'heroic mothers' (*ba me anh hung*) who lost several sons in war, sits in the communal house compound and has become the main focus for rites dedicated to village war dead.

The problem of war dead in Vietnam persists to this day, especially for those whose loved one's remains have never been recovered. The number of the missing apparently runs into the hundreds of thousands.[10] Many families continue to organize trips to southern and central Vietnam to search for remains. In early 1996, for example, the skeletons of two soldiers were brought back to Thinh Liet and buried in the local cemetery near their mothers. Given the widespread practice of secondary burial, the local ritual corpus is well-suited to putting such soldiers to rest. Concern with finding soldiers' remains is visible in the public media as well. Vietnamese television has broadcast a number of shows that followed both family and military efforts to locate remains. The magazine 'The New World' (*The Gioi Moi*) even published an article in May 1996 that described a 'new method for finding the burial place of soldiers.' This was a form of divination in which a family member placed one chopstick in the ground and tried to balance an egg on top of it. If the egg did not fall, the deceased's remains were directly below. This method apparently succeeded in finding the remains of several soldiers, including one who had been missing since December 1946 (Xuan Cang and Ly Dang Cao 1996:8–11).

Conclusion

Dead soldiers remain an important part of social life in Thinh Liet commune. Every year families and the local administration perform rites to commemorate and remember those who fell in battle. Public concern about war dead in the commune has been so great that in 1999 local residents forced the administration to move the war dead monument to a new location because many felt the old site, which faced the Giap Nhi communal house, was geomantically inauspicious and therefore disrespectful to the dead. The rites that the living conduct for the war dead, however, reveal that two distinct ontologies of war dead exist. Official rites commemorate the dead and restate the nobility of their deaths, but do not engage their souls nor admit of their souls' existence. Many of the officials performing the rites do privately admit to their existence, but the rites they perform as officials do not address this issue. Family rites mobilize a different ontology. In these rites, the dead soldiers' souls live on, and must be cared for and turned into benevolent ancestors. Despite these different ontologies, residents do not forego one set of rites and exclusively engage in the other. The rites are instead complementary. Families appreciate the honor and nobility official rites give to their loved ones who made the ultimate sacrifice, while their home rites ease their own concerns and help them give their loved ones peace.

CHAPTER SEVEN

Is Ho Chi Minh our Guardian Spirit?

Renegotiating Sacred Space and the Ritual Roles of Women

A survey of recent press coverage of contemporary Vietnamese cultural practices creates the impression that a revival of 'traditional' ceremonies has begun in communities across Vietnam (see Minh Phuc 1998; Nhat Binh 1998; Tuyet Minh 1998). Journalists have fanned out across the country to document and celebrate the return of practices long suppressed by the government. The folk song contests of Bac Ninh are now championed as venerable manifestations of traditional culture and other village ceremonies receive similar praise. Thinh Liet commune is no exception to this trend. In January 1993, a video crew from Hanoi Television spent several days in the commune recording the first 'village worship' (*te lang*) ceremony for the Giap Nhi village guardian spirit since 1946. The crew filmed a group of senior village men, wearing blue mandarinal robes and caps, solemnly worshiping the spirit in the communal house as a large assembly of villagers looked on. The year before, an elderly male villager had produced a long lost charter describing the ritual's proper conduct, which the men carefully followed. In the evenings of the previous thirty five days, the officiants had assembled in a local home to master the ritual's performance.

Despite its assertion of the resurrection of tradition, the documentary did not directly draw attention to a number of the ceremony's 'non-traditional' aspects. The chief officiant was not the village's highest ranking mandarin, but instead a party member who had retired to his natal village after serving as the director of Hanoi Television. (Of the nineteen other men who participated, ten were retired officials and six were party members). The participants' rank order was not determined by the year they had participated in the 'enter the village' (*vao lang*) initiation rite. In fact, there was no predetermined rank order for them, nor had there been an enter the village rite since the early 1950s. The invocation read by the chief officiant was not written in Sino-Vietnamese characters by a high-ranking mandarin. The ceremony did not involve the slaughter of any animals or feasting, even though the ritual charter dictated the slaughter of

189

several pigs and their later consumption by village men. The rites were not followed by a status-generating competition between the 'twelve chiefs,' a group of high status 54 year old men who had previously been responsible for coordinating and organizing communal house rites (see Malarney 1993:156–62). Money to conduct the rites did not come from the village budget, but instead from individual donations. Bystanders also talked during the rites, an offence formerly punishable by fine.

The most remarkable feature of the rites that the documentary failed to draw attention to was the participation of women. Compared to men, women in Vietnam had historically been, to borrow a phrase A. Thomas Kirsch used regarding Thai women, 'religiously "disadvantaged"' (Kirsch 1985:304). Even though at an everyday level women were more religiously and ritually active, they were at a definite disadvantage because men had monopolized the most prestigious religious roles, dominated the ecclesiastical hierarchies, and reserved for themselves the role of defining religious orthodoxy. The definitions of such largely female practices as spirit mediumship as superstitious had after all been propagated by male-dominated institutions. In such local practices as ancestral and communal house rites, female disadvantaging was also visible in the fact that although the outcome of the rites had direct consequences for women, they were dependent upon men to serve as the primary ritual officiants. The Thinh Liet documentary, however, inadvertently showed that the terms of female religious disadvantaging had changed and women could now conduct rites in the Giap Nhi communal house. Perhaps more significantly, the documentary also failed to note that the year before the female-dominated Giap Nhi Buddhist Association had organized its own 'village worship' in the communal house without the permission of local party officials. Held on the 15th of the 2nd lunar month, the stipulated date, this ceremony featured a large procession as well as exclusively female officiants. All other claims notwithstanding, this ceremony was in reality the first village worship conducted in the Giap Nhi communal house since 1946.

This chapter's purpose is to analyze changes in Thinh Liet communal house rites in order to understand the transformations in male and female ritual roles that have occurred since the 1940s. Revolutionary policies had brought an end to communal house rites in Thinh Liet. This orthodoxy, however, began to break down in the 1980s as residents began reasserting the sacredness of the communal houses. Since then, organized ritual activity has returned to Thinh Liet communal houses, but in an unexpected change, local women have stepped forward to assume roles in the rites formerly denied them. This chapter examines the various social and political factors that have produced the current situation. It should be well noted that Thinh Liet's case appears to be somewhat unique. In most other northern Vietnamese villages male control over communal house rites has remained (cf. Kleinen 1999:163–4; Luong 1993:271). Nevertheless, the resolution of such important questions as what sort of rites should be performed in the communal house, who can participate in those rites, and to which spirit those rites should be dedicated, illustrate the manner in which revolutionary policies have indirectly created a new structure for defining communal house rites that is, from a gender perspective, more egalitarian than before.

Communal Houses Under the Revolutionary State

At the conclusion of the land reform in January 1955, Giap Nhi and Giap Tu's communal houses lay empty. The former structure, though damaged during the war and land reform, was largely intact. Importantly, the inner sanctum (*hau cung*), where the guardian spirit's altar sat, had been left untouched, and many ritual objects, as well as the scroll that contained the guardian spirits' identities, remained. The Giap Tu communal house was in ruins. The altars were destroyed, the spirit charters gone, and little remained of the former structure. As discussed in Chapter 1, government policy endeavored to desacralize the communal houses and convert them into mundane spaces. At both sites, officials permitted the free entry of women and young men into the communal houses, but prohibited the conduct of any rituals on their premises. All administrative functions in the communal houses also ceased. These policies helped neutralize the structures' former exclusive and sacred associations. For the next twenty five years, the local administration maintained complete control over the communal houses and furthered the linked processes of desacralization and conversion to mundane usage. In the early 1960s, not long after the establishment of the agricultural cooperatives, the Giap Nhi cooperative appropriated the communal house and converted it into a rice warehouse. In a similar vein, the administration filled in a pond and tore down a geomantically auspicious set of three arches that formerly stood before the communal house in order to create a large, open area for drying paddy. The communal house's facade was then completely redone in 1980 when the administration put a large, two story brick addition on the front to serve as a meeting hall for official organizations. Giap Tu's history was similar. Renovations were carried out on the structure during the early years of collectivization, but only to convert it into another rice warehouse. Later on, the administration built a pre-school in the communal house's compound, filling it with scores of loud and rambunctious children.

Discontent and the Indications of Supernatural Efficacy

Thinh Liet residents did not universally support the campaign to desacralize the communal houses. Their inappropriate usage troubled many people, and others warned that misfortune would befall those who desecrated the sites. The devastation of the Giap Tu communal house prevented its covert utilization as a sacred site, but the treatment of Giap Nhi's revealed a deeper ambivalence. When the administration carried out the assortment of changes to the communal house, the inner sanctum was left untouched. Most villagers were forbidden from entering the room, but officials never emptied the room of its contents. The reason for this is unclear, but was most likely related to secret persuasion of local officials by their senior kin who found the administration's actions objectionable. Furthermore, the designation of Lao Tsu as Giap Nhi's guardian spirit by the revered ancestor Bui Huy Bich of the numerically and politically dominant Bui lineage could also have created a measure of reluctance to anger the ancestors as well as the guardian spirit. No one has yet to declare that the guardian spirit was clandestinely propitiated during the 1960s or early 1970s, but the sacred infrastructure remained hidden in the back of the warehouse.

Silent discontent with the policy continued into the late 1970s, when the first stirrings of popular desire to reconsecrate the communal houses appeared. In 1977, Giap Tu residents began very minor, individual propitiations in the communal house. Residents then restored a small altar area. Official opposition to any larger-scale re-emergence focussed on the proposed non-existence of supernatural entities. Guardian spirits did not exist, therefore residents should not waste their energies and resources propitiating them. This remained the status quo for several years until an unexpected event occurred in the early 1980s. The reconstruction of the Giap Tu communal house as a warehouse had involved the construction of one small building at the back of the compound where the inner sanctum had been located, and one larger building before that. The inner building was used to store small implements, while the outer building was the main warehouse. Late one evening a local youth, considered a hooligan by other villagers, climbed onto the outer building's roof. In what he perceived to be an amusing prank, he stood at the roof's edge and urinated onto the inner building and the ground below. When he awoke the next morning, much to his surprise, he was unable to relieve himself. The condition persisted throughout the day, resulting in a trip to a local hospital. Unfortunately, the doctors could not help him. The problem continued into the following day, and involved another trip to the hospital, but still no resolution. Giap Tu residents relate that at this point another village family contacted the young man's family and declared that the cause of his blockage was the guardian spirit's anger from the urination incident. If the family assembled a small set of offerings and asked the guardian spirit's forgiveness, the problem would end. The family did, and as expected, the young man could freely urinate again.

Exact details of this story are difficult to confirm, but what is clear is that this incident assumed an important role in public discourse about the need to restore the communal house as a sacred site. Contrary to the party's claims, the young man's blockage served as proof of the Giap Tu guardian spirit's continued efficacy and the necessity to properly worship the spirit. Armed with this incident to support them, Thinh Liet residents increased the pressure on local leaders to restore the communal houses, and by the mid-1980s they began to respond. By the late 1980s, the local cooperatives vacated the communal houses in both Giap Nhi and Giap Tu. Each also donated significant sums of money to begin their restoration. The agricultural cooperative of Giap Tu donated three million dong ($300) for the communal house renovation and another three million for chairs, tables, and a new drum. By the end of the 1980s, villagers had reclaimed the communal houses, but ritual practice was still confined to individual propitiation of the spirit, usually on the first and fifteenth of every lunar month.

Gender and the Politics of Resurgence

On 14 May 1991 (1st of the 5th lunar month), the people of Giap Nhi organized an 'entering summer' (*vao he*) ceremony in their communal house. The ceremony began early in the morning. Before nine o'clock, twenty to thirty people had filed into the communal house, many carrying aluminium trays upon which they had heaped glutinous rice and often a cooked pig's head. At nine o'clock, a local man lit a string of firecrackers before the entrance and announced the ceremony's commencement. The ceremony inside was quite simple and gave many indications that a ritual orthodoxy had yet to be established. Unlike pre-revolutionary rites, there was no ritual hierarchy nor specific set of officiants. When the ceremony began, the people already assembled performed a brief set of organized supplications, but over the next several hours residents came in as they wished. They carried offerings of their own choosing, though again usually trays with rice and other items, which they placed on the main offering platform. Most strikingly, some ninety percent of the participants were women, dressed in the long brown robes and black headbands seen at Buddhist temples. A number of men stood on the side, often remarking that men knew more about organizing communal house rituals, but they remained spectators. The women also propitiated in the ways they felt most comfortable. Some simply bent slightly over and quickly raised and lowered incense sticks clasped between their palms three times, while others performed elaborate kowtows in which they repeatedly knelt down and stood up before the altar. Others sat on the mats before the altar for long periods, engrossed in prayer. Participants also came for different reasons. In the anteroom, some women purchased, for five hundred dong, large sheets of brown paper with '*so cau phuc tho*' inscribed on them in red letters. On these sheets, which had been printed by the Hanoi Buddhist

193

Association, participants wrote people's names. They then placed them on the altar, said a brief prayer, and later burned them. In doing so, they asked the Buddha and the Boddhisatva Avalokitesvara (*Quan The Am*) to bring peace, safety, and longevity to the person whose name had been inscribed. They also asked that 'The country be at peace, the people warm and full' (*To quoc hoa binh, nhan dan am no*). Other participants noted that they had come to bring health and happiness to their family members, particularly the elderly. Others sought to make merit (*cong duc*) for themselves by donating money to the communal house. Confusion also existed over which spirit they worshiped. One woman mistakenly declared that the Giap Nhi guardian spirit was Confucius. Such confusion aside, the presentation of petitions to members of the Buddhist pantheon represented a major innovation.

Women had stepped forward to lead the return to communal house ceremonies for several reasons. As discussed in Chapter 3, most women never renounced their links to the supernatural throughout the reform period. An examination of official publications on ritual reform and the campaign against superstitions illustrates that throughout the period, cadres had the least success in persuading women, particularly the elderly, to abandon their religious practices. In Thinh Liet, elderly women had exercised a behind-the-scenes influence on the conduct of the reform campaign. In the fifth neighborhood of Giap Nhi, for example, sat a large spirit shrine (*dien*) maintained by members of the Bui lineage. Official policy mandated the conversion of this structure to a useful purpose, such as housing, but lobbying by elderly female lineage mates on their male juniors in the administration prevented its enforcement. Women had similar success in influencing the course of funeral reforms. Women also enjoyed a structural advantage compared to men. Despite its claims to institutionalize gender equality in Vietnam, the party and government remained heavily male dominated (see Porter 1993:37). Thinh Liet had the exceptional occurrence of a woman serving as President of the Communal People's Committee in the 1980s, but her case aside, men still dominated the local party and administrative apparatus. Consequently, women had greater freedom in social and cultural affairs. Fear of official criticism or punishment prevented a number of males who might have logically stepped forward to lead the resurgence from doing so.

Without such political encumbrances, many women openly championed the resacralization cause without fear of serious retribution. The most vigorous lobbyists in the wake of the urination incident were elderly women. Importantly, women were the most organized religiously. As discussed in Chapter 4, the female-dominated Buddhist Associations had continued to clandestinely exist from the 1950s onward. Their main function had been secret night-time chanting in people's homes on the night before burial in funeral ceremonies. When the reform policies began to relax, this group assumed a more public role, first in chanting at funerals, and later in organized worship at the temple. They also began appropriating communal houses as venues where village women could perform religious rites.

Giap Nhi as Leader of the Resurgence

The Thinh Liet Buddhist Association was strong in both Giap Nhi and Giap Tu, but the members of the former village pushed more vigorously for a return to communal house ritual. In many ways, Giap Nhi's lead followed historical precedent. Of all villages in Thinh Liet, Giap Nhi was always the most educated and politically powerful. Giap Nhi set the cultural standard for all villages in the commune, and its communal house served as the de facto center of all commune-level rituals. The week-long celebrations of all villages in pre-revolutionary Thinh Liet, for example, concluded with two days of festivities at the Giap Nhi communal house. Leaders from the other villages attended the Giap Nhi ceremony, while Giap Nhi leaders attended no others, and at the final feast in Giap Nhi, leaders of the other villages were obliged to sit at trays below those of the Giap Nhi leaders. The conduct of the 'entering summer' ceremony in 1991 was one of the first large ceremonies organized in either communal house. Over the following months, other large ceremonies were held in both communal houses, particularly at the turning of the lunar new year in January 1992.

The first 'village worship' was held on 8 March 1992, the 15th of the 2nd lunar month. Preparations for the ceremony had begun weeks before with the repainting of the communal house interior and the refurbishment of a number of ritual objects inside that had been left unattended since the land reform. This included refinishing two wooden cranes, a large wooden buffalo, and a large wooden horse. Early in the morning of the 15th, village women had prepared the altars with flowers and set up tables and chairs in an anteroom to receive guests. The ceremony began at 8:00 am when a village man ignited a string of firecrackers before the communal house entrance. Over the next ninety minutes, large numbers of older women slowly filled the area before the communal house. Some entered inside. At around 9:15 am, a loud and vigorous woman in her fifties dressed in a gold tunic and black headband started marshaling people into a procession line before the communal house entrance. Except for three men playing a flute, gong, and lyre respectively, the procession consisted only of women, dressed in the brown and black outfit worn to temples. As the lead woman barked out orders for where to stand, it became clear that the main principle determining the procession's order was relative age as the oldest women went to the front, their juniors to the back. This principle of genealogical seniority has defined the seating and ritual order for lay participants in Thinh Liet Buddhist rites up to the present day (see also

Luong 1993:271–72). In a clear reference to local concerns regarding purity, pollution, and ritual propriety, the leader elicited a chuckle from more than one bystander when she warned all of the women that they should not enter without first lighting incense sticks, asked if they had bathed before coming, and then yelled out that all menstruating women should leave the procession and not enter the communal house. No one left the line. Once the people were in their appropriate places, the procession headed off at 9:30 am.

The oldest women led the way, many of them holding colorful flags attached to short sticks. The procession, which now numbered several hundred people including onlookers, worked its way down Giap Nhi's main thoroughfare, then turned left on the narrow street that connected, via a short bridge over the Set River, Giap Nhi with Giap Tu. Just before the river's edge, the procession stopped and the lead elements entered a family compound. The stop in the family compound was the symbolically critical part of the journey. Historically, the village worship ceremony represented a form of regeneration in the village. The first segment of this process was the pre-ceremonial cleaning of the communal house, the last segment the replenishment of purified water in the communal house and the 'changing of the clothes' (*thay quan ao*) of the guardian spirit. This latter metaphor referred to the replacement of a pair of mandarin-style paper boots and hat that villagers kept on a chair on top of the cabinet for the guardian spirit in the communal house's inner sanctum. The rite's performance was an annual responsibility and its completion in the village worship entailed the reinvigoration of the cult for another year. Historically, villagers classified the replenishment of the water and changing of the clothes ceremonies as 'retrieval' (*ruoc*) ceremonies. This meant that the ceremony involved the formation of a procession to obtain the necessary item and then its transport back to the communal house. In the pre-revolutionary 'water retrieval' (*ruoc nuoc*) ceremony, a group of young men carried a palanquin supporting an empty vat to the village of Phap Van in Thanh Tri district. There, they filled the vat with water from a local well, and carried it back to Giap Nhi. Performance of this ceremony ended in the 1940s. The changing of the clothes ceremony was accomplished through the performance of the 'votive paper objects retrieval' (*ruoc ma*), another reference to collecting the paper boots and hat. For this rite, the 'twelve chiefs' selected a family renowned for its skill in making votive paper objects, and contracted out one pair of boots, one hat, and two 'gold trees' (*cay vang*). They could select whomever they desired. In different years they obtained the items from Giap Nhat, Giap Luc, and even Cho Mo in Hanoi's southern outskirts. The Giap Nhi home at which the March 1992 procession halted was that of a family famous for the production of votive paper objects. During the years of the strict enforcement of the policies against superstitions, the family had

196

clandestinely continued to produce paper objects. Following the relaxation of cultural policies in the late 1980s and early 1990s, they had emerged as one of the two most skilled producers in Thinh Liet. Working from the historical example familiar to them, the Giap Nhi women organizing the village worship had placed an order with the family for the boots, hat, and trees. Given the difficulties of hauling water from distant Phap Van, and the close proximity of a well right next to the Giap Nhi communal house, the women had decided to forego the water retrieval ceremony, making the retrieval of the paper objects the centerpiece of their ceremony.

Once inside the family compound, women from the procession picked up the hat, boots, and two gold trees, along with three trays of glutinous rice with a cooked pig's head on each. When men performed the ceremony, the only individuals entitled to carry the objects back to the communal house were members of the twelve chiefs who were physically healthy and had both sons and daughters, with preference given to those of highest rank in the group. In line with the previously mentioned concern with pollution, the five women selected to carry back the objects were elderly, unmarried widows. These women were considered 'cleaner' (*sach se hon*), a reference to the fact that they would not have been exposed to the pollution of sexual intercourse, and, given their age, had probably ceased menstruating, a question the ethnographer did not feel comfortable confirming directly. After picking up the items, the procession reversed its course and returned to the communal house with the sacred items in the forefront.

The formal segment of the ceremony concluded when the elderly women placed the trays and paper objects on altars inside the communal house. They placed the hat and boots on an altar directly adjacent to the inner sanctum, the rice and pig-head trays on the large offering platform in the center of the communal house, and the golden trees on both sides of the platform. By this point, the communal house was packed, with a noticeable predominance of women over men. Many people had come individually, carrying their own trays of food that they placed on the altars. Some also brought belts of firecrackers that they lit before entering, creating an unceasing wave of explosions throughout the morning. After propitiating the guardian spirit, the trays became sanctified food (*loc*) that the individuals later took home to share with their families as eating loc is said to bring good fortune. Many people also came and donated money to the communal house. In the anteroom next to the entrance sat several women who collected money and recorded each donor's name. Such donations were 'meritorious work' that would help bring good fortune. The majority of donations ranged from 2,000 to 10,000 dong, but word spread quickly throughout the communal house that one Giap Nhi resident living abroad had donated 500,000 dong. These individual donations, most of which had been made possible by the recent improvements in

Thinh Liet's economy, had proven crucial as Giap Nhi alone had collected several million dong in donations that they had used to sponsor rituals and renovate the communal house. Unlike in the pre-revolutionary period in which the public budget subsidized communal house rituals, residents' voluntary contributions were now the foundation for local ritual life, thus economic development has helped create the conditions for ritual growth.[1] In addition to individual participation, each of the five Giap Nhi neighborhoods had also slaughtered one pig that they brought into the communal house, 'to present to the guardian spirit.' They then had a feast for their residents over 50 years old. In an ironic appropriation of revolutionary rhetoric, the feasts took the name of 'Unity Meals' (*Com Doan Ket*), the name formerly used for the annual banquets for agricultural cooperative members. Previously, these meals had been held on the Vietnamese National Day, but that year they had chosen to switch back to the schedule linked to the traditional ritual cycle.

The participation of men in the ceremonies was rather complicated. Inside the communal house were large numbers of men, but only women actually went forward to propitiate the guardian spirit. Most men simply stood on the sides and watched, sometimes offering up such discontented opinions as, 'anything goes, now that the administration lets it.' A number of local men had been reluctant to involve themselves in the preparation or festivities. Some of these had 'followed the revolution' (*theo cach mang*) and their friends noted that it was 'difficult for them to change back.' Another small group remained aloof because they had participated in the damaging of the communal house during the land reform. Such men were said to 'feel awkward' (*nguong*). Male influence was present, however, behind the scenes. One main focus of pre-ceremonial debate was the colors women would wear during the ceremony. When attending Buddhist temple ceremonies, Vietnamese women wear the previously mentioned brown and black outfits. When participating in spirit medium ceremonies (*dong bong*), women forego the modest colors of the temple and don bright silk tunics of green, gold, and red. Many Thinh Liet residents consider dressing in bright colors slightly inappropriate, hence the common criticism of a brightly clad woman as 'very dong bong.' Many of the women active in organizing the entering summer ceremony were also active in spirit medium ceremonies. Their clothing preference for the day was their bright red tunics, but the men objected. Bright colors in the communal house, they argued, were if not bad, then at least 'inappropriate' (*khong hop*). Such colors were spirit medium colors and the boundaries should not be blurred. Moreover, some other colors the women sought to wear, such as blue or purple, were male mandarin colors, and therefore also inappropriate. The vast majority of women acceded to the male requests not to wear bright colors and wore their regular temple outfit. The leading woman, however, was not persuaded by such arguments. She wore her gold tunic. Afterwards, a number of men openly complained about this choice as gold is the color of kings, princes, and princesses. Subsequently, gold tunics on women have become visible in many communal house ceremonies.

Is Ho Chi Minh Our Guardian Spirit?

The return of the village worship ceremony in Giap Nhi was not only a stimulus to other villages in the commune to proceed with the organization of their own ceremonies. It also clearly displayed the fact that communal house rites had become an area of contestation and negotiation between men and women. In reconstructing the rites, groups from both genders attempted to impose their ideas upon ritual organization, each with varying degrees of success. While Giap Nhi's case initiated this process, it was even more vividly played out in Giap Tu where a public debate regarding the identity of the village guardian spirit began in late 1990 and did not end until early 1996. The origins of this debate trace back to the loss of the spirit charter either by chance in the early twentieth century or through its destruction in the battle fought between Giap Tu guerrillas and French forces in February 1947. Spirit charters were a codification of the village guardian spirit's identity as well as the identity of any other lesser spirits worshiped in the communal house. Elite village men read out their biographies in communal ceremonies, and the mandarinate periodically scrutinized the charters in order to ensure their accordance with official ideology. Despite the rather portentous ideas put forth regarding the sacredness of the village guardian spirit, their identities did periodically change, either through local activities or through a spirit's promotion or demotion by the government. In some cases, this change was the result of actions by a determined individual, such as the appointment of Lao Tsu as the Giap Nhi guardian spirit by the high-ranking mandarin Bui Huy Bich. A more common cause of change was the recognition that the guardian spirit had lost its effectiveness and no longer adequately cared for the community. One such case occurred in the early twentieth century when another Thinh Liet mandarin, Bui Trac, visited another village in Thanh Tri district. Trac visited the village on official business, but, unbeknownst to him, he arrived on the day of the annual village wrestling festival. This was a tournament organized by the village in which local men, dressed only in loincloths, wrestled each other for village honors. On the day of his visit, the ground was wet and muddy, covering the men with dirt as they wrestled. As he walked into the tournament area, Trac came upon a group of dirty men dressed in loincloths, causing him to exclaim, 'What kind of guardian spirit would allow such an event to be held!' Local leaders apparently took Trac's words to heart, and began to question their spirit's efficacy and legitimacy. Not long after this incident, Trac died, and the village leaders installed his spirit as their guardian spirit.

199

The 1947 damaging of the communal house, its subsequent neglect for almost forty years, and the death, suffering, and hardship that befell villagers throughout that period, produced a similar sense of doubt among many Giap Tu men regarding their guardian spirit's efficacy. Historically, the Giap Tu spirit was a doctor of herbal medicine who had lived in the village. As is standard in the appointment of a guardian spirit, he had performed a 'meritorious work' that had brought great benefit to the community. In his case, he had played a major role in limiting the spread of a village epidemic and treating its victims, all without payment. The loss of the charter, and the four decades of ritual inactivity, ruptured the transmission of knowledge of his identity. In 1991, some villagers were aware of his name, *Ong Duc Tam Lang* or simply *Ong Lang*, because of a prohibition against mentioning his name, which was a homonym for a type of sweet potato (*khoai lang*) grown locally. Villagers had to refer to khoai lang as *khoai giay* in order to avoid violating the taboo, thereby maintaining knowledge of his name. Details regarding his biography, beyond being a doctor and his role in the epidemic, were not widely known. During dozens of interviews, no one could definitively state when he had lived or any details of his life, something unthinkable in Giap Nhi. Furthermore, in 1991, a number of interviewees were even unclear about the doctor element in his biography, a deficiency that would disappear by mid-1992 as a codified version of his biography began to circulate.

When renovations began on the Giap Tu communal house in the late 1980s, a number of issues animated local discussions. Apart from rededicating the building to the guardian spirit, local women also wanted a place in the village where the elderly of both genders could gather to conduct 'rites' (*le*). They argued that it was too difficult for many of them to regularly make the trip to Set Temple. The real argument, as evident in the destination, was that the trip to the temple was too difficult for elderly women to make, thus a space in the village was needed for female practices, mostly of a Buddhist nature. The political climate at this time, however, was still quite delicate. Village men, though sympathetic to female concerns, feared taking a step that might lead to punishment or criticism. The secretary of the commune's party cell had declared that if the women started building altars in the communal house he would send officials to destroy it. The men also feared the possible conversion of the communal house into a space for Buddhist rites. Thus, when the initial communal house renovations were completed in 1988, they implemented an innovative solution. The main altar inside the communal house was flanked by one altar on each side. The central altar was traditionally dedicated to the guardian spirit. When the men refurbished the altars, they placed an incense urn dedicated to the worship of the souls of village dead on the right side. On the left, they placed a second urn dedicated to the worship of the souls of revolutionary martyrs. And in the center, they placed a large, white plaster bust of Ho Chi Minh. This statue's placement, the variety of which one commonly sees in government offices, and its accompaniment by an urn for war dead, allowed local men to steer clear of political sanction by claiming that the restored communal house was dedicated to paying appropriate respect to local people who had given their lives for the fatherland, while also commemorating the revolution's greatest hero.

Supporters of the Ho bust placement, almost exclusively older men with party backgrounds, could initially claim that the statue was there for strictly commemorative purposes, but by 1991 their position had evolved into an assertion that Ho Chi Minh should become the Giap Tu guardian spirit. The former spirit, they argued, was ineffective, and no person in Vietnam had greater 'meritorious work' with the people than Ho. He was therefore a logical choice. The idea that a political leader could become a tutelary spirit after death has deep roots in Vietnamese history (see Malarney 1996a). A number of cults have developed around heroic leaders, particularly those who succeeded in freeing Vietnam from foreign domination. Tran Hung Dao has the most vibrant cult, but Trieu Au and the Trung sisters' also have active cults (see Taylor 1983:336). The selection of Ho as a guardian spirit accorded with this pattern. Ho had succeeded in ridding the country of foreign occupation, thus the powers he possessed while alive transferred to the supernatural realm, where humans can draw upon them for assistance and protection. Some Thinh Liet residents even asserted that Ho had supernatural links in his lifetime, saying that he was a living god (*than song*) sent by the heavens to help liberate Vietnam.[2] Worship of Ho in the communal house, the men declared, was just another manifestation of the widespread worship of 'national heroes' (*anh hung dan toc*).

Not all segments of Giap Tu society willingly accepted the designation of Ho as the new guardian spirit. Young people, absorbed in raising children and making ends meet, were ambivalent about the matter, but elderly women opposed the action vigorously. Their objections took many forms. At the simplest level, they did not like the plaster bust. The communal house was a sacred place of worship, they argued. The bust created an atmosphere similar to a government office, making any engagement or communion with the sacred difficult. At another level, many felt that the designation was part of male conspiracy, orchestrated through such official organs as the village unit of the Fatherland Front, to constrain female religious practices. By mid-1991, the Giap Tu communal house had become a site for the regular conduct of Buddhist rites. A charismatic young nun from Set Temple had started to lead chanting sessions there that large numbers of local women attended. The insertion of Ho as the guardian spirit, they felt, was part of a broader effort to remove traditionally unsanctioned practices from the communal house and

201

thereby prevent women from using the communal house for their own religious needs. Finally, many women contended that there was no reason to install a new guardian spirit since the village already had one. Claims by local men about the herbal doctor's purported ineffectiveness received little support. Events such as the young man's blockage demonstrated the spirit's continued efficacy, thus the responsibility of village residents was to properly worship and propitiate that spirit. To do otherwise could bring negative consequences.

The impasse lasted for over a year. To help defuse the situation, men from the Elderly Association and women from the Buddhist Association met several times to negotiate a settlement. The future presence of women in the communal house was by this point assured, but the disposition of the altars remained undetermined. In late 1991, both sides reached a mutually agreeable solution. The men accepted the removal of the plaster bust, but Ho's presence would be maintained through the construction of a cabinet for the main altar that would serve as the seat of the guardian spirit. The choice of the cabinet had interesting historical associations. Reluctant to design a cabinet of their own, villagers hired a carpenter to travel to the village of Nhi Khe, the natal village of Nguyen Trai, a famous fifteenth century national hero. There, the carpenter studied the cabinet that sits on the main altar in his shrine, and returned to construct an exact replica to house Ho's spirit. The feature of the large, black and gold lacquer cabinet that facilitated its acceptability was its folding front doors. The men hung a lacquer portrait of Ho inside. If the assembled congregation sought to worship him, they could open the cabinet doors. If they felt it inappropriate, they could simply close them. Men and women could therefore carry out their desired practices in the same sacred space. Nevertheless, the portrait's placement in the cabinet was a definitive assertion that Ho was the village guardian spirit.

Giap Tu residents installed the new cabinet with the Ho portrait in February 1992. Although there was never a formal installation ceremony, most villagers came to accept Ho as if not the main village guardian spirit, then at least as one of the guardian spirits, along with the herbal doctor. During this same month residents organized the innovatory rite dedicated to those killed in the 1947 battle with the French. In fitting syncretic fashion, the nun from Set temple served as the main ritual officiant and local women chanted in the communal house, even though men were also in attendance. When the ceremonies concluded at mid-day the souls of the dead were officially installed in an urn in the communal house. These rites constituted one of the first large-scale ceremonial events held in the Giap Tu communal house.

From 1992 to 1996, ritual practices within the communal house alternated between Buddhist chanting led by the Set Temple nun, chanting led by a male Giap Tu spirit priest, and more orthodox rites dedicated to the guardian spirits. Women dominated the former two events, and large numbers of them also visited the communal house on the 1st and 15th of every lunar month. Other significant ritual days were the first day of the lunar year, the 'entering summer' ceremony, and the traditional day of the village worship, the 13th of the 2nd lunar month. When women performed rites on these days, they adhered to a fixed hierarchy in their propitiations, beginning with the herbal doctor guardian spirit, moving to Ho Chi Minh and former village mandarins, and finishing with prayers and chants addressed to the Buddha. This order illustrated the many discordant layers of ritual practice in the communal house. Unlike Giap Nhi, Giap Tu never organized a large village worship ceremony during this period. Rites were held on the stipulated day, but instead of such large scale activities as a procession or a feast, only a modest number of male and female villagers conducted rites in the communal house on that morning. Many arrived later according to their own schedules. The comparatively undeveloped ritual schedule did not, however, indicate collective disinterest. During the same period, villagers donated several million dong to finance extensive renovations as well as the purchase of furniture and new items for the altars. In 1994, residents added a new roof to cover the open space between the communal house's inner and outer sections, thereby transforming it into one continuous, enclosed structure. This added greatly to the available floor area. Compared to the relatively open space of the early 1990s, the communal house had become much more somber and solemn.

Despite the peaceful coexistence that had evolved over the issue of Ho Chi Minh as guardian spirit, discontent still existed among a number of village women. In early 1996, their position received unexpected support from the communal administration. Although no one was willing to openly declare from what level it had originated, pressure was put on the administration to end all cultic activities devoted to Ho. Giap Tu had not been alone in initiating such a cult. In December 1995, the government disbanded a Ho cult in a village in Vinh Phu province, northwest of Hanoi, where the organized worship of Ho as the 18th king in the mythical Hung dynasty had begun (Mydans 1996:A4).[3] Concerned about the proliferation of such unorthodox rites, high level officials appear to have learned of the Giap Tu practices and ordered their cessation. Giap Tu responded by taking down the Ho portrait and hanging it in another building in the communal house compound. Orders to remove the portrait spurred on a broader debate regarding the disposition of the altars. The communal house, with its diverse practices, had become like 'a house the master has left' (*nha vang chu*). There was no proper order or structure. Things were just done according to whim or desire. An initial focus of dispute was the war dead altar. Although everyone agreed that villagers should pay proper respect to those who had given their lives for the nation and revolution, some deemed the communal house an inappropriate place for such activities. Therefore, the altar to the war dead was cleared, resulting in no exclusive place to commemorate them in the village until Giap Tu residents constructed a war dead monument in the communal house compound in 1997. Some of the final arguments supporting the altar's removal revealed the extent of change that had already occurred. Village women who opposed the war dead altar matter of factly declared that the communal house was for worshiping the village guardian spirit and conducting Buddhist chants, not for propitiating souls of war dead. The fact that fifty years ago Buddhist rites were uniformly excluded from communal houses remained unspoken. At present, the doctor of herbal medicine has returned as Giap Tu's official guardian spirit and his spirit rests in the black lacquer cabinet on the main altar. Some male villagers are still not content and in 1997 unsuccessfully attempted to gain popular support for the installation of the spirit of a famous general from the pre-modern period. The altar on the main altar's left is now dedicated to the guardian spirit of the communal house land, while that on the right is for the people who originally built the communal house. Although the removal of the Ho portrait from the cabinet might indicate the end of cultic practices devoted to his spirit, the octogenarian keeper of the communal house noted that many people still come to the communal house to pay their respects and ask Ho's spirit for assistance.

Redefining Communal House Rites

The January 1993 village worship ceremony conducted by the Giap Nhi men represented a deliberate attempt to reclaim their communal house as a space for organized male ritual. Local men had not been particularly happy with the female ceremony and then, surprisingly, an elderly male villager discovered a copy of the village worship charter from the 1940s. One point not presented in the telling of this story was the fact that the charter had undoubtedly long been hidden in his home, most likely tucked away in a safe place by a family member during the land reform. The men pursued a different course than the women when they began organizing their ceremony. They first formed a 'ceremony association' (*hoi te*) and then, in one man's words, 'asked the opinions of the party,' an expression for asking permission from the administration. No serving officials participated, but they immediately gave their permission, albeit conditionally. They supported the ceremonial aspects, but these had to focus on ritual activities considered part of the people's legitimate 'religious practices' (*tin nguong*) and not 'superstitions,' an indirect way to constrain the introduction of some practices favored by women. They also objected to feasting because, in standard party fashion, they considered it wasteful, but they also feared it might produce public drunkenness that could lead to arguments and insults that might 'erode solidarity' (*mat doan ket*). Feasting was therefore banned, though snack foods were acceptable, and local drunks were warned to be on their best behavior.

The invocation of the idea of legitimate 'religious practices' (*tin nguong*), as well as the statement by the local authorities that they were 'giving permission for the renovation of the people's "traditions"' (*truyen thong*), illustrated the extent to which official attitudes toward communal house rites had changed. As noted in Chapter One, one of the more remarkable characteristics of official documents on ritual reform is that they contain very little discussion of communal house rites. While the government sought to appropriate weddings, funerals, death anniversaries, and other ceremonies to advance official ideology, communal house rites received little direct mention. In some cases 'festivals' (*hoi*) were mentioned, but most documents did not declare whether these festivals were organized in communal houses, shrines, or temples. What was clear was that the government only reluctantly allowed their organization and that they sought to control them. A 24 January 1958 government instruction (*chi thi*) declared people could organize festivals, but they needed to receive official permission first. The festivals were also not to include any 'outdated practices' (*hu tuc*) or superstitions. Instead, the festivals were only to celebrate 'national heroes' (*anh hung dan toc*) (Vietnam, Government Gazette 1958:31–2). A 1974 speech by the Minister of Culture Hoang Minh Giam indicated that the organization of festivals had continued, and that cadres were to preserve the same anti-superstitious, patriotic character (Vietnam, Ministry of Culture 1975:33–4). A year later, the government revealed that village festivals specifically had continued, but as they stated, 'With regard to village festivals (*hoi lang*) in the countryside, those that have not been organized for a long period of time cannot be reorganized' (Vietnam, Ministry of Culture 1975:43), while those with a patriotic or 'religious' (*ton giao*) character could remain. By the early 1990s the government's attitude had changed. Communal house rites had begun returning all over the country. Officials accepted them, but then attempted to gain control over them by again advocating the retention of patriotic elements and exclusion of unsanctioned elements. In a peculiar way, communal house rites thus re-emerged in the official cultural agenda. By 1996, a scholar could even publish such a book as 'Religious Practices Regarding Vietnamese Village Guardian Spirits' (*Tin Nguong Thanh Hoang Viet Nam*) and conclude it by asserting that communal house rites and the worship of guardian spirits should be further developed in order to unite all of the people in building a strong and rich nation (Nguyen Duy Hinh 1996:411).[4] Changing government attitudes toward communal house rites and their redesignation as worthy cultural practices allowed Thinh Liet officials to permit the reorganization of the ceremonies, but at the same time established their boundaries so that residents could only perform certain types of rites.

Giap Nhi men were very pleased with their ceremony's outcome. The thirty five days of practice served them well. The mandarinal attire and carefully performed rituals created the desired atmosphere of solemnity, and the ceremony had gone off without incident. Since 1993, the men have continued to exclusively perform the village worship on the 15th of the 2nd lunar month, although women do enter the communal house and can make offerings afterwards. The appropriation of this ceremony has not entailed the removal of all female-organized practices in the communal houses. In both Giap Nhi and Giap Tu, women regularly gather for chanting, particularly on the 1st and 15th of every lunar month, and have also taken over the entering and exiting summer ceremonies. The former ceremony in particular has become one of the grandest female ceremonies in Giap Nhi. Unlike the 1991 ceremony's rather disorganized character, contemporary ceremonies have a more strictly defined ritual structure with women dressed in bright gold tunics lining up in rows in the anteroom as a senior woman leads the syncretic Buddhist/guardian spirit ceremony. Although men still object to the women's choice of colors, they have become a standard part of the ceremony. Since 1996 local officials have also lost their reluctance to participate in the rites and now play important roles. Although I have not attended any of these later rites, participants have commented that the President of the People's Committee now leads the Giap Nhi procession during the retrieval rites. Unlike the practices of even five years ago, communal house rites have become a domain of legitimate activity for all residents.

Conclusion

Contemporary Thinh Liet communal house rites constitute a major departure from their pre-revolutionary antecedents. No longer the home of an exclusive adult male guardian spirit cult, the communal house has become a male and female ritual space. The rites performed there now involve people from across the population and draw on the diverse practices of different local groups. The rites' financing has also changed from an obligatory part of the local budget to voluntary, and therefore meritorious, contributions. Men and women are united in the idea that some rites in the communal house should be dedicated to the guardian spirit, but beyond that they disagree. Most men argue that communal house rites should focus exclusively on the guardian spirits, but women have inserted a significant element of Buddhist practice into the ritual repertoire. More than one Thinh Liet man has commented that 'a communal house is not a place for Buddhist rites.' A large number of Giap Tu men lament what they see as the conversion of their communal house into a temple. Many men in both villages also refuse to participate in Buddhist rites in the communal house, though they might at a temple.

For many women, however, the communal house is a sacred space for all villagers, thus they should be allowed to perform whatever rites they desire within. In examining this change analytically, it is clear that in Thinh Liet, the revolutionary policies designed to desacralize communal houses and end elite male control over their rituals resulted in the destruction of the status quo ante in which one particular social group defined communal house orthodoxy. What had previously belonged to local men became common property and women actively created a role for themselves in it. In the process, not only have they become important agents in the struggle to define local orthodoxy, they have also become the relative equals of men. Whereas fifty years ago, Thinh Liet women were 'religiously disadvantaged' compared to local men, they now enter the arena as legitimate actors with a powerful voice in the definition and conduct of communal house rites. The recent actions of Giap Nhi men to take over their village worship and of Giap Tu men to install a new guardian spirit both indicate that local men are not willing to capitulate to their female co-villagers. The officiation by the President of the People's Committee and the more clearly defined ritual roles in Giap Nhi rites might also potentially indicate that the relative egalitarianism of the earlier rites will be replaced by more hierarchical forms. Such issues aside, what is clear is that as the years pass both male and female Thinh Liet residents will continue to play a role in defining communal house orthodoxy.

Conclusion
Morality and Meaning in a Changing World

The epigraph for this book comes from a passage in Dostoevsky's novel *The Possessed*, in which the character Shatov attempts to delineate the features that define a nation's distinctiveness. A nation is only a nation, he argues, when it has its own distinctive god. Rome, he asserts, was distinctive because it had its own god, the state. France was a true nation because of its embrace of atheism. And a socialist state would become a nation through the exclusive enshrinement of science and reason. A nation is convinced of its own truth, and once it begins to share its god, which he describes as 'the synthetic person of the whole nation,' its distinctiveness is lost. A nation must therefore defend its own god, give it definitive pride of place, and relentlessly rule out all other gods. The passage, written in the 1860s, was strangely prophetic as it inadvertently anticipated what would become one of the most important components of revolutionary socialist states, their efforts to 'drive all other gods from the world.'

One of this study's main objectives has been to describe the other gods that the Vietnamese Communists wanted to drive from the world, how they attempted to do that, and what they hoped to install as their own new God. It is indisputable that Vietnamese revolutionary policies have fundamentally altered the cultural world and conceptualizations of 'reality' for the residents of Thinh Liet commune. Revolutionary policies introduced their own sets of facts about the true nature of the world, and many of these have achieved a remarkable degree of public acceptance. Forced marriage is bad, voluntary marriage is good, policy families should be cared for, war dead should be remembered, Ho Chi Minh is a worthy moral example to follow, polygamy is feudal, children should not be symbolically debased in funerals, the list goes on and on. For a large portion of the Thinh Liet population, these assertions have achieved the fusion of 'facticity and validity' of which Habermas spoke. They are simply true statements and in some cases have entered into the realm of taken for granted knowledge. Other assertions have become a part of local reality, but the link between facticity and validity is much more tenuous and open to debate. Feasting is wasteful, supernatural causality does not exist in human life, material items are not needed to reproduce sentimental relations, astrological auspiciousness is not required for a ritual's success, science can cure society's ills, and so forth. Such ideas are part of Thinh Liet's reality. Residents cannot simply 'wish them away,' but some might reject them, others might agree with them, and others might simply be ambivalent. The existence of this latter category illustrates that despite the often extraordinary lengths to which Vietnamese authorities went, they were never able to completely impress their vision upon the people of Thinh Liet. As the commune's history has shown, people have often brought their own meanings, values, and agendas to social life, and these have sometimes taken precedence over elements from the official cultural agenda. Phrased another way, the gods of the revolution never completely supplanted those that preceded them.

This concluding chapter constitutes a reflection upon a deeper question raised by the history of cultural and ritual reform in Thinh Liet: why were official reforms only partially successful? As this study has shown, the Vietnamese state applied tremendous pressure to achieve its goals, but in some cases they fell short, and this failure has been highlighted in recent years with the resurgence of ritual practice. Nevertheless, there were people who accepted the reforms and the assertions they involved, and others who were simply ambivalent. Such a turn of events requires an explanation that can account for all of these cases. The one I will develop here will focus on two main factors: morality and agency. As I will argue, the revolutionary reform campaign problematized two of the most fundamental aspects of Thinh Liet life: what did it mean to be a moral person and what were the nature and limits of human agency. Thinh Liet society had its own definitions on these points prior to the revolution, but the revolutionary campaigns introduced their own. Residents therefore had to deal with two sets of definitions, and frequently had to choose between them. In choosing, however, residents were also making significant statements about who they were, what their society should be, what existed in the world, and what human agents could do within that world. They were also invoking specific forms of authority and legitimacy in making those claims. As I hope to show, in their ritual practices, residents provide answers to these questions, but as there is still not a definitive set of assertions accepted by all residents, Thinh Liet cultural life remains complex and contradictory.

Debating the Good Society and the Good Self

The philosopher Charles Taylor, in his monumental study *Sources of the Self: The Making of Modern Identity*, argues that being human in human society always involves morality. Humans exist in what he calls 'moral

209

space' and human agency is inextricably tied to morality (Taylor 1989:27). The implication of this linkage of agency and morality is that humans 'exist in a space of questions about strongly valued goods' (Taylor 1989:31). Taylor's position follows in the tradition of moral philosophy from Plato onward as it asserts that humans in social life always face such basic questions as what is a good society, what is a good life, what is a good person, and others. The totality of these 'goods' constitute what Taylor refers to as 'moral frameworks' (Taylor 1989:26). The existence of moral frameworks has two important consequences in Taylor's thought. First, he notes that they 'provide the background, explicit or implicit, for our moral judgments, intuitions, or reactions' (Taylor 1989:26). Thus, when we make moral discriminations, they are informed or influenced by the moral frameworks that we internalize in our lives. Second, and perhaps more significantly, Taylor argues that it is through morality and moral frameworks that humans construct their identities and define who they are. Ultimately, all humans face the question of 'Who am I?' And the process of answering this question involves moral discriminations. He states, 'To know who you are is to be oriented in moral space, a space in which questions arise about what is good or bad, what is worth doing and what not, what has meaning and importance for you and what is trivial and secondary' (Taylor 1989:28).

In answering this latter question, people must decide what is good or bad, honourable or dishonourable, admirable or contemptible, and worthy of emulation or worthy of rejection. This process has a second dimension in that people must also look at their own actions and determine whether they have lived up to the demands these moral concepts impose. The ability to answer this question in the affirmative is critical to the construction of one's own sense of pride, dignity, or self-worth, while the failure to do so can produce an 'acute form of disorientation' or 'identity crisis' (Taylor 1989:27). Failure, in effect, can produce extremely painful and disturbing consequences for the individual. Taylor's thinking highlights an extremely important point about morality and the self. On the one hand, it is profoundly informed by extant moral frameworks, but on the other, the creation of a sense of moral worth is a processual phenomenon that humans engage in through lived social practice. Stated more simply, it is by *doing* things that people define themselves and either construct or destroy their sense of pride, worth, or dignity. By doing or not doing specific socially recognized things, people make public statements, that they and others recognize, as to who they are. All humans are involved in what Richard Madsen has described for Chen village as 'a constant interplay between word and deed' (Madsen 1984:2), and it is out of this interplay that one's identity and sense of worth is constructed.

Taylor recognized that moral frameworks are socially constructed and that they can vary between societies and over time. Madsen's work in

China employed a similar idea, but he also recognized another complicating factor: human societies can feature more than one moral framework. Revolutionary Chen village featured two dominant moral frameworks, or what he referred to as 'moral paradigms.' One paradigm preceded the revolution and the other had been introduced during the revolution. Each had its own vision of the good society and good person, and each also made powerful demands on how residents were to live their lives. Madsen noted of Chen village that as a result of revolutionary change, 'villagers had to make a long series of excruciating moral decisions' (Madsen 1984:3). These included such dilemmas as how to treat those classified as enemies of the revolution, how to participate in the new revolutionary social organizations, and for political leaders, how to develop their leadership style. In making such decisions, residents strove 'not for theoretical consistency but for a felt integrity' (Madsen 1984:2). They sought to attain an inner sense that what they were doing was correct and appropriate. And as his study showed, the inability to live up to the moral code through which people defined themselves was disturbing for many.

Revolutionary Thinh Liet also featured two distinct moral frameworks, one revolutionary and one non-revolutionary. Each of these frameworks articulated their own vision of the good society. The former envisioned a community that existed within a revolutionary nation-state. It was built around such principles as democracy, gender equality, 'collective mastery,' the equitable distribution of resources, rationality, science, party leadership, and commitment to revolutionary agendas. This vision of the good society was distinguished by its futurity. Past and present society fell far short of the ideal, thus commitment, discipline, and concerted effort were required of all residents to create it. The latter vision of the good society did not involve a nation-state or revolution. It instead centered on the 'spirit of the village' (*tinh lang*) and its associated exhortations to 'live with morals' (*song dao duc*). This vision valued honesty, respect, age-based hierarchy, mutual assistance, kinship ties, relations between co-residents, and affective 'sentimental' relationships. The past, in this vision, was not problematic. It was not idealized, but it did provide the blueprint for the proper realization of the present and future.

Both of these visions mobilized their own systems of authority and legitimacy. In the revolutionary case, authority and legitimacy derived in part from the charisma of its main definer, Ho Chi Minh. It also derived from the residual prestige that the party earned in forcing the French to leave Vietnam. Both of these also drew on the semi-millenarian nature of official ideology. Vietnam needed to transcend its troubled and backward past to build a better future, and the state was to play a leading role in this process. If residents submitted to this vision and enthusiastically participated in the oft-mentioned process of 'building socialism' (*xay dung xa hoi chu nghia*), a brighter future and better society could be realized.

This argument about the past and future were vital to the revolutionary vision. The pre-revolutionary vision's authority and legitimacy derived from the past and the ancestors. People were inheritors of traditions that needed to be maintained because they were traditions, which itself carried some weight, but this was further reinforced by the notion that to not maintain them could be an insult to the ancestors. And in certain cases, the ancestors or other spirits would punish those who failed to maintain those traditions and practices. In this case, the past legitimized and did not need to be transcended.

Each of these visions also made specific behavioral demands that defined the good person within the good society. Social action in the revolutionary society was to be oriented toward the state and its goals. One was to enthusiastically increase production, devote oneself to the emulation campaigns, participate in the war effort, work for the collectivity, and implement the cultural reforms. Conversely, one was to avoid such stigmatized practices as 'familism' (*chu nghia gia dinh*), 'localism' (*chu nghia dia phuong*), or 'small-peasant production,' which all prioritized the local over the state, as well as the range of feudal practices discussed in earlier chapters. The non-revolutionary moral framework centered people in the context of family, kin, and co-resident obligations, and valorized their fulfilment, even if they contradicted the state's claims. Thus, familism, localism, and small-peasant production all had their virtues, if they helped one's family, kin, or co-residents. Many antecedent cultural and ritual practices were also important because they provided a practical demonstration of the fulfilment of people's obligations. Such was the situation with the conduct of funeral or death anniversary ceremonies according to the pre-reform model. In both of these conflicting frameworks, resource utilization was also an extremely important measure of a person's moral commitments. Raising and slaughtering a pig for sale to the state made a very different moral statement than raising that same pig but secretly slaughtering and consuming it in a wedding feast.

Following the introduction of the new and contradictory revolutionary moral framework into Thinh Liet life, residents often found themselves forced, like the residents of Chen village, into 'a long series of excruciating moral decisions.' Some of these were similar to those faced in Chen village, such as how to interact with former mandarins or landlords, or, for officials, how they were going to develop their leadership style (see Malarney 1997). Others, such as the implementation of the ritual reforms, were different. It is important to note that the introduction of the revolutionary agenda did not create a moral dilemma in *every* aspect of Thinh Liet life, and on a related point, Thinh Liet residents did not have a hide-bound commitment to their cultural past. To the contrary, in some cases residents had the social space to basically ignore certain aspects of the revolutionary agenda, such as the requirement to register a marriage or use an officially-approved

212

grave stone, thus these did not generate dilemmas. Other changes were relatively easily accepted, such as the elimination of arranged marriage, the reduction of premarital meetings and exchanges, the more expansive issuance of wedding invitations, the reduction of the mourning period, the burial of the corpse within 48 hours, the elimination of symbolic abasements in funerals, the general simplification of all rites, and others. Contemporary Thinh Liet rites are very different from their pre-revolutionary antecedents and many of these changes derive directly from the reform campaign elements that residents have accepted and reproduced.

Certain elements, however, did become foci of moral controversy, notably in such family-based rites as weddings, funerals, and death anniversaries. These centered around three main points: the participation of officials, the severance of ritual interaction with the ancestors, and the elimination of feasting and its associated exchange relations. These points became foci of such intense moral controversy because it was in the performance or refusal of revolutionary reforms that residents were forced to make public statements regarding the framework they used to define themselves. When a family had to perform a major family ritual, they had to decide what had precedence for them and how they would deal with that. The rituals forced residents to answer the question, 'Who am I?' A party member? A committed revolutionary? Or a loving mother? A devoted father? A filial son or daughter?

For some residents during the reform period, the exclusive form of moral authority in the commune was the non-revolutionary framework that centered on 'living with morals.' Earning this appellation required them to perform the socially-prescribed acts mentioned above. Most importantly, it required them to fulfill their exchange relations in order to obtain the prized social label of 'living with sentiment.' It also necessitated that they organize their family rites along pre-revolutionary lines so they could be recognized socially as a good son, daughter, parent, sibling, or kinsperson. The response to the revolutionary changes for the people in this group, who were often older women and sometimes men advanced in years by the late 1950s, involved no equivocation. Some stated outright that the reforms were 'not right' (*khong dung*). Reformed ceremonies were 'without sentiment' (*vo tinh cam*) and people who carried them out did not 'remember their ancestors' (*khong nho to tien*) or 'know their moral debts' (*khong biet on*). For the advocates of this position, the reforms required a moral decision, but they could definitively make their choices and confidently define themselves and their priorities according to the non-revolutionary framework.

Ranged against the opponents was another group of residents who vigorously supported the reforms. This group, composed largely of men with party backgrounds, saw the cultural and ritual reforms in positive terms. Their positions and arguments were supported by an array of

213

officially-produced facts. Vietnam was a country that had been held back for centuries by an array of retrograde practices that wasted resources and oppressed people. If Vietnam was to progress, these practices had to be eliminated and a new culture created. Instilling this in social life would require difficult and unpopular choices, but such was the way forward. Support for their arguments was easy to find. In the 1950s and 1960s Thinh Liet commune, like the rest of North Vietnam, was poor, had only a rudimentary educational system, was basically unindustrialized, and had an under-productive agricultural system. By remaking social life, a new society could be built. Conversations with reform supporters demonstrate their vigor and commitment. In their cases, they made their choices and defined themselves first and foremost as committed revolutionaries whose primary allegiances were to the state and its policies. Many comment that this position frequently made them unpopular with their kin and co-residents, but they were ready to endure such difficulties. Some justified this through grand commitments to building socialism, but others saw themselves in more prosaic terms. Quoting Ho Chi Minh, many stated that they were committed to the party and its goals because that was the way to make the Vietnamese 'warm, full, and happy' (*cho am no, hanh phuc*).

Stuck in between these two poles of confident commitment was the great mass of Thinh Liet residents who really had to make the difficult moral decisions. By carrying out rituals as the party described and submitting to the new moral discipline devised by the state, they marked themselves socially as a people committed to following revolutionary guidelines, and also as those who subsumed other claims of moral authority to the state's powerful claim. By conducting a ritual as the government dictated, they became a good person in revolutionary terms. Conversely, if they conducted a ritual in an officially unsanctioned manner, they become a good person according to the non-revolutionary framework. Every death and every wedding, therefore, presented residents with a choice. Did they adhere to the line established by the party and conduct themselves according to those moral rules? Or did they, even in the face of official pressure or coercion, draw upon a different moral discourse to do what they considered proper? The reforms raised deep and often troubling questions of who and what kind of person they were. The inability to fulfill moral obligations to kin and co-residents could create discomfort, but a stern response from committed officials was equally upsetting. Residents recall that moral pressure to live in accordance with both frameworks persisted throughout the reform years. Official pressures have already been discussed in detail, but public life also featured an abundance of uncomplimentary comments about the reforms and some residents showed no reluctance to speak frankly about their dissatisfaction with the policies, their consequences, and those who implemented them. These pressures often extended into the home as well. A man might have been an official with the local party cell, but he was also a son, grandson, nephew, and other things. Parental pressure, frequently exerted by mothers or other senior female kin, could serve as a powerful inhibitor on the behavior of some officials. Members of a Giap Nhi lineage recall how lineage members who were both party members and officials dearly wanted to shut down a spirit shrine owned by their lineage mates, but pressure from their elders prevented them. The best they could do was limit the open performance of rites in the shrine, while clandestine spirit rites carried on. People also remember with great irritation how many officials aggressively interfered in other people's rituals, but when it came to the wedding of their child, or the death of their parent or family member, they willingly bent the rules and organized the largest ritual possible. The case of the official whose parents died in the mid-1980s constitutes the favored example of this problem. Failure to live up to the non-revolutionary framework could have negative consequences. But, any pressure one received at home was often matched in public life by the scathing commentary and interference of strident local officials.

The combination of pressures from these two directions created a large middle ground in which the vast majority of residents, including the less committed and perhaps more politically savvy officials, worked things out as best they could within the shifting boundaries of what was possible at any particular moment. For the officials, it was clear after the first few years that they would have to selectively approach the reforms and be willing to make some concessions if they wanted some of the reforms to succeed, and they often gave ground on those matters that took place within family homes. The continued presence of the Buddhist Association speaks to this, as do the quick return of weddings to the participants' homes and the continuation of rites dedicated to dead souls. Vietnamese speak of 'leaving it alone' or 'pretending to not see what you see' (*mac ke*), and many Thinh Liet officials employed this approach throughout the reform campaign in order to help them balance the conflicting moral claims.[1] Some residents also took a pick and choose approach to balance the disparate claims. This came out clearest in the case of men who accepted sumptuary restrictions, but then pressed for the retention of other practices, such as the return of ancestral rites in wedding ceremonies or the performance of funeral music. Another interesting case was that of the Thinh Liet cooperative chairman who, while ensuring that residents met their pork quotas, tacitly allowed them to slaughter several animals when they asked permission to slaughter one for a feast. This same man would later hold the commune's largest feast. Many residents felt that the revolutionary reforms had positive things to offer, thus some measure of balancing of the conflicting claims was needed. Other residents maintained the public appearance of supporting the reforms, but then covertly engaged in unsanctioned practices. The Buddhist Association's clandestine chanting represented the best example,

215

but so was the covert maintenance of spirit shrines and the secretive production of votive paper objects. The case of the Giap Nhi votive paper object producer expelled from the party was an interesting case of this. A former land reform cadre, he enthusiastically endorsed the revolution at first, but over time the claims of his family tradition and the necessity of caring for the ancestors led him secretly back to producing the items while still in the party. Finally, some residents carried out the reforms even when they did not want to, and then felt bad about it afterwards. Many in this category could not achieve the sense of 'lived integrity' described by Madsen. This was particularly the case during the early years when cadres most vigorously enforced the reforms and people had little choice but to follow official instructions. However, the fact that over time the rites changed demonstrates that local officials were being pressed to reduce the moral dilemmas the reforms raised for people.

The past decade has witnessed the re-establishment of the non-revolutionary moral framework's dominance in Thinh Liet. With its re-establishment, residents have largely solved the three main dilemmas raised by the reforms: officials have been removed from critical roles in the ceremonies;[2] ritual interaction with the ancestors has returned; and, perhaps most importantly, feasting and exchange relations between co-residents have blossomed. Still, as has been demonstrated throughout this study, this framework's re-attainment of dominance has not entailed the elimination of the revolutionary framework. It still has its full or partial supporters, particularly with regard to criticisms of ritual over-complexity and perceived wastefulness, and represents a legitimate moral perspective in social life. Regardless of where people stand, however, such rituals as weddings, funerals, and death anniversaries remain important arenas of moral action as residents make assertions of who they are and how they will prioritize and fulfill their moral obligations. Some decide in favor of the non-revolutionary framework predicated upon the authority of family and communal relations, others publically assert that their primary allegiance lays with the state and its policies, others seek to balance the two. Taylor commented that, 'Our identity is what allows us to define what is important to us and what is not' (Taylor 1989:30), and many residents come up with complex answers because both family and revolution can be important. Certain aspects of the reforms can be appealing, such as an elimination of wastefulness, but it is equally important to organize a proper wedding for a child or funeral for a parent.

This same moral dynamic is also present today in the amount of resources residents devote to ritual practice. It is indisputable that improvements in the economic situation of many Thinh Liet families have enabled them to organize and conduct rituals much grander than they could ten or twenty years ago. The quality and quantity of ritual items has increased; the ritual infrastructure, such as altars and the buildings that house them, has been improved; and the size and cost of feasts has grown significantly. Many people now have the ability to organize larger and costlier rituals, and therefore do, thus recent economic changes have been vital for the growth and expansion of ritual. It is tempting to describe this growth, particularly in its more extravagant forms, as the consequence of a competitive impulse for conspicuous consumption, status display, or the 'eat jealousy, live hatred' mind set of some residents. This has undeniably been an important factor, particularly in such cases as the growth in wedding feast size or the push for higher prestige items at feasts. But it is an incomplete explanation for three reasons. First, most Thinh Liet residents regard the resources they devote to ritual activities, particularly to fund renovations of sacred sites or the conduct ritual practices therein, as a morally beneficial activity or 'meritorious work' (*cong duc*). Some residents devote large sums of money, but even many extremely poor people will devote a few hundred dong. Those who make such donations agree on their importance, while many see it is as a responsibility and take pride in its fulfilment. It is difficult to find anyone, even among the most devoted revolutionaries, who argue against the moral dimension of these expenditures, a point evident in the administration's recent embrace of communal house renovations and rituals. Second, as Thorstein Veblen noted when he developed the conspicuous consumption concept, consumption involves moral valuation and must occur in socially appropriate ways for it to have any social value; or, to use his language, to create honor, nobility, and reputability for the consumer (Veblen 1994:70). Veblen also noted that 'the failure to consume in due quantity and quality becomes a mark of inferiority and demerit' (Veblen 1994:74). Weddings, funerals, and death anniversary ceremonies in Thinh Liet by definition involve socially-prescribed consumption. Their nature and content have changed, and continue to change, but the linkage between appropriate consumption and moral valuation remains strong. As discussed in earlier chapters, many families are very sensitive to the evaluations and commentary that follow rituals and seek to avoid criticism or ridicule. They want to be known as filial children, good neighbors, or devoted parents, thus consumption levels have by default increased as residents, sometimes reluctantly, seek to achieve a socially respectable form and level. As many say, residents 'live according to public opinion' and pressure to match precedent is strong.[3] Finally, Thinh Liet ideas regarding the appropriate level of consumption are powerfully informed by 'wealth gives birth to ritual form' concept. This idea places added pressure on the wealthier because for them to perform their rituals in a manner regarded as stingy or cheap brings social opprobrium, which again pushes up consumption levels. As Thinh Liet's economy has improved over the past decade, higher incomes have become intertwined in this complex web of those who conspicuously consume simply to assert their status and those who more

217

simply seek to fulfill what they consider as moral responsibilities and be regarded in morally positive terms in the community.

Lurking beneath all of these various differences on how to conduct these rituals is a set of diverse ideas, some of which are not directly articulated as such, that describe what the good society in Thinh Liet should be. Ritual practices feature so prominently in this discourse because they give public expression to three of the most morally charged aspects of Thinh Liet life: how does one appropriately interact with one's ancestors; how does one appropriately interact with one's relatives and co-residents; and how does one appropriately utilize and consume one's resources. All three of these points were foci of official action and local resistance. In Thinh Liet today, as people organize and conduct their rituals, they make assertions of who they are, what is important to them, and what their society should be. The assertions people make, as has been shown, are diverse and often contradictory, but nevertheless important. Is Thinh Liet going to be a community that adheres to the revolutionary line and commits itself to the construction of socialism? Is it going to be a community that prioritizes local desires and values over the state's claims? Or is it going to be a community that balances both? The answer to this is complex and dynamic, and a definitive answer has yet to be achieved because, to put it simply, residents still do not fully agree on what it should be. As we reflect on these changes, it is clear that explanations based upon morality are most compelling with the cases of weddings, funerals, and other mortuary rites, but do not explain the retention of other rites. To understand why spirit mediumship and other related rites that involved contact with the spirit world persisted and later blossomed requires an examination of another aspect of the existential situation of Thinh Liet residents.

Making Sense of a Chaotic World

In *Economy and Society* and other writings, Max Weber predicted that the growth of modernity would be accompanied by the 'disenchantment' of the world. As science and rationality came to occupy an ever greater part of human life and consciousness, they would progressively eliminate non-secular systems of understanding and explanation, and human understandings of the world and how it operates would become increasingly rational or 'scientific' in character. While Weber saw the advancement of modernity as a gradual process, socialist revolutions took this trend to its furthest limits and attempted to forcibly implement it in a relatively short period of time. Weber's idea at a certain level seemed to make sense. The world had entered 'an age in which the divine, at least in its classical forms, ha(d) receded into the background of human concern and consciousness' (Berger 1969:2). The power and authority of organized religion was visibly weakened, individual religious affiliation was shrinking, and reliance on non-empirically verifiable systems of explanation was in decline. All of this seemed to confirm Weber's thesis, but as critics began to argue, perhaps Weber and others had overstated the argument and failed to acknowledge less traditional forms of religiosity or other ways in which the supernatural played a role in human life (see Berger 1969; Kendall 1996; Weller 1994).

Thinh Liet's recent history would seem to support Weber's critics. Despite the revolution's vigorous secularization drive, the majority of residents never accepted the idea that the world is void of supernatural forces or entities. People continued to engage supernatural forces through horoscopy, tests for astrological auspiciousness, and the numerous forms of divination associated with ritual practices. People also continued to engage supernatural entities in spirit medium rites, soul-calling ceremonies, weddings, funerals, death anniversary ceremonies, healing rites, rites devoted to prosperity and good luck, the burning of votive paper objects, and numerous other ways as well. Try as they may, the cadres could never fully convince all residents that such things did not exist, and interaction with the supernatural remained a constant thorn in the cadres' sides. In recent years, as the number of Thinh Liet spirit shrines has grown and the formerly hidden spirit medium groups have become more public, the failure of the cadres' efforts seems even more pronounced. The question this raises then is why? Why were so many Thinh Liet residents unwilling to accept what Ann Anagnost has described for China as 'the official construction of the world' (Anagnost 1987:41)? Why did they instead retain a set of ideas and values that run counter to that construction, and why have these ideas been increasingly mobilized in ritual practice over the past decade? There are several answers to this question, but I will argue that the most important answer lies in the nature of revolutionary ideology itself.

In his book *Marxism and Christianity*, Alisdair MacIntyre addressed the question of the similarities between Marxism and Christianity. MacIntyre argued that in spite of its secular or atheistic creed, Marxism bore a substantial resemblance to Christianity. The roots of this resemblance lay in two main places. First, like Christianity, Marxism provided 'an interpretation of existence' (MacIntyre 1968:2). Marxism might be secular in nature, but through the employment of such concepts as alienation, estrangement, objectification, class struggle, and others, it provided a set of concepts through which people could understand how the world came to be the way it is and how it works. These concepts did not invoke divine forces, but instead foregrounded the idea that society and culture were human creations. They were the product of human social practice. They also foregrounded the material. Explaining the world and how it works depended on explanations based upon 'this-worldly causation,' particularly those constructed by 'science,' while Christianity and other religions depended upon 'other-worldly causation' (MacIntryre 1968:108). The point that MacIntyre makes, but does not fully develop, is that Marxism, like every cultural system, provides a set of explanations about the world and its constitution. In order to establish the legitimacy of its explanations, it mobilized the authority of science and material causation.

The second resemblance that MacIntyre describes is the fact that both Marxism and Christianity have a millenarian dimension. Each system, though grounded in the present, makes very strong claims about human agency and its ability to influence the future. Marxism's basic logic is that since human society is the product of human social practice, humans have the ability to understand it, change it, and, most importantly, improve it. The present is not immutable. Through the application of Marxist principles, humans can transcend the limitations of the present and construct a better future. Quoting Marx, MacIntyre commented that Marxism 'draws its poetry from the future' (MacIntyre 1968:112). In this system, the future becomes the focus of contemporary social action because Marxists should devote themselves to 'liberating the present from the boundaries of the past' (MacIntyre 1968:115), and thereby construct a better future. Given the recognition of the human creation of social phenomena, humans are no longer powerless agents. Instead, they have the ability to impress their will upon the world. MacIntyre concluded that Marxism 'rescue(s) individual lives from the insignificance of finitude ... by showing that he has or can have some role in a world-historical drama' (MacIntyre 1968:112). No matter how bad the situation might be on earth, humans can, through concerted social action, construct a better world for themselves.

For a number of Thinh Liet residents, particularly male party members who came of age in the 1940s, 1950s, and 1960s, Marxism and revolutionary ideology did constitute a kind of quasi-millenarian religion. For these people, the revolution provided an opportunity to create a better society and a better future. Their past had not been a particularly good one, thus many actively participated in the revolutionary struggle to create the new society. One of the strongest impressions one gets from conversations with such people, even after you strip away the layer of post facto nostalgia that many have for those years, is the sense of possibility that many felt during that time. The old order had been torn down, and the future had enormous potential. The negative and retrograde cultural aspects of that order had also been diagnosed and isolated, thus with concerted, guided action, a better society could be made. The enthusiasm of some who embraced this line of thought endured through the years. Throughout this study, numerous cases have been presented of men who, even in the 1990s, confidently declared that there were no supernatural forces or entities, that the world could be understood through material causation, and that Vietnamese society would be much better off if people abandoned superstitious ideas and practices. People needed more science in their lives and ways of thinking. As long as people did not accept the idea that only science can produce true facts, Vietnam would retain backwards ideas and practices.

Such cases, however, are rare. It was clear from the beginning that many people, notably women, did not accept the party's position, and over time even those who once did gradually shifted away from it and returned to a position opposed by the party. There have been a number of celebrated cases of this in Thinh Liet. Several former high ranking officials have recently constructed spirit shrines (*dien*) in their homes to propitiate spirits. Included here is an American war veteran and former full colonel (*Dai Ta*) in the People's Army. The former land reform cadre returned to his family's traditional occupation of producing votive paper objects. A former secretary of the Thinh Liet party cell was also expelled from the party because he became a spirit priest. He is now regarded as the most skilled in the commune. Another Dien Bien Phu veteran, party member, and former official recently completed an expensive renovation of his family's spirit shrine (*dien*). And then there was the death bed conversion of the man who had supported the party line, but demanded Buddhist funeral rites as death approached.

Looked at in the aggregate, one reason for the change of heart of these men and the opposition of others comes back to the very simple issue of explanation. As MacIntyre argued, Marxism does provide an interpretation of existence, but ultimately it, like the science and empiricism that it champions, simply cannot answer every question that humans face. Science can give humans technical control over nature, or even the means to analyze and improve their societies, but it often proves inadequate in addressing fundamental existential concerns. Habermas recognized this point when, in a discussion of science in modern industrial societies, he commented that, 'even a civilization that has been rendered scientific is not granted dispensation from practical questions' (Habermas 1974:255). Science may help humans better manipulate the natural world, but it struggles to provide answers to such questions as why is there suffering, why is there evil, what will happen to me after death, or why did the seemingly impossible actually occur? Events of the latter variety have taken on tremendous rhetorical importance in Thinh Liet. Why did the men who desecrated the Giap Nhat spirit shrine all meet early and unfortunate ends? Why did biomedical techniques fail to relieve the blockage of the young man who urinated on the Giap Tu communal house? Why did the young woman who sold meat in front of the Giap Nhi communal house die an early death? Why does Giap Nhat continue to have a comparatively lower birth rate for males? And perhaps most important of all, how did a small, impoverished nation with a rudimentary economy and minimal industry take on and defeat a fading colonial power and then one of the world's richest countries with one of the most powerful armies? As many reflective Thinh Liet residents note, it is difficult to construct compelling empirical or material explanations for all of these events, though particularly the latter. In such cases, many residents have therefore engaged other systems of knowledge and explanation, with their own ontologies and causal notions, that the revolution did not endorse or advocate. However, as the case of the Giap Tu mother who has never found any meaning or reason for her teenage son's accidental death in the army demonstrates, even these systems can have their limits.

While the explanatory failures of revolutionary ideology partially explain its rejection, a second and related question that requires an answer is why did residents continue to mobilize unsanctioned bodies of knowledge in unsanctioned ritual practices. People not only employed such knowledge in conversation or disputes, they also employed it in the rituals they performed. This was particularly evident in ritual teleology. Rituals are always performed for a reason and with a particular goal or goals in mind that express human desire for the future. MacIntyre described how Marxism had a shared orientation toward the future and its principles, at least in theory, provided another way in which humans could impress their own will upon the future. Through it, humans could create their own social world as they desired. Although this ability to influence the future was a significant and motivating feature for some Thinh Liet residents, just as with its explanatory failures, revolutionary ideology did not provide the means for people to assert control over all aspects of their lives and futures. True, it could help make gender relations more egalitarian or the distribution of resources more equitable, but it could not help people ward off misfortune, put a soul to rest, or cope with the vagaries and vulnerabilities of their lives. However, certain ritual practices and their associated bodies of knowledge could help them cope with these concerns. The basic point here is that many residents could not abandon ritual practice because it constituted a vital component in their personal repertoire of methods for making sense of, ordering, and exerting control over both their present and their future. These practices, and their associated bodies of knowledge and explanations, were critical to the effort to assert some measure of control and predictability over potentially chaotic and unpredictable phenomena in life. For residents of Thinh Liet commune, like everyone else in the world, life at times is simply unpredictable. Crops fail, floods destroy fields and gardens, people become ill and cannot be cured, people die young, families hover near poverty, the list goes on and on. Since the Renovation policy's introduction, this uncertainty and vulnerability has intensified. Under the collective economy residents were guaranteed at least some minimal level of subsistence, in addition to access to education and medical care.

Now, all subsistence guarantees are gone, and families must pay for almost all education and medical care costs. Many previous safety nets have disappeared and people are basically left to fend for themselves. In this atmosphere of uncertainty and potential disaster, many residents have marshalled ritual practice as a way to control chaos, fix the problems of the present, and ensure a positive future. This can be seen clearly in some of the more instrumental ritual acts residents perform. Young students visit shrines or temples so that they can pass university entrance exams. Petty traders visit the Goddess of the Treasury's shrine to guarantee success in business. People of all ages and genders consult spirit mediums to cure illness or determine the cause of repeated misfortune. In all of these cases, people reach out to the supernatural through ritual in order to engage it and make it respond according to their desires. It is very important to note that the participants do not necessarily 'believe' in the existence and efficacy of these spirits or forces. Some people are indeed quite convinced that they exist, and they are the ones who are most likely to present stories of benefits the supernatural can bring. Many others basically take the attitude that they are not sure if it works or not, but it just might, so it cannot hurt anyway. Like their more committed contemporaries, their involvement in ritual is one way that they attempted to impress their own volition on the future.

In a discussion of religious change in Taiwan, Robert Weller commented, 'The new religious growth in Taiwan and other modern states reflects a need for meaning that these states cannot meet' (Weller 1994:159). He further noted, 'A secular state has problems even addressing some of the issues with which religion deals, like the meaning of death or the problem of evil' (Weller 1994:160). Shatov in *The Possessed* had come to the same conclusion when he noted that, 'Reason has never been able to define good and evil, or even to separate evil from good, if only approximately.' This was also the case in Thinh Liet. Socialist ideology *was* extremely successful in explaining some aspects of existence and as this study has shown, official ideology does constitute one of the dominant systems for explaining matters as diverse as the consequences of cultural feudalism, the class struggle in colonial Vietnam, or the role of status endogamy in creating inequality. But despite the persuasiveness of the 'official construction of reality' in numerous domains of social life, it could not address all of the troubling questions that residents faced. They therefore searched for answers in other bodies of knowledge and systems of meaning not entirely concordant with official ideology, and then mobilized these ideas and values in ritual practices. Socialist ideology granted humans only limited agency. It gave them the power to create a new society, but it left them powerless to confront and hopefully control the unpredictability of life. It also did not help them address such concerns as putting the souls of their loved ones to rest. Unsanctioned ritual practices and their

223

associated knowledge therefore persisted, and the social world of Thinh Liet for many residents remains at least partially 'enchanted.' Weber, like Marx before him, had failed to recognize that whatever explanatory power they might have, science and reason still cannot answer every question that humans face, nor do they necessarily empower people to compellingly deal with indeterminacy in their lives. As long as they do not, humans will continue to rely upon other systems of knowledge and meaning that help answer those questions and give them the capacity to cope with them.[4]

Conclusion

In her recent book *Disrupted Lives*, Gay Becker commented that, 'The effort to create order is, in essence, what anthropologists study' (Becker 1997:5). As a discipline, anthropology attempts to comprehend how it is that human beings give order to the ever-present chaos and indeterminacy of life. Whether through cultural narratives, ritual practice, bodies of religious knowledge, or other methods, humans must constantly address the at times bewildering totality of experiences they encounter at the quotidian level and turn them into some comprehensible pattern. The creation of order, as Becker argues, is part of the creation of meaning. She makes this linkage explicit when she notes that anthropology examines 'the ways in which people strive to create order out of chaos and thereby render life meaningful' (Becker 1997:5). In rendering life meaningful, the emphasis is not necessarily on answering the grand question of 'What is the meaning of life,' but a more basic concern with rendering sensible such questions as whether the phenomena one encounters in life are comprehensible, whether one's past can be compellingly linked to one's present, and whether one can at least partially understand the kind of future to which one's present will lead. Becker's particular focus is on the narratives people construct in order to take discordant life events and render them into a meaningful form that makes the events comprehensible and also creates a sense of continuity between past, present, and future (see also Good 1994:135–165). The assumption underlying her argument is that the creation of order and meaning in life are a fundamental part of being human.

As we reflect on the many changes in Thinh Liet commune over the past decades, it is important to come back to this very basic anthropological point. Thinh Liet's history over the past one hundred years may have unfolded against the background of colonization, resistance to colonial rule, warfare, socialist revolution, and ultimately independence and peace, yet despite such a grand history, the characters and participants who filled the stage in this drama were all, ultimately, human. They were people who faced such basic questions as 'Who am I?,' 'What is my place in the world?,' 'What powers and abilities do I have or can I draw upon?,'

'What is a good society?,' or 'What is a good person?' They also had to answer more difficult questions such as 'Why is there suffering?,' or 'Why is there misfortune?' The Vietnamese revolution had produced its own set of facts and assertions about reality and how the world works, but as I have argued in this chapter, the answers it provided were in some cases were not fully compelling. Revolutionary ideology was an excellent tool for analyzing and remaking society. Its lived realization could also for some create the sense that they were engaged in something meaningful and important. However, it had its limits. It could not help to explain why a child died young or a soldier died in battle. It could not explain what happened after death, except to give what for many was the unsatisfying answer that death marked the end of everything. It could not give extra assistance to attain personal or financial success. It also did not provide people with the means to carry out such fundamental obligations as caring for the dead. Some people were comfortable with the minimal definitions that the revolution propagated regarding what existed and how the world worked, but for many these were not enough. At the deepest level, revolutionary ideology only empowered humans to change and modify those things that could be empirically isolated and verified, but existence regularly confronts humans with events and phenomena that fall beyond this realm. For these and other events to have some meaningful order, which is to say that they were comprehensible and that human agency had the capacity to address and deal with them, Thinh Liet residents needed other understandings of reality and the position of humans within it. Thus, in spite of official desires for it to become the definitive understanding of reality, revolutionary ideology could only enter into dialogue with the other understandings that preceded it. These different understandings continue to confront and contend with each other. As history unfolds, they will continue to inform and animate how the people of Thinh Liet commune understand and make sense of their world.

Notes

Introduction

1 Luong notes, by contrast, that officials in the village of Hoai Thi attempted to reform longevity ceremonies (Luong 1993:272). Both Luong (1993) and Endres (1999) discuss how the ritual life of the women in the communities they studied tended to focus on the Buddhist temple, yet the dynamics of female ritual life in Thinh Liet, as will be discussed in Chapter 7, were different. It is important to keep these cases in mind as it demonstrates the variability of ritual reform and change in different northern Vietnamese communities, as well as the need to consider each case in its own terms.

2 Fitting examples of this phenomenon from the extremely broad literature on the subject can be found in Evans 1991 and 1998, Humphrey 1983, Kligman 1977, Madsen 1984, Potter and Potter 1990, Siu 1989 and 1990, and Rubie Watson 1994.

3 Michael Lambek's work on the uneven distribution of Islamic and other forms of knowledge in Mayotte society provides another excellent example (see Lambek 1990; Lambek 1993).

4 Non-revolutionary societies have also taken a state functionalist approach to ritual, as can be seen in Bloch 1986, Cannadine and Price 1987, Hobsbawm 1983, and Kertzer 1988. Vietnamese emperors and the pre-modern Vietnamese state, which featured a Ministry of Rites (*Le Bo*), were also intensely concerned with maintaining orthodox ritual practice in their realm as they assumed that proper ritual performance would produce the correct values and attitudes in the participants (for examples see Tran Trong Kim 1954:244–246 and Woodside 1971:27–28). Like their revolutionary successors, officials at the Ministry of Rites often had difficulties in getting the people to follow their edicts. This was evident as late as 1920 when the ministry attempted to pressure the governor of Ha Dong province, Hoang Trong Phu, to persuade local residents to reduce their ritual expenditures. Phu, as shown in a 29 May 1920 letter, felt that it would take years to ever convince the people to do so, a sentiment that Communist cadres would echo decades later (Ha Dong #2854).

5 Popkin's usage of *xa* as village and *lang* as hamlet applies better to areas of central and southern Vietnam (see also Woodside 1970:153). It is also worth noting that during the colonial period, administrative records referred to the multi-village community as *Tong Thinh Liet, Canton de Thinh Liet*, and also *Xa*

Thinh Liet. This unit had its own chief executive, the *Chanh Tong* or *Chef de Canton*, a position of limited power normally occupied by a high-ranking elite male. The importance and independence of the villages was evident in the fact that each village had its own budget, its own 'Village Chief' (*Ly Truong*), and its own 'Council of Notables' (*Hoi Dong Ky Muc*). The latter two administered the village and dominated village political life. Each was exclusively restricted to village residents.

6 The figures given to me by the administration often did not add up. Thus, all should be regarded as approximate.

7 The establishment of the Communal People's Committee in 1954 involved the elimination of the Council of Notables and the post of Village Chief. Compared to its predecessor, the revolutionary commune represented a stronger and more centralized administrative structure. In the mid-1990s, the communal administration reinstalled a new form of village-level executive, the *thon truong*, in order to make the administration more sensitive to local residents' needs.

8 The vagueness of the *gia dinh* contrasts with the bureaucratic specificity of the 'household' (*ho*), the residentially-defined unit used for administration. Thinh Liet residents are registered in households and the communal administration keeps careful count of their number.

Notes to Chapter 1

1 See Hanoi, Land Reform Committee 1956:35–39 for a list of the regulations.

2 These numbers differ slightly from those in Malarney 1993:260–261. Follow up interviews in January 1994 produced three more landlords as well as different sizes of land holdings. It should also be noted that people's individual recollections of the number of landlords and their holdings varied, sometimes significantly. Given that there is no official list to verify these figures, all land holding figures in the text should be treated as rough estimates. Thinh Liet's People's Committee possesses a copy of a land register from 1940, but political considerations prevented me from examining it.

3 Given that families generally do not like to reveal their former landlord classifications, I have chosen to list only their first names. In the text, all land holding figures are given in hectares after converting them from the northern Vietnamese system of reckoning land area in which one *mau* (3600 square meters) is composed of ten *sao* (360 square meters).

4 In reality, this number was likely higher than two.

5 The classifications also revealed the linkages between local elite families. The wealthy Uy, a former member of the Giap Nhi Mandarin Association, was affinally related to five other Giap Nhi landlords. Among these were two former village chiefs, one village administration member, and a respected local teacher. Many other landlords had similar relations.

6 Communal land (*dat cong*) was land owned by villages, lineages, or other social groups. It is discussed further below.

7 One important historical question that has yet to be adequately resolved is the extent of Chinese involvement in the Vietnamese land reform and cultural campaigns. A number of Thinh Liet natives recall seeing Chinese cadres during the land reform in the outskirts of Hanoi, but their numbers and the nature of their involvement remain unclear.

8 In the time period when land reform was being conducted the Communist Party had yet to completely solidify its hold on power in North Vietnam. Its main rival was the VNQDD. Many active or alleged agents of the VNQDD were

dispatched by the Communists in the years immediately following the French withdrawal.

9 At that point in time, the Vietnamese Communists went under the name of the 'Vietnam Workers' Party' (*Dang Lao Dong Viet Nam*).

10 A 1921 administrative report indicates the existence of 14.3 hectares (39 *mau* 8 *sao*) of communal land, which stretched along the Set river and its banks, and was owned jointly by the commune's six villages. The report was written as a result of a dispute over the land's ownership. Residents made no mention of this land, leading me to believe that the cadastral service ultimately divided it up equally between the villages as they requested. The receipt of 2.38 hectares would help explain how Giap Nhi, which according to a 1911 report had only 1.37 hectares (3 *mau* 8 *sao*) of communal land, had by the 1940s the approximately 3.6 hectares of contemporary residents' recollections (Ha Dong #1705; Ha Dong #3403).

11 These again are rough estimates derived from a combination of administrative records and residents' recollections. One obvious problem is that, according to contemporary officials, both Giap Nhi and Giap Tu have more productive land than they did before the land reform. This could partially be explained by Giap Nhi's appropriation of some Giap Tu land, and Giap Tu's appropriation of Set Temple land, during the land reform. Still, the numbers are difficult to reconcile as the commune has lost land to factories and housing projects.

12 In 1998, some villagers began to propagate a new story about the loss of the spirit scroll, stating that it had in fact been lost since the beginning of the twentieth century. It seems highly unlikely that Giap Tu residents would have done nothing about this for such a long period of time, particularly when conflicts over ritual conduct did occur in the commune. Furthermore, with educated Giap Nhi next to them, it also seems unlikely that residents would have willingly accepted such an embarrassing fact. The same people assert that the communal house was not burned by the guerrillas during the 1947 battle. This story does not add up because the inner sanctum of the communal house was completely destroyed somehow, none of the original altars remain, and residents were in uniform agreement that Giap Tu's treatment of their communal house during the land reform and later was less violent than in Giap Nhi. Their statement that it occurred during collectivization is therefore unconvincing. Nevertheless, the reasons why they would want to propagate this new version remain unclear.

13 There is an interesting discrepancy between the amount of attention given to the reform of communal house rites versus weddings, funerals, and other more family-centered rites. Nguyen Hong Phong argued in 1959 that the worship of guardian spirits had been corrupted by the former elite (1959:159–60) and in 1962 Tuan Cau wrote of the conversion of communal houses to recreation houses (*cau lac bo*), but over the following decades detailed regulations were never released, revised, and re-released as occurred with the other rites. Kirsten Endres' work in the Ministry of Culture archives has revealed a number of important dynamics of this period that were not published by officials (see Endres 2001). This is further discussed in Chapter Seven.

14 I have yet to discover any mention of reforming or changing lineage rites in party or government documents.

15 One of the alleged reasons for denying me access to the 1940 land register was to prevent the spread of information regarding the size and location of former communal land plots so no one could make a claim for that land. By the late 1990s that issue had yet to become a focus of controversy.

Notes to Chapter 2

1 It is appropriate to include a brief discussion of the complex semantics of *dao duc* in Vietnamese. At the most refined level, '*duc*' is the equivalent of 'virtue' in English and *dao duc* can be defined as 'the way of virtue,' or either ethics or morality. However, in spoken Vietnamese people rarely use *duc* by itself. For example, to comment on the moral worth of another person, they use the term *dao duc*. As a result, Vietnamese generally does not differentiate between virtue, morals, or ethics with different terms as in English. It is instead determined contextually. In the text, I have employed 'ethics' or 'morality' according to whichever is appropriate.

2 This volume was written under his earlier name Nguyen Ai Quoc, or Nguyen the Patriot.

3 People began using the respectful term 'great grandfather' (*cu*) in his final years of his life. This term is very popular today.

4 This idea was part of the mass mobilization in the land reform as discussed in Chapter 1.

5 Official documents employed both 'New Ways' and 'New Life' for this agenda. For consistency's sake, I will use New Ways in the text.

6 Tan Sinh 1977 provides a good discussion of the New Ways' early formulations.

7 During the war years a number of Thinh Liet families fled to areas controlled by the Viet Minh and participated in reformed ritual practices. Such reforms did not take place in Thinh Liet.

8 Tran Phu (1904–1931) was the first General Secretary of the Indochinese Communist Party. Nguyen Thi Minh Khai (1910–1941) was a female revolutionary active in the south. Ly Tu Trong (1913–1931) was also a revolutionary active in the south, reportedly from the age of ten. Hoang Van Thu (1906–1944) was a high-ranking party official. Tran Phu died of illness in prison, while the French executed the other three. Hoang Van Thu was executed at the Tuong Mai rifle range adjacent to Thinh Liet.

9 *Quoc ngu*, or 'national language' is the romanized Vietnamese script used today. Its usage became common during the colonial period as it replaced the system of Sino-Vietnamese characters used previously (see DeFrancis 1977).

Notes to Chapter 3

1 At the same time, the government encouraged the use of Chinese and Vietnamese herbal medicines, though for chronic and not acute conditions.

2 This spirit has other names such as *Ong Nuc Bep*, *Ong Dau Rau*, and *Vua Bep*.

3 Nguyen Van Khoan mentioned in 1930 that women were much more active in these activities than men (Nguyen Van Khoan 1930:109–110). The previously mentioned physiognomist commented that the vast majority of those who came to him were 'Women of the age where they had to worry about their families, children, finances, and those I took the worst advantage of were not exempt from concerns of love and fate' (Ha Nam Ninh 1976:37).

4 The musical instruments played minimally include a flute, a 'two-chord fiddle' (*dan nhi*), a drum, and other small percussion devices (*phach*). For a full discussion of contemporary spirit mediumship, particularly from the musical side, see Norton 1999.

5 Some people also assert that the persistence of ideas regarding a period of matriarchy in Vietnamese history derive from her prominence.

6 Chua Huong is a popular destination for couples seeking supernatural assistance in conceiving a child.

Notes to Chapter 4

1 It should be noted, though, that conflict could emerge between being filial to one's father and loyal to the Emperor.

2 The reason for reforming funeral rites is difficult to determine. Revolutionary France implemented reforms to make funerals more modest (Mosse 1990:40), but cadres in the Soviet Union delayed funeral reform because it was too difficult and potentially divisive (Lane 1981:82). Chinese cadres vigorously implemented such reforms, thus it is likely that Chinese influence, combined with their own history of government assertiveness in funerary rites, played a dominant role in Vietnam.

3 Other provinces also used this adage to justify their reforms (see Vietnam, Ministry of Culture 1975:58 (for Hanoi) and 72 (for Hai Hung).

4 In order to help understand the material in this chapter, Vietnamese funerals follow this basic structure: 1) Death, the preparation of the corpse, and its placement in the coffin. 2) The *phat tang* phase in which mourning attire is distributed to family and kin. 3) The *phung vieng* phase in which other villagers arrive at the house of the deceased to pay their respects to the deceased, share the sadness (*chia buon*) of the bereaved family, and give them prestations. 4) The delivery of the final funeral orations and the commencement of the funeral procession (*dua dam*) that takes the casket from the deceased's house to the gravesite. 5) The funeral feast.

5 In the case of death outside the home, local practices forbid bringing the casket back into the home for funeral rites.

6 This latter requirement produced a peculiar type of wedding, called a 'running from mourning wedding' (*cuoi chay tang*), in which an engaged couple hastily married in the time between the death of a parent and the conduct of the obviously delayed distribution of the *tang* ceremony.

7 *Toi* can be translated as crime, offence, sin, or demerit, but it is important to note that in Thinh Liet, the Buddhist idea of demerit, while present, is not nearly as strongly developed as the ideas of merit and demerit found in the Theravada Buddhist societies of Southeast Asia.

8 Luong has also noted that in Son Duong and Hoai Thi villages the Women's Buddhist Associations (*hoi chu ba*) were the only officially unsanctioned social organization to persist throughout the cooperative years (Luong 1993:289).

9 These figures can be interpreted in another fashion. If the figure of 4,066,800 days of labor lost is divided by an average figure of a cooperative worker working 250 days per year, the lost days of labor equal that of 16,267 cooperators. If an average cooperative engaged 500 cooperators on its workforce the number would then equal the annual labor totals of 32 cooperatives (see Malarney 1996:557).

10 During this period, the average cost per tray was 45,000 dong ($4.50) and an average funeral feast cost approximately $200.00 to $225.00.

11 Families also receive prestations at weddings, but they record those separately. One never repays a funeral prestation at a wedding nor visa versa.

12 The political biography of the cooperative chairman most responsible for allowing illegal slaughter is examined in detail in Malarney 1997. This case provides a useful example of some of the values and commitments embraced by different local officials, how they chose to conduct themselves as officials, and what the political consequences of those choices were.

13 For the past several decades the Vietnamese government has encouraged cremation and even set up a foreign-manufactured crematorium at the Van Dien cemetery southwest of Thinh Liet. Although some city residents choose this method, virtually no Thinh Liet residents do.

14 The strictly commemorative aspect of the rites also served in some cases as a justification for not needing to perform the rite according to the lunar calendar (see Vietnam, Ministry of Culture 1975:104).

Notes to Chapter 5

1 Women were expected to show the three obediences (*tam tong*) in life: obedience to their fathers when young, to their husbands when married, and to their sons when a widow.

2 The marriage data presented in this chapter derive from a survey of 509 marriages conducted in 1991–2. Respondents were chosen randomly from all three villages, and in some cases parents reported marriage data for their children who were not present or no longer living in Thinh Liet. The survey focused on age of marriage, arranged versus voluntary marriage, and village endogamy versus exogamy. Cases ranged from the early 1900s to 1991. Given the problems of this approach, and because these cases represent a limited percentage of the total number of marriages this century, the figures should be considered more descriptive than exact.

3 It is difficult to determine the extent of Chinese influence on the formulation of the Vietnamese law, but some influence was there as evident in the 1957 publication of a Chinese primer, *Husband and Wife in the New Society* (*Vo Chong Trong Xa Hoi Moi*) (Ton Minh 1957).

4 The government tacitly allowed men with multiple wives at the time of the law's introduction to keep their wives.

5 A more detailed description of the reform campaign can be found in Malarney 1993 and 1998. It should also be noted that Thinh Liet's history of wedding reform was unique and should not be regarded as representative of all communities in the north. To give one example, officials in the neighboring community of Yen So succeeded in organizing numerous wedding in their People's Committee in the period from 1970–75. Thinh Liet had none.

6 While aware of the many terminological complexities involved in describing marriage payments, I have chosen to use the term 'brideprice' in accordance with Helen Siu's restricted usage of the term for Chinese marital transfers. She comments that brideprice is used to describe 'transfers from the groom's side, whatever their destination' (Siu 1993:167).

7 *Mung* prestations vary from village to village. Luong reports that villagers in Son Duong village generally refuse cash gifts (Luong 1993:279).

8 It is an interesting comment on the uneven success of official reforms that many families now are comfortable conducting a death anniversary ceremony according to the solar calendar, yet many also choose to hold their weddings on auspicious days.

Notes to Chapter 6

1 As dictated in the Land Reform Law, Section 28. It should be noted, however, that this law describes each of these cases and does not use the term 'policy families.'

2 Translation of the term *Pho Ban Chinh Sach Xa* is difficult because technically, by designating the official as a 'deputy' (*pho*), there would be a corresponding superior. However, this was not the case with this position. Since the position was devoted exclusively to the government's social policies for families with members in the military, I have chosen to translate it as 'Social Policy Officer' in order to reduce confusion.

3 The example of '*vinh du*' in a Hanoi-published dictionary *Tu Dien Viet-Anh* reads, '*Hi sinh cho To quoc la mot vinh du*: It is an honour to lay down one's life for the fatherland' (Nguyen Q. Thang and Nguyen Ba The 1991:762).

4 A number of recent studies have shown that despite the Vietnamese government's master narrative of the glory of war and sacrifice, many Vietnamese who lived through the war years have far more ambivalent or even critical understandings of the period (see Ho-Tai 2001). Unlike the official heroic narrative, there were people who dodged the draft, deserted, or resented the military's willingness to sacrifice soldiers' lives, even in Thinh Liet.

5 There are situations when a young person dies, but is thought to be of particular sacred potency. In such cases an altar might be built inside of the family home to worship that spirit and bring its blessings to the family. In Thinh Liet commune, no such altars have been built for dead soldiers.

6 The Vietnamese government has never released figures for the number of its soldiers killed in the American War, thus during the war years Vietnamese had no precise knowledge of the number of their soldiers killed.

7 Paper votive objects were not universally present in all ceremonies as they were suppressed by the government.

8 One group that has been written out of this heroic narrative are those who served in the South Vietnamese military. Although tens of thousands of men gave their lives fighting for the south, they are not part of the government's commemorative effort.

9 The 15th of the 7th lunar month is the Vietnamese All Soul's Day.

10 One number frequently mentioned is 300,000 missing, but this can never be verified.

Notes to Chapter 7

1 Luong also observed in Hoai Thi that economic improvements created the conditions for the intensification of ritual practices (Luong 1993:271).

2 Such ideas are also shared by some Hanoi residents. One such story is that rain will at least briefly fall every September 2 as the heavens weep on the anniversary of Ho's death. Another is that an examination of older Ho portraits will reveal a second pupil in his right eye, a mark that indicates divinity.

3 Some Vietnamese regard the Hung dynasty as Vietnam's first, though scholars consider it mythical.

4 I am grateful to Kirsten Endres for alerting me to this passage.

Notes to Conclusion

1 Malarney 1997 examines in greater detail the question of how different officials dealt with the moral claims of revolution and locality.

2 The only exception is the representative of the Elderly Association delivering an oration before going to the grave site in an elderly person's funeral, yet this role complements and does not replace other speeches delivered by family members.

The association plays a positive role in the lives of many elderly residents and helps out with their funerals, thus their continued involvement is regarded as beneficial.

3 But as previously shown, *not* consuming can make an equally important moral statement for those who follow the revolutionary moral framework.

4 The fact that ritual should be part of the manner in which Thinh Liet residents attempt to make sense of and order their changing world is not unique. The scholarly literature from other Asian societies illustrates that despite urbanization, industrialization, and other aspects of modernization, people have not renounced the supernatural nor ritual actions toward it. Aihwa Ong described how female workers at electronics factories in Malaysia demanded the performance of rites by spirit specialists (*bomoh*) in order to eliminate what they considered to be supernatural dangers in the factories (Ong 1988). Robert Weller demonstrated how the growth of innovative spirit cults in Taiwan has been linked to attempts by the economically vulnerable to ensure some financial stability and ideally prosperity (Weller 1994). Laurel Kendall, in a similar vein, described the growth of shamanic ceremonies in Korea organized by economically vulnerable women to either ensure prosperity or diagnose why they are struggling (Kendall 1996). And William La Fleur and Helen Hardacre have both analyzed the emergence of *mizuko kuyo* rites in Japan that women perform in order to put the soul of a miscarried or aborted fetus to rest (La Fleur 1992; Hardarcre 1997). These examples, and others, all point to continued ritual congress with the supernatural.

Bibliography

Anagnost, Ann. 1987. 'Politics and Magic in Contemporary China.' *Modern China* 13(1):40–61.

Asad, Talal. 1980. 'Anthropology and the Analysis of Ideology.' *Man* (n.s.) 14:607–27.

Bao Ninh. 1991. *The Sorrow of War*. London: Secker and Warberg.

Barth, Frederik. 1975. *Ritual and Knowledge among the Baktaman of New Guinea*. New Haven: Yale University Press.

Becker, Gay. 1997. *Disrupted Lives: How People Create Meaning in a Chaotic World*. Berkeley: University of California Press.

Beresford, Melanie. 1988. *Vietnam: Politics, Economics, and Society*. London: Pinter Publishers.

Berger, Peter L. 1969. *A Rumor of Angels: Modern Society and the Rediscovery of the Supernatural*. Garden City: Anchor Books.

Berger, Peter L. and Thomas Luckmann. 1966. *The Social Construction of Reality: A Treatise in the Sociology of Knowledge*. Garden City: Doubleday and Company.

Binns, Christopher. 1979. 'The Changing Face of Power: Revolution and Accommodation in the Development of the Soviet Ceremonial System: Part I.' *Man* (n.s.) 14:585–606.

—— 1980. 'The Changing Face of Power: Revolution and Accommodation in the Development of the Soviet Ceremonial System: Part II.' *Man* (n.s.) 15:170–187.

Bloch, Maurice. 1986. *From Blessing to Violence: History and Ideology in the Circumcision Ritual of the Merina of Madagascar*. Cambridge: Cambridge University Press.

Bloch, Maurice and Jonathan Parry. 1982. 'Introduction: Death and the Regeneration of Life.' In Maurice Bloch and Jonathan Parry, eds., *Death and the Regeneration of Life*, pp. 1–44. Cambridge: Cambridge University Press.

Confucius. 1979. *The Analects*. Great Britain: Penguin Books.

Croll, Elisabeth. 1981. *The Politics of Marriage in Contemporary China*. Cambridge: Cambridge University Press.

Do Huy. 1978. 'Con Nguoi Moi – Tinh Cam Tham My Moi' (The New Person – The Beautiful New Sentiment). In Pham Nhu Cuong, ed. *Ve Van De Xay Dung Con Nguoi Moi* (On the Problem of Creating the New Person). Hanoi: Nha Xuat Ban Khoa Hoc Xa Hoi.

Dinh Thu Cuc. 1976. 'Buoc Dau Tim Hieu Ve Qua Trinh Hinh Thanh va Phat Trien Tu Tuong Lam Chu Tap The Cua Nguoi Nong Dan Viet Nam' (First

Steps for Understanding the Process of Realizing and Developing Collectivist Ideology Among the Vietnamese Peasantry). *Nghien Cuu Lich Su* (Historical Research) 2:34–45.

Dumont, Louis. 1970. *Homo Hierarchicus: The Caste System and Its Implications.* Chicago: University of Chicago Press.

Dumoutier, Gustave. 1904. *Le rituel funeraire des Annamites: Etude d'ethnographie religieuse.* Hanoi: F.H. Schneider.

Durkheim, Emile. 1965. *The Elementary Forms of Religious Life.* New York: The Free Press.

Ebrey, Patricia Buckley. 1991. 'Introduction.' In Patricia Buckley Ebrey and Rubie S. Watson, eds., *Marriage and Inequality in Chinese Society,* pp. 1–24. Berkeley: University of California Press.

Endres, Kirsten W. 1998. 'Culturalizing Politics'. *Doi Moi* and the Restructuring of Ritual in Contemporary Rural Vietnam.' In Bernhard Dahm and Vincent Houben (eds.), *Vietnamese Villages in Transition. Background and Consequences of Reform Policies in Rural Vietnam,* pp. 197–221. Passau: Passau Contributions to Southeast Asian Studies.

—— 2001. 'Local Dynamics of Renegotiating Ritual Space in North Vietnam: The Case of the *Dinh*'. *Sojourn* 16(1): 71–103.

Evans, Grant. 1991. 'Reform or Revolution in Heaven? Funerals among Upland Tai.' *Australian Journal of Anthropology* 2(1):81–97.

—— 1998. *The Politics of Ritual and Remembrance: Laos Since 1975.* Honolulu: University of Hawaii.

Evans-Pritchard, E.E. 1976. *Witchcraft, Oracles, and Magic Among the Azande.* Oxford: Oxford University Press.

Fauchois, Yann. 1989. *Religion et France Révolutionnaire.* Paris: Herscher.

Fforde, Adam. 1989. *The Agrarian Question in Vietnam, 1974–1979.* New York: M.E. Sharpe.

Fleck, Ludwik. 1979. *Genesis and Development of a Scientific Fact.* Chicago: University of Chicago Press.

Freedman, Maurice. 1958. *Lineage Organization in Southeastern China.* London: The Athlone Press.

Good, Byron. 1994. *Medicine, Rationality, and Experience: An Anthropological Perspective.* Cambridge: Cambridge University Press.

Goodkind, Daniel. 1995. 'Rising Gender Inequality in Vietnam Since Reunification.' *Pacific Affairs* 68(3):342–359.

Goody, Jack. 1973. 'Bridewealth and Africe in Africa and Eurasia.' In Jack Goody and S.J. Tambiah, *Bridewealth and Dowry,* pp. 1–57. Cambridge: Cambridge University Press.

Ha Nam Ninh, Cultural Service. 1976. *Day! Thuc Chat 'Hoi Phu Giay'* (Here! The Real Essence of 'Hoi Phu Giay'). Ha Nam Ninh: Ty Van Hoa Ha Nam Ninh.

Ha Tay, Cultural Service. 1967. *Xay Dung Nep Song Van Hoa Moi* (Building the New Ways of the New Culture). Ha Tay: Ty Van Hoa Ha-Tay.

—— 1970. *Xay Dung Nep Song Van Hoa Moi* (Building the New Ways of the New Culture). 1970. Ha Tay: Ty Van Hoa Ha Tay.

Habermas, Jurgen. 1971. *Toward a Rational Society: Student Protest, Science and Politics.* Boston: Beacon Press.

—— 1973. *Legitimation Crisis.* Boston: Beacon Press.

—— 1974. *Theory and Practice.* London: Heinemann Educational Books Ltd.

—— 1979. *Communication and the Evolution of Society.* Boston: Beacon Press.

—— 1990. *Moral Consciousness and Communicative Action.* Cambridge: Polity Press.

235

—— 1998. *Between Facts and Norms: Contributions to a Discourse Theory of Law and Democracy.* Boston: MIT Press.

Hanoi, Culture and Information Service. 1973. *Giang Bien Xoa Bo Hu Tuc Ma Chay Cuoi Xin* (Giang Bien Rids Itself of All Bad Marriage and Funeral Customs). Hanoi: So Van Hoa Thong Tin Ha Noi.

—— 1975. *Xay Dung Nhung Phong Tuc Tap Quan Moi* (Building New Customs). Hanoi: So Van Hoa Thong Tin Ha Noi.

Hanoi, Land Reform Committee. 1956. *Thang Loi Cai Cach Ruong Dat O Ngoai Thanh Ha Noi* (The Victory of the Land Reform in the Outskirts of Hanoi). Hanoi: Uy Ban Cai Cach Ruong Dat Ha Noi.

Hardacre, Helen. 1997. *Marketing the Menacing Fetus in Japan.* Berkeley and Los Angeles: University of California Press.

Hefner, Robert. 1985. *Hindu Javanese: Tengger Tradition and Islam.* Princeton: Princeton University Press.

Hiebert, Murray. 1996. *Chasing the Tigers: A Portrait of the New Vietnam.* Tokyo: Kodansha International.

Ho Chi Minh. 1984. '*Sua Doi Loi Lam Viec*' (Correcting the Way We Work). In *Ho Chi Minh, Toan Tap: 1945–1947. Tap 4* (Ho Chi Minh's Complete Works: 1945–1947, Volume 4), 439–530. Hanoi: Nha Xuat Ban Su That.

—— 1988. *Ve Tu Cach Nguoi Dang Vien Cong San* (On the Behavior of Communist Party Members). Hanoi: Nha Xuat Ban Su That.

Ho-Tai, Hue Tam (ed.) (2001) *The Country of Memory: Remaking the Past in Late Socialist Vietnam.* Berkeley: University of California Press.

Keesing, Roger. 1987. 'Anthropology as Interpretive Quest.' *Current Anthropology* 28(2):161–9.

Kendall, Laurel. 1994. 'A Rite of Modernization and its Postmodern Discontents: Of Weddings, Bureaucrats, and Morality in the Republic of Korea.' In Charles F. Keyes, Laurel Kendall, and Helen Hardacre, eds., *Asian Visions of Authority: Religion and the Modern States of East and Southeast Asia*, pp. 165–92. Honolulu: University of Hawaii Press.

—— 1996. 'Korean Shamans and the Spirits of Capitalism.' *American Anthropologist* 98(3):512–527.

Kim Cuc. 1960. *Doi Song Moi* (The New Ways). Hanoi: Nha Xuat Ban Pho Thong.

Kim Phong. 1946. *The Nao La Doi Song Moi* (What Are the New Ways?). Hanoi: Nha Xuat Ban Nuoc Nha.

Kirsch, A. Thomas. 1985. 'Text and Context: Buddhist Sex Roles/Culture of Gender Revisited.' *American Ethnologist*, pp. 302–20.

Kleinen, John. 1999. Facing the Future, Reviving the Past: A Study of Social Change in a Northern Vietnamese Village. Singapore: Institute of Southeast Asian Studies.

LaFleur, William R. 1992. *Liquid Life: Abortion and Buddhism in Japan.* Princeton: Princeton University Press.

Lambek, Michael. 1990. 'Certain Knowledge, Contestable Authority: Power and Practice on the Islamic Periphery.' *American Ethnologist* 17(1):23–40.

—— 1993. *Knowledge and Practice in Mayotte: Local Discourses of Islam, Sorcery, and Spirit Possession.* Toronto: University of Toronto Press.

Lane, Cristal. 1981. *The Rites of Rulers: Ritual in Industrial Society – The Soviet Case.* Cambridge: Cambridge University Press.

Lao Cai, Culture and Information Service. 1964. *Cai Tao Phong Tuc Tap Quan* (Reforming Customs). Lao Cai: Ty Van Hoa Thong Tin Lao-Cai.

Lavely, William. 1991. 'Marriage and Mobility under Rural Collectivism.' In Patricia Buckley Ebrey and Rubie S. Watson, eds., *Marriage and Inequality in Chinese Society*, pp. 286–312. Berkeley: University of California Press.

236

Le Duan. 1965a. *Giai Cap Vo San Voi Van De Nong Dan Trong Cach Mang Vietnam* (The Proletarian Class and the Problem of the Peasantry in the Vietnamese Revolution). Hanoi: Nha Xuat Ban Su That.

—— 1965b. *On the Socialist Revolution in Vietnam.* Vol I. Hanoi: Foreign Languages Publishing House.

Levi-Strauss, Claude. 1962. *The Savage Mind.* London: Weidenfield and Nicolson.

Luong, Hy Van. 1989. 'Vietnamese Kinship: Structural Change and the Socialist Transformation in Twentieth-Century Vietnam.' *Journal of Asian Studies* 48:741–56.

—— 1992. *Revolution in the Village: Tradition and Transformation in North Viet Nam, 1925–1988.* Honolulu: University of Hawaii Press.

—— 1993. 'Economic Reform and the Intensification of Rituals in Two Northern Vietnamese Villages, 1980–90.' In Borje Ljunggren (ed.), *The Challenge of Reform in Indochina*, pp. 259–292. Cambridge: Harvard Institute for International Development.

MacIntyre, Alasdair. 1968. *Marxism and Christianity.* Notre Dame: University of Notre Dame Press.

Madsen, Richard. 1984. *Morality and Power in a Chinese Village.* Berkeley: University of California Press.

Malarney, Shaun Kingsley. 1993. *Ritual and Revolution in Viet Nam.* Unpublished Ph.D. dissertation. University of Michigan.

—— 1996a. 'The Emerging Cult of Ho Chi Minh? A Report on Religious Innovation in Contemporary Northern Viet Nam.' *Asian Cultural Studies* 22:121–131.

—— 1996b. 'The Limits of "State Functionalism" and the Reconstruction of Funerary Ritual in Contemporary Northern Viet Nam.' *American Ethnologist* 23(3):540–560.

—— 1997. 'Culture, Virtue, and Political Transformation in Contemporary Northern Viet Nam.' *The Journal of Asian Studies* 56(4):899–920.

—— 1998. 'The Consequences of the Revolutionary Reform of Marriage and the Wedding Ceremony in Northern Vietnamese Village Life.' *Asian Cultural Studies* 24:127–42.

Malinowski, Bronislaw. 1922. *Argonauts of the Western Pacific.* London: Routledge and Kegan Paul.

Marr, David. 1981. *Vietnamese Tradition on Trial, 1920–1945.* Berkeley: University of California Press.

Marx, Karl. 1987. *The Eighteenth Brumaire of Louis Bonaparte.* New York: International Publishers.

Marx, Karl and Frederick Engels. 1970. *The German Ideology.* New York: International Publishers.

Minh Phuc. 1998. 'Traditional Vietnamese Tet: Working Hard to Fully Enjoy the Tet Holiday.' *Vietnam Economic News* 3:68–9.

Moise, Edwin. 1983. *Land Reform in China and North Vietnam: Consolidating the Revolution at the Village Level.* Chapel Hill: University of North Carolina Press.

Mosse, George L. 1990. *Fallen Soldiers: Reshaping the Memory of the World Wars.* Oxford: Oxford University Press.

Murray, Martin. 1980. *The Development of Capitalism in Colonial Indochina (1870–1940).* Berkeley: University of California Press.

Mydans, Seth. 1996. 'Vietnam, a Convert, Pursues Capitalism Devoutly.' *The New York Times* April 5: A4.

237

Nam Ha, Cultural Service. 1971. *Chi Thi Ve Hoi He va Quy Uoc Ve To Chuc Dam Cuoi, Dam Ma, Ngay Gio, Ngay Tet va Ngay Ky Niem Lon* (Instructions on Public Festivals and Conventions on the Organization of Weddings, Funerals, Death Anniversaries, Tet and Important Commemorative Days). Nam Ha: Ty Van Hoa Nam Ha.

Needham, Rodney. 1972. *Belief, Language, and Experience.* Oxford: Basil Blackwell.

Ngo Van Cat. 1980. *Viet Nam Chong Nan That Hoc* (Viet Nam Against the Disaster of the Lack of Education). Hanoi: Nha Xuat Ban Giao Duc.

Nguyen Ai Quoc School. 1955. *Tai Lieu Hoc Tap Ve Cai Cach Ruong Dat* (Materials for Study on the Land Reform). Hanoi: Truong Nguyen Ai Quoc.

Nguyen Duy Hinh. 1996. *Tin Nguong Thanh Hoang Viet Nam* (Religious Practices Regarding Vietnamese Village Guardian Spirits). Hanoi: Nha Xuat ban Khoa Hoc Xa Hoi.

Nguyen Hong Phong. 1959. *Xa Thon Viet Nam* (Vietnamese Villages). Hanoi: Nha Xuat Ban Su Dia.

Nguyen Ngoc Huy and Ta Van Tai. 1987. *The Le Code: Law in Traditional Vietnam.* Vol. I. Athens, Ohio: Ohio University Press.

Nguyen Q. Thang and Nguyen Ba The. 1991. *Tu Dien Nhan Vat Lich Su Viet Nam* (Dictionary of Characters from Vietnamese History). Hanoi: Nha Xuat Ban Khoa Hoc Xa Hoi.

Nguyen Van Khoan. 1930. 'Essai sur le dinh et le culte du genie tutelaire des villages au Tonkin' (Essay on the Dinh and the Cult of Village Guardian Spirits in Tonkin). *Bulletin de l'Ecole Francaise d'Extreme-Orient* 30(1–2):107–139.

Nhat Binh. 1998. 'Greeting Tet in Rural Vietnam: Impressions of the Central Region's Tet Traditions.' *Vietnam Economic News* 5:72.

Ninh Binh, Cultural Service. 1968. *Cong Tac Xay Dung Nep Song Moi, Con Nguoi Moi va Gia Dinh Tien Tien Chong My, Cuu Nuoc* (The Task of Building the New Ways, New Person and the Progressive Family in the Struggle Against America to Rescue the Nation). Ninh Binh: Ty Van Hoa Ninh Binh.

—— 1970. *Quy Uoc Nep Song Moi* (Conventions on the New Ways). Ninh Binh: Ty Van Hoa Ninh Binh.

Ninh Binh, People's Court. 1967. *Kien Quyet Chong Cac Te Nan Xa Hoi Thuong Xay Ra Trong Dip Tet* (Be Resolute Against the Social Evils Which Usually Occur During Tet). Ninh Binh: Toa An Nhan Dan, Vien Kiem Sat Nhan Dan, Ty Cong An Ninh-Binh.

—— 1970. *Tet Tiet Kiem, Lanh Manh, Lam Theo Loi Bac* (A Frugal, Wholesome *Tet,* Carried Out According to Uncle's Words). Ninh Binh: Toa An Nhan Dan Tinh Ninh Binh.

Norton, Barley. 1999. *Music and Possession in Vietnam.* Unpublished Ph.D. dissertation. University of London.

Ong, Aihwa. 1988. 'The Production of Possession: Spirits and the Multinational Corporation in Malaysia.' *American Ethnologist* 15(1):28–42.

Ortner, Sherry B. 1994. 'Theory in Anthropology Since the Sixties.' In Nicholas B. Dirks, Geoff Eley, and Sherry B. Ortner, eds., *Culture/Power/History,* pp. 372–411. Princeton: Princeton University Press.

Pham Xanh. 1990. *Nguyen Ai Quoc Voi Viec Truyen Ba Chu Nghia Mac-Le Nin O Viet Nam (1921–1930)* (Nguyen Ai Quoc and the Task of Disseminating Marxist-Leninism in Viet Nam (1921–1930)). Hanoi: Nha Xuat Ban Thong Tin Ly Luan.

Phan Ke Binh. 1990. *Viet Nam Phong Tuc* (Vietnamese Customs). Saigon: Nha Xuat Ban Thanh Pho Ho Chi Minh.

Phi Ha and Thanh Binh. 1960. *De Xay Dung Mot Che Do Hon Nhan va Gia Dinh Kieu Moi* (Building a New Marriage Regime and a Family of the New Style). Hanoi: Nha Xuat Ban Thanh Nien.

Pike, Douglas. 1986. *PAVN: People's Army of Vietnam*. New York: Da Capo Press.

Popkin, Samuel. 1979. *The Rational Peasant: The Political Economy of Rural Society in Vietnam*. Berkeley: University of California Press.

Porter, Gareth. 1993. *Vietnam: The Politics of Bureaucratic Socialism*. Ithaca and London: Cornell University Press.

Schutz, Alfred. 1973. *Collected Papers I: The Problem of Social Reality*. The Hague: Martinus Nijhoff.

Siu, Helen F. 1993. 'Reconstituting Dowry and Brideprice in South China.' In Deborah Davis and Stevan Harrell, eds., *Chinese Families in the Post-Mao Era*, pp. 165–88. Berkeley: University of California Press.

Son La, Cultural Service. 1975. *Mot So Van Ban Ve Xay Dung va Thuc Hien Nep Song Moi* (A Few Documents on the Building and Realization of the New Ways). Son La: Ty Van Hoa Son La.

Sperber, Dan. 1975. *Rethinking Symbolism*. Cambridge: Cambridge University Press.

Spiro, Melford. 1970. *Buddhism and Society: A Great Tradition and its Burmese Vicissitudes*. Berkeley: University of California Press.

Ta Van Thanh. 1990. *Tim Hieu Ve Cach Mang Tu Tuong Va Van Hoa* (Understanding the Ideological and Cultural Revolution). Hanoi: Nha Xuat Ban Su That.

Tambiah, S.J. 1970. *Buddhism and the Spirit Cults in North-east Thailand*. Cambridge: Cambridge University Press.

Tan Sinh. 1977 (1947). *Doi Song Moi* (The New Ways). Hanoi: Nha Xuat Ban Lao Dong.

Taylor, Charles. 1989. *Sources of the Self: The Making of Modern Identity*. Cambridge: Harvard University Press.

Taylor, Keith Weller. 1983. *The Birth of Vietnam*. Berkeley: University of California Press.

Thanh Hoa, Cultural Service. 1975. *Ke Chuyen Nhan Dan Ta Len An Hu Tuc* (Stories of Our People Denouncing Outdated Customs). Thanh Hoa: Ty Van Hoa Thanh Hoa.

Toan Anh. 1968. *Nep Cu: Lang Xom Viet Nam* (Old Ways: The Vietnamese Village). Saigon: Nha Xuat Ban Khai Tri.

—— 1969. *Nep Cu: Hoi He Dinh Dam, Quyen Thuong* (Old Ways: Village Ceremonies, Volume I). Saigon: Nam Chi Tung Thu.

Ton Minh. 1957. *Vo Chong Trong Xa Hoi Moi* (Husband and Wife in the New Society). Hanoi: Nha Xuat Ban Thep.

Tran Do. 1986. *Van Hoa Van Nghe Trong Cach Mang Xa Hoi Chu Nghia O Viet Nam: Muc Tieu Va Dong Luc* (Culture and Literature in the Socialist Revolution in Viet Nam: Goals and Motive Forces). Hanoi: Nha Xuat Ban Van Hoa.

Tran Phuong. 1967. *Cach Mang Ruong Dat O Viet Nam* (The Land Revolution in Viet Nam). Hanoi: Nha Xuat Ban Khoa Hoc Xa Hoi.

Tran Quoc Vuong, Le Van Hao, and Duong Tat Tu. 1976. *Mua Xuan va Phong Tuc Viet Nam* (Spring and Vietnamese Customs). Hanoi: Nha Xuat Ban Van Hoa.

Tran Thanh. 1958. *Lam The Nao De Cung Co va Phat Trien Phong Trao Doi Cong Hop Tac* (How to Strengthen and Develop the Cooperative Labor Exchange Movement). Hanoi: Nha Xuat Ban Su That.

Tran Trong Kim. 1954. *Viet Nam Su Luoc* (Summary of Vietnamese History). Saigon: Tan Viet.

Truong Chinh and Vo Nguyen Giap. 1974. *The Peasant Question (1937–1938)*. Data Paper No. 94, Southeast Asia Program, Department of Asian Studies. Ithaca: Cornell University.

Tuan Cau. 1962. '*Tu Cai Dinh Lang Xua Den Cau Lac Bo Ngay Nay*' (From the Communal House of the Old Village to the Recreation Club of Today). *Van Hoa* 71:5–13.

Turner, Victor. 1967. *The Forest of Symbols: Aspects of Ndembu Ritual*. Ithaca: Cornell University Press.

Veblen, Thorstein. 1994 (1899). *The Theory of the Leisure Class*. In *The Collected Works of Thorstein Veblen*, Vol. 1. London: Routledge/Thoemmes Press.

Vickerman, Andrew. 1986. *The Fate of the Peasantry: Premature 'Transition to Socialism' in the Democratic Republic of Viet Nam*. New Haven: Yale University Southeast Asian Studies Program.

Vien Nghien Cuu Han Nom. 1981. *Ten Lang Xa Viet Nam Dau The Ky XIX* (Names of Vietnamese Villages and Communes at the Beginning of the 19th Century). Hanoi: Nha Xuat Ban Khoa Hoc Xa Hoi.

Vietnam, Government. 1962. *Dau Tranh Chong Doi Phong Bai Tuc Cai Tao Thoi Quen Cu Xay Dung Nep Song Moi* (Struggle Against Bad Practices and Corrupt Customs, Reform Old Habits and Build the New Ways). Hanoi.

Vietnam, Government Gazette. 1946. *Sac-Lenh so 44 ngay 3 thang 4 nam 1946 lap ban trung-uong van-dong doi song moi* (Decree No. 44 of 3 March 1946 to Establish the Central Committee for Propagation of the New Ways). 20 April: 222.

—— 1953. *Sac Lenh so 149-SL ngay 12–4–1953 quy dinh ve chinh sach ruong dat*. (Decree 149-SL of 12–4–1953 on regulations regarding land policy). 15 May: 47–50.

—— 1958. *Chi Thi So 047-TTg ngay 24–1–1958 ve tet Nguyen Dan* (Instruction No. 047-TTg of 24 January 1958 on Tet Nguyen Dan). 5 February: 31–2.

—— 1960. '*Luat Hon Nhan Va Gia Dinh*' (Law of Marriage and Family). 4:54–7.

Vietnam, Institute of Philosophy. 1973. *Dang Ta Ban Ve Dao Duc* (Our Party Discusses Ethic). Hanoi: Nha Xuat Ban Khoa Hoc Xa Hoi.

Vietnam, Ministry of Culture. 1975. *Doi Song Moi* (The New Ways). Hanoi: Bo Van Hoa.

—— 1979. *Nhung Van Ban Ve Viec Cuoi, Viec Tang, Ngay Gio, Ngay Hoi* (Documents on Weddings, Funerals, Death Anniversaries, and Public Festivals). 1979. Hanoi: Nha Xuat Ban Van Hoa.

Vietnam, National Peasant Liaison Committee. 1957. *Lay Doi Cong Hop Tac Lam Trung Tam Day Manh San Xuat Nong Nghiep (Tai Lieu Huan Luyen Doi Cong Cho Can Bo Xa va To Truong Doi Cong)* (Take Cooperative Labor Exchange as a Centre to Strengthen Agriculture (Instructional Materials on Labor Exchange for Communal-Level Cadres and Chiefs of Labor Exchange Groups)). Hanoi: Nha Xuat Ban Nong Thon.

Vietnam, Prime Minister's Office. 1957. *Chinh Sach Phan Dinh Thanh Phan Giap Cap O Nong Thon* (Policies for Determining Classifications in the Countryside). Hanoi: Van Phong Thu Tuong Phu.

Vu Huy Phuc. 1993. '*Vai Nhan Xet Ve Nang Suat Ruong Dat O Mien Bac Thoi Ky 1954–1960*' (A Few Observations on Land Productivity in Northern Viet Nam, 1954–1960). *Nghien Cuu Lich Su* (Historical Research) 4:19–23.

Watson, Rubie S. 1991. 'Afterword: Marriage and Gender Inequality.' In Patricia Buckley Ebrey and Rubie S. Watson, eds., *Marriage and Inequality in Chinese Society*, pp. 347–68. Berkeley: University of California Press.

Weber, Max. 1978. *Economy and Society*. Vol. I and II. Berkeley: University of California Press.

Weller, Robert. 1994. 'Capitalism, Community, and the Rise of Amoral Cults in Taiwan.' In Charles F. Keyes, Laurel Kendall and Helen Hardacre, eds., *Asian Visions of Authority: Religion and the Modern States of East and Southeast Asia*, pp. 141–164. Honolulu: University of Hawaii Press.

Wolf, Margery. 1985. *Revolution Postponed: Women in Contemporary China*. Stanford: Stanford University Press.

Woodside, Alexander Barton. 1971. *Vietnam and the Chinese Model*. Cambridge: Harvard University Press.

Xuan Cang and Ly Dang Cao. 1996. *'Tim Mo Liet Si Bang Phuong Phap Moi?'* (Discovering the Graves of War Dead By a New Method?). *The Gioi Moi*, pp. 8–11. Hanoi, October 1996.

Archival Sources

Ha Dong Province Files (Ha Dong)

#488 *Recensement de la population de 1921. Etats de recensement des villages du Canton Thinh Liet, huyen Thanh Tri.*

#583 *Etats de recensement de la population des villages de Thinh Liet, huyen de Thanh Tri, 1926.*

#1704 *Affaires Indigenes, Huyen de Thanh Tri, Canton de Thinh Liet, Village de Giap Nhi(2), 1904–1906.*

#1705 *Affaires Indigenes, huyen de Thanh Tri, canton de Thinh Liet, village de Giap Nhi(3), 1907–1919.*

#2854 *Projet de reforme concernant les ceremonies rituelles, 1920.*

#3403 *Contestation entre les villages Giap Nhat, Giap Nhi, Giap Tu, Giap That d'une part et le village de Giap Bat d'autre part au sujet d'une mare commune, 1921–24.*

Democratic Republic of Viet Nam National Assembly Files (QH)

#39 *To Trinh Ve Du Luat Hon Nhan Va Gia Dinh, 21.5.59.*

Index